I first met Pat Boone in October 1956 in New York City on the Arthur Godfrey Show. At the time we were both college boys and now, 45 years later, we can both call ourselves 'survivors of the fifties'!

Pat is a direct descendant of Daniel Boone, the great explorer and frontiersman. He is also the son-in-law of one of the greatest country and country gospel singers of all time – Red Foley. Daniel Boone, like me, was a North Carolinian long before he blazed a trail through the wilderness of the Great Smokies to Kentucky, where Red Foley was born. They have a saying in North Carolina and Kentucky: 'Walk your talk.' Pat Boone is a great balladeer, but he's also a powerful witness, a living, singing testimony to his Christian faith. His career and his musical ministry have been an inspiration to many.

GEORGE HAMILTON IV, Nashville, Tennessee

Pat Boone and I have been good friends for nearly half a century, but that never ruled out an amicable rivalry for chart placing. In fact, for a decade or so, just as Pat and Elvis chased each other up and down the charts in the USA, Pat and I were similarly competing up and down the British and European charts. Our deep respect for each other has grown since that time.

Thinking back, it seems that Pat and I shared much in common. In the fifties, at the same time that Pat was enjoying massive hits with songs such as 'Love Letters In The Sand', 'A Wonderful Time Up There', 'Speedy Gonzales' and 'April Love', I was simultaneously enjoying my early achievements in the European charts. Both of us have had success in secular as well as Christian movies. Pat's box office hits included the adventurous *Journey to the Centre of the Earth*, and who could forget the passionate drama of *The Cross and the Switchblade*? I remember listening to Pat's rich voice singing the title songs of movies such as Friendly Persuasion and Anastasia, charting him on both sides of the Atlantic.

Throughout his extensive career in show business, Pat navigated himself well through the hefty storms that sought to sink his personal integrity. To his credit, his commitment to Christ remains a lighthouse for many, as Paul's book illustrates, and he remains a powerful Christian communicator in concerts, movies and books. Speaking of Christian movies, another shared experience has been his involvement in travelogues on the Holy Land, commenting on important biblical sites with the help of appropriate songs.

Like mine, Pat's Christian views are often courted on TV chat shows, giving him the opportunity to offer well reasoned answers to questions about his faith. Pat was always a giver, and his unstinting commitment to charity work has been widely commended. Personally, it's a privilege for me to be counted among his friends.

SIR CLIFF RICHARD OBE, London, England

PAT BOONE

The Authorized Biography

April Love: The Early Days of Rock 'n' Roll

Paul Davis

Introduced by Sir Cliff Richard & George Hamilton IV

ZONDERVAN™

GRAND RAPIDS, MICHIGAN 49530 USA

ZONDERVAN™

Pat Boone
Copyright © 2001 by Paul Davis

First published in Great Britain in 2001 by HarperCollins*Publishers*

First published in the United States in 2002 by Zondervan

Requests for information should be addressed to:

Zondervan, *Grand Rapids, Michigan 49530*

Paul Davis asserts the moral right to be identified as the author of this work.

A catalogue record for this book is available from the British Library.

ISBN 0-00-710088-4

Scripture quotations are taken from the *King James Version* (KJV) of the Bible.

Printed and bound in the United Kingdom

02 03 04 05 06 07 08 /❖CPD/ 10 9 8 7 6 5 4 3 2 1

To
My dear wife Hazel

Our wonderful children and grandchildren,
Anita and Ed McGirr (and Nathanael and Rachel),
Wes and Sue Davis, Laura and Paul Ewers

Our faithful parents, Helen and Tom Davis,
Rosie and Walter Scott

Our loving church, Leighton Christian Fellowship,
England and worldwide

All our friends in the world of music

ACKNOWLEDGEMENTS

Thanks to Pat and Shirley Boone, Janet Saint Pierre, Ed Rhinehart, Charlie Shaw, Maureen Mata, George Hamilton IV, Jerry Arhelger, Judy Donald, Alan Coates, Chris Bujnovsky, Hazel Sutherland, Terry Smith, Tony Byworth, Jim Long, Steve Revell, David Diggs, Garth Hewitt, Jimmy and Carol Owens, Mary and Ed McGirr, Arthur Rowley, Jeffrey Kruger, Bill Latham, Sir Cliff Richard, Wes Davis, Laura Ewers, Hazel Davis, Kelly Hancock and Johnny Cash.

CONTENTS

FOREWORD

BY PAT BOONE

PAUL DAVIS HAS DONE an amazing and extremely complimentary job of gathering information, talking to friends and associates
and compiling a detailed history of my life and career so far. I say
'complimentary' because there are many details and conversations
I frankly do not remember now, but Paul unfailingly ensures that I
am seen in a favourable light! I can only surmise that he has talked
in depth to many of the other people who were involved at various
junctures in my life and career, and has taken down their recollections. Some of these episodes and conversations have slipped
completely out of my own memory bank. Bear in mind, however,
that a lot of water has flowed over the dam, and I do have an occasional 'senior moment' these days. I hate to admit it, but it's true.

Perhaps the reason Paul has a better recall than I do is that this
life of mine has flown by, so far, in such a blurring, heady stream
that many details have simply failed to stick in my brain. These
days, I am frequently delighted when someone I have known in
previous years reminds me of happy moments with hilarious
details that I have not thought much about, if at all, since they
happened. In some ways, it is good that a person stays so busy,

xi

involved in so many activities, that even the disappointments do not matter much. In other ways, it is sad not to savour and file away some of the real high points for later times of reminiscence.

I have found this book fascinating reading! Sometimes I think I am reading about someone else and his family, but that is surely a tribute to Paul's enthusiasm for the music I have made and the life I have lived, with lots of help from family and friends and the good Lord Himself. I hope you enjoy reading about it all.

Pat Boone
Beverly Hills, California

INTRODUCTION

MILESTONES

EVERY POPULAR MUSIC FAN knows Pat Boone's special, velvet-smooth sound. For 50 years his voice has graced songs embracing every conceivable human sentiment. No lover could forget the sweet romance of 'April Love'. No military serviceman could avoid the hopeful sentiment of 'I'll Be Home'. No teenager could deny the adolescent empathy of 'Twixt Twelve And Twenty'. No believer could fail to be stirred by the high spirits of 'A Wonderful Time Up There'. No art lover could resist the sheer beauty of 'Friendly Persuasion'. No fun seeker could fail to smile at the ticklish comedy of 'Speedy Gonzales'. All these classics became high-scoring hits under the influence of the rich Boone vocals. Taking the pop charts by storm, Pat's early hit parade success brought him 13 gold records and a fervent following.

Pat's recording successes were all the more remarkable because of his unlikely mixture of peppy rock'n'roll, spirited gospel toe-tappers, tender country love songs, earthy rhythm and blues, majestic hymnal favourites and well loved pop standards. Such artistic diversity was unique and it was this that kept his popularity flying consistently high for so long. Against all the critics'

xiii

predictions, Pat scored his first million-seller with the Fats Domino classic 'Ain't That A Shame'. Then he switched direction with beautiful, haunting ballads such as 'Friendly Persuasion' and 'Love Letters In The Sand'. Under the shadowy threat of atomic warfare at the height of the Cold War, with military service still compulsory, plaintive songs such as 'I'll Be Home' and 'Remember You're Mine' notched up a steady chart domination in many parts of the globe. Many more hits followed, such as 'Don't Forbid Me' and 'April Love'. Then, in 1961 and 1962, he scored with two very divergent themes – the sad, suicidal saga of 'Moody River', followed by the gimmicky and comical 'Speedy Gonzales'. Two more gold discs were added to his trophy shelf.

In those dizzy, busy days, Pat's hit records barely kept pace with Hollywood film acclaim, as his fans flocked to see him act and sing on the silver screen. His movie money-spinners ranged from *Bernadine* (with Terry Moore, Janet Gaynor and Dean Jagger), *April Love* (with Shirley Jones), *State Fair* (with Ann Margaret, Alice Faye and Bobby Darin) and *Mardi Gras* (with Tommy Sands, Sheree North and Gary Crosby) to *Journey to the Centre of the Earth* (with James Mason, Arlene Dahl and Diane Baker).

Looking back at the chronicle of popular music in the second half of the twentieth century, it is safe to say that no one enjoyed a more enviable reputation in both the popular music and gospel music fields than Pat Boone. Nowadays he is recognized as one of the most influential of the veteran popular song stylists. Fans, critics and fellow performers all acknowledge that his name became synonymous with excellence in that field.

A trailblazer in audio recordings, movie acting, book writing and as a 'teens and twenties' counsellor of sorts, Pat set for himself ever-rising standards in diverse pursuits. Whether it was in music, writing or acting, many other aspiring performers tried to copy his success. None succeeded with such flair in all three fields. Then and now, Pat is acknowledged as a moral role model, and as someone with quick wit and persuasive wisdom, balanced with a genuine depth of humility and patience. Many are surprised that he still patiently meets and shakes hands with so many people with childlike delight and professional dedication. Long after most stars would have made their legitimate excuses and slipped out through the back door of the stage and onto the golf course, Pat is still chatting away, seemingly oblivious of time. Above and beyond his musical gifts, he also has the rare talent needed to communicate powerfully through speech – be that story-telling, poetry, writing, acting, preaching or teaching. And he still delights in recounting simple, life-changing verities wherever an audience is available to listen.

The show-biz dream all started when he was a youngster in the Tennessee city of Nashville, known as 'Music City USA'. There, playing in his family's living room, he would listen attentively to the songs on the radio. It was the golden age of classic crooners such as Bing Crosby, Frank Sinatra, Perry Como and Nashville's own Eddy Arnold. All these greats exuded sophistication and professionalism. Nashville was also the home base of a less polished genre, although the performers were every bit as professional. The famed Grand Ole Opry broadcasts on the radio could boast their own high-quality country crooners, including Ray Price, George Morgan, Jim Reeves and the man who became Pat's father-in-law, Red Foley. Deservedly, Pat reached the very top of his chosen profession. Now his superstar reputation is both global and legendary.

He has an outrageous sense of humour and dislikes being described as 'holy' or 'saintly'. Such terms, he says, belie his down-to-earth empathy with 'everyday' people. Despite that earthy sense of humour and his plain speaking, Pat has always been known for his Southern charm and Christian courtesy. He remains a lifelong and ardent follower of the Christian faith. Throughout the years, he says, he has always tried to use his professional giftings to 'bring lost souls to the Lord Jesus, bridging the gap between heaven and earth'. Never confrontational for the sake of it, his witness for his faith remains tolerant, gentle and gracious.

Pat's commanding presence has been a show-biz constant since 1954. He still serves the popular and gospel music causes with great skill and conscientiousness. Despite advancing years, he is dedicated to his entertainment role, and is increasingly recognized worldwide as a Christian statesman and spokesman. He is, for instance, now an official Christian Ambassador to Israel. Without hesitation or solicitation, many of his associates also happily testified to me that Pat still sacrificially gives quality time and dedicated effort to ordinary people and charitable enterprises.

Inside and outside the USA, the exposure given by Pat to Christian music in secular quarters should not be overlooked. He continues to play his part in a thriving Christian music industry and touring circuit. After half a century of constant personal appearances, the rigours of being on the road have not dulled his zeal. He also hosts a weekly gospel TV show and two weekly radio programmes. One of these has been going for 20 years: *The Pat Boone Show* features contemporary Christian music and is now syndicated nationally to nearly 200 stations. The other radio show is a popular music programme called *Pat Boone's Then and Now*, syndicated nationally to 170 stations and featuring music from the 1950s through to the present day.

At the beginning of the new century, Pat lives in the same Beverly Hills mansion he has occupied for the past 40-odd years with his wife Shirley, and cheerfully continues an active popular and gospel music concert schedule. He still performs frequently in live concerts and church services nationwide and abroad. The trophy cases in his Sunset Boulevard office and his home overflow with industry and fan awards of every shape and size.

Deservedly riding high on the unique heritage of their father and grandfather, the four Boone daughters also carry the family banner onwards. Close friends consider that Pat and Shirley are twice blessed: firstly in each other, and secondly in having such a close and loving family, as well as dear friends. Some friends feel that Shirley is often the more spiritually discerning of the couple.

At times, she has certainly been the family's spiritual pioneer, and she is genuinely pleased that her spouse continues to use his God-given talents to witness to so many people around the world.

For myself, I would like to document my grateful thanks to Pat for his co-operation with my work on this biography. He would describe this book as an 'Ebenezer' – the word for a landmark or milestone in the Bible. Pat believes in recognizing devotional landmarks. 'These were always important to the ancient nation of Israel,' he says. '"Stones of Help"' (or Ebenezers) were erected as testimonies to the times when God helped His people. The Bible says, "Then Samuel took a stone, and set it between Mizpeh and Shen, and called the name of it Eben-ezer, saying, Hitherto hath the LORD helped us" (1 Samuel 7:12). Simple as they were, stone Ebenezers served a useful national and personal purpose.'

This book can be seen in that context, outlining one Ebenezer after another in Pat's life. Looking back over his lengthy career, Pat is grateful for the times when God's help was evident to him. 'We human beings have short memories when it comes to calling back to mind times when God has helped us. That's why God encouraged the Old Testament people to take time to raise their Ebenezers of Praise, tangible reminders of God's interventions. We too, as God's people today, need reminding from time to time of God's goodness to us in our lives. He has many times stood by us faithfully, as He promised, in sunshine and in rain, in joy and pain, and through thick and thin. Every time we turned to Him He was truly a very present help in time of trouble. We should take time to remember.'

CHAPTER 1

TENNESSEE SATURDAY NIGHT

Now listen while I tell you 'bout a place I know
Down in Tennessee where the tall corn grows!
Billy Hughes

PAT BOONE MAY BE a famous name, known around the world
for his music, but he has an even more legendary ancestor, a man
with a name which is synonymous with all that was good and
heroic about the American pioneers. Courageous adventurer
Daniel Boone is a huge figure in American folklore, rivalling Davy
Crockett in the popularity stakes. He was a frontiersman, trapper,
surveyor, builder and judge of great renown and today he still
features in story books, traversing the Cumberland Gap and the
Appalachian Mountains to establish the Wilderness Road to
Kentucky.

'Defiance', Daniel Boone's final home, lies in the peaceful
Femme Osage Valley, 25 miles from St Louis, Missouri. He arrived
in that untamed region in 1799 with about 100 other families
from Kentucky. At the time, Missouri was a Spanish 'syndic' (a
territory under the syndicated government rule of Spain).
Supervised by Daniel himself, the building of 'Defiance' was
started in 1803. The area was well known for its blue limestone
quarries, and these provided the stone for the two-and-a-half-
foot-thick walling. Constructed to withstand freezing snow and

1

searing heat, the house was also armed with built-in gun posts as protection against the Indians. Inside, furniture, beams, fireplace mantels and doors were all made from the plentiful local walnut timber. The house stands to this day, and visitors can see authentic furniture and mementos contributed by Boone descendants, who abound in those parts. In the grassy grounds stand the remains of the Judgement Tree under which Daniel held civil and military court.

An independent man, Daniel had a reputation for being someone who disliked the public – even though he was obliged to meet them daily in his capacity as a judge. Such was his dislike of 'being around people' that he made it a point not to live within five miles of others. This might have led to a very lonely existence, were it not for the fact that he and his wife produced 10 children! The house itself was always alive with activity. In his latter years, Daniel became a national hero, well respected and renowned. He died in a small bedroom at the family homestead in 1820 at the ripe old age of 86, by which time stories of his exploits as a younger man had already found a firm footing in the nation's folklore.

One hundred and fourteen years later, a proud descendant of the great pioneer, Pat Boone was born in the small country town of Jacksonville on 1 June 1934 – a bakingly hot day in the drought-gripped Sunshine State of Florida.

Pat's maternal grandparents, Julian (JC) and Lela Pritchard, had set up a construction business working in and around Jacksonville. With no privileged college education, JC was self-taught, gaining experience first-hand by working on the railroad and in carpentry, and by building his own house. He became an entrepreneur and owner of a thriving construction company. His marriage to Lela produced four children, although one died in infancy. Their eldest daughter Margaret was born on 10 May 1909. She was a bright girl with a gentle, caring nature and it was no surprise to JC and Lela when their daughter enrolled at Florida State University to train as a nurse. At the same time, Margaret's brother Morris also enrolled to study architecture. It was Morris who introduced Margaret to a fellow student named Archie Boone.

Archie Altman Boone was a few years older than Margaret, having been born in Nashville, Tennessee, on 6 April 1906, the only child of Ernest and Etta Lou Boone. The Boones later moved to Clovis, New Mexico, where Ernest pursued a butcher's trade as well as doing some homesteading. Life was unfulfilling in Clovis, however, so the family relocated to Kentucky. Then they moved on again to the warmth of Florida and to the schooling in architecture hankered after by the ambitious Archie.

Archie and Margaret knew each other for six years before they became romantically involved. Margaret's oldest brother and Archie were best friends, almost as close as brothers. During the summer Archie would work for Margaret's building contractor father. He quickly became one of the family – even to the extent of JC calling him 'son' and Lela doing his laundry. In time the fledgling friendship between Archie and Margaret developed into a marriage that would last for the next 67 years. The couple were married on 6 October 1932 in Brunswick, Georgia. Meanwhile, in Boston, the Great Depression was causing would-be president Franklin D. Roosevelt concern as he put final plans together to introduce a five-day week and federal aid to the unemployed if he was elected. Archie and Margaret certainly needed the strength of a loving marriage as they supported each other through the economic turmoils and war tragedies that followed.

When Pat was born, his parents were in their prime, making the most of their early twenties. The day before the baby's birth, Archie found himself in dire need of a haircut. Sitting patiently in line at the barber's, he joined in the light-hearted banter. He told his Jacksonville neighbours about his close kinship with the renowned Daniel Boone. Adventure comics and Hollywood movies were still featuring the hero even in the early twentieth century, and many a movie at the Jacksonville theatre had depicted wildly elaborate versions of Daniel Boone's historic exploits.

The other men in the shop fell to joking about poor Archie's lack of similarity to his heroic ancestor. John the barber, clearly feeling more charitable towards his customer, offered to wait and let Archie go home to fetch his 'pioneer's coon-skin hat', so that he could cut both sets of hair at once.

Refusing the kind offer, Archie settled himself in the barber's chair, and attention turned from Old Man Boone to the new Boone baby, expected at any time. Archie explained how worried he was about his wife, with the baby due the next day. 'She'll be glad when it's all over, John.'

'Sure she will! Are ya gonna call the little fella Daniel Boone?'

'No, John, we think our first's gonna be a baby gal. Though whether it's a boy or a girl, one thing's for sure: the young 'un's gonna be the *great-great-great-great-grandchild* of ol' Daniel!'

When the baby arrived the next day after a long and exhausting labour in the Florida heat, its parents were taken completely by surprise. Against all their expectations, the baby was a healthy boy. On his birth certificate the first child of Archie and Margaret was burdened with the lofty-sounding, hastily chosen name of Charles Eugene Boone. They had been so sure the baby was a girl that they had selected no male names in advance. For weeks before the birth, the excited parents had been convinced that the restless baby in Margaret's womb was a girl, and they had firmly decided to call her Patricia. Margaret had shared this certainty with friends and family, who all started knitting baby garments in pink. These were hurriedly substituted for a more appropriate blue upon the arrival in the world of Charles Eugene!

According to family legend, the midwife had unwittingly prophetic words to say as she handed the newborn baby to his mother for the first time. After slapping the new arrival gently to stimulate his breathing, the midwife was surprised at the volume of noise the crying baby produced. Charles Eugene continued to exercise his lungs to full effect as she cleaned him up. Barely audible over the din, the midwife laughed, 'Well, Margaret, I guess this beautiful young 'un took you by surprise. And judging by the noise he's makin', he's got a mighty fine pair of lungs – he'll be a good singer one day, you mark my words!'

Archie came in to see his wife and baby. 'Oh, congratulations Mama, that boy's beautiful!' he exclaimed. 'Now I can look forward to some baseball in our backyard...'

Margaret sighed. 'Archie, I was kinda looking forward to calling our baby Pat...'

'We can still call the baby Pat!' said Archie as inspiration struck. 'It's a name that'll double up for either a boy *or* a girl.'

Thus, undaunted by the gender surprise, the new parents gave the nickname 'Pat' to their firstborn son. The name stuck so firmly that, even more than 60 years later, he will answer to no other.

Pat has absolutely no recollection of sunny Jacksonville. Archie and Margaret moved to Nashville, Tennessee, in 1935 when he was only a year old. The move enabled Archie to take up a job in a small construction company with his Uncle Jack. The first Boone house in Nashville was in Donelson, not far from the Hermitage, the home of the early American hero Andrew Jackson. Later the family moved to Gale Lane and then to a 10-acre plot in Lone Oak Road in a quiet, residential quarter of the town. (It was not always such a peaceful area. The 'lone oak' was an old site for horse-thief executions – a hanging tree, to be exact.)

Music City was to have a huge influence on the growing boy. Even today, after spending a year in busy London, several years in bustling New York and some decades in glitzy Southern California, Pat still considers himself to be a Tennessean. Whenever Nashville is mentioned, his thoughts leap back to that happy childhood home. 'You may take the boy out of Tennessee, but you'll never take Tennessee out of the boy!' he says. 'I might have been born in Florida, but I grew up in Nashville. That's where most of my boyhood memories live. It was there that I caught my first crawdads, learned to whistle, sold buttercups on the side of the road, camped out on my first Scout hike, smoked Indian cigars, milked my only cows, sold my only calves, picked a ukulele ... Nashville was where I used to sit on the porch-swing talking to Mama and Daddy, discussing the day's events. And it was there I learned to pray. Yes, all of that and much more is Nashville to me.'

For Archie and Margaret's generation, hard work was a God-ordained way of life. They earnestly tried to foster love and Christian values in their children, joining the local Church of Christ. Highly conservative and exclusive, the Church of Christ stressed the necessity of water baptism for salvation – upholding the strong conviction that all doctrine should arise solely from Scripture and nothing else. An often quoted motto was, 'Speak where the Bible speaks and be silent where it is silent.' The Church nurtured the young Pat not only in the disciplines of faith but also with a passion for music. As a toddler at the Sunday gatherings, sitting on his mother's knee, he would listen closely to the grandiose hymns. Too young to read the words, he would whistle along to the tunes instead. Often the families in the seats around the Boones would turn mid-song to smile at the toddler's original accompaniment. Pat also showed off his whistling skills in the local stores, much to the amusement of other shoppers. Tickled as they were by his skill, no one ever dreamed that this infant would one day rise to the top of the music profession.

Pat never lost touch with those first musical experiences in the Nashville church. Using his worldwide success as a platform, he would later include a considerable amount of Christian music in his secular song repertoire. He would even revert to some of those old hymnal favourites from his boyhood church, introducing the songs to millions of people around the globe.

Without doubt, Christian music made a significant contribution to Pat's emotional development. He was continually drawn to this musical genre – it was all around him from the start, and was an integral part of Nashville life and culture. His mother sang hymns around the house, then Pat began to learn the words and melodies of his first Sunday School songs, and from then on he developed a passion for the most majestic hymns. 'Everything seemed very evangelically orientated back then. Most of our community were very involved in church activities in one way or another. Popular music and gospel music were intimately coupled down South. I'll always be beholden to the legacy of those old sacred songs. Culturally, they blended into my entertainment world, uniquely mixing Christian values with leisure. Traditionally, white spirituals were channelled down through successive generations. Entertainers and evangelists amalgamated them into the mainstream of popular music and hymnody. Still today, cross-pollination of musical styles continues. I've called upon all these diverse traditions to form my own repertoire.'

Early on in their marriage, Archie and Margaret had covenanted to commit themselves to a Christian lifestyle, come what may. Always smartly but simply dressed, Mother and Father Boone were slight in bodily stature but strong in moral influence – typical 'middle America' stock – and they worked hard to instil the same morality in their children, Pat, his brother Nick and sisters Margie and Judi. At times, the close family did have to weather severe storms. Margaret suffered a couple of devastating and painful miscarriages after the birth of her two daughters, and the years of the Great Depression were desperately tough for everyone. Yet they seemed to survive every blow with dignity and fortitude – and there was always, it seems, a song to be sung!

As often happens in a marriage, Providence seems to bring together two people with different, and often opposing, character traits. This was certainly true of Pat's parents. He remembers his father as a gentle, philosophical man, someone to whom his children could turn for sound counsel. An early riser, he would be awake at 5.30 a.m., making time for Bible reading before he went off to work at his contracting company. Pat's mother, on the other hand, was less philosophical and rather more practical in her approach. Her no-nonsense character was the weightiest influence in the children's lives, as their father was out at work most of the time. It nearly always fell to her to mete out discipline when necessary – which was very often in the case of the two boys. What Mama said, Mama meant!

Today Pat confirms his deep appreciation of his parents. 'Humanly speaking, Mama and Daddy were insignificant individuals, but their devout Christian life played a crucial part in my early development. I can see them now in our humble homestead on Sunday morning. Early in the day, after making the beds and eating breakfast together, they would prepare us as a family for church in a disciplined fashion. It was a divine rendezvous that they made sure they never missed. The weekly Sunday worship was their time to express their personal thanksgiving. Also, midweek, they would lovingly remember family and friends in prayer. Mama would sometimes tearfully gather up her anxieties and express them in prayer. At other times, while cooking or doing the family laundry, she'd sing a well-loved hymn – perhaps "Abide With Me".'

After the Sunday worship was ended, with their spiritual priorities met, Pat's parents were clearly refreshed and ready for whatever the week ahead might bring. Pat looks back nostalgically on those childhood years. 'As Dolly Parton's song put it so well, those were "the good ole days when times were bad"! Sometimes life was certainly good, but it was also tough and often challenging. Our parents learned the secret of satisfaction.' Such a positive and optimistic outlook rubbed off on the Boones' children. On chilly winter evenings the family routinely gathered around the crackling fire. No matter how tired they were, one parent would read out the allotted portion from the family Bible. Then they would all sing a hymn together. 'Rock of Ages' was one of Pat's favourites.

> Rock of Ages, cleft for me,
> Let me hide myself in Thee…
> > Augustus Montague Toplady

Margaret and Archie took care to nurture their eldest son's growing personal relationship with his Maker. It was a safe and encouraging environment for Pat to develop his faith – firmly held family convictions were reinforced by what he learned at church meetings. He was encouraged by everyone around him to use his God-given musical talents to good purpose, both in his local church and later in his international recordings and concerts. He could have asked for no better start in life.

After decades of a stable and happy partnership, Margaret and Archie were asked what qualities made a good marriage. Margaret said that she believed in keeping the doors of communication open and being willing to talk. The couple admitted that they had completely different personalities which often led to little arguments, but over the years, they said, they had learned the art of forgiving each other quickly and not holding grudges. Archie admitted to being a procrastinator, whilst Margaret was the one who always thought ahead and made plans. Both believed that an ability to compromise was one of the keys to their strong marriage. Having a good sense of humour helped too. They had also agreed never to argue in front of their children, keeping their discussions for a nightly walk around the driveway after the children had gone to bed. The couple shared a vibrant Christian faith, an important rallying point in their marriage. The outward sign of this was their love of others. Many needy people were brought into the Boone home, enriching the lives of all concerned. Last, but not least, they believed that praying together about everything was the most essential element of their lasting marriage.

Living through the Great Depression could not have been easy, and that troubled time must have tested even the strongest relationship. America's working classes experienced desperate hardship, with many struggling to find employment following the Wall Street Crash of 1929. The chilling wind of economic deprivation continued to blow strongly across the country for many years. It forced every working family, including the Boones, to adapt as best they could to the reality – or at the very least the threat – of unemployment. For Archie, a trained architect, earning a basic living and providing for his large family was a strenuous, sacrificial task that bit deep into family time. Never afraid of hard work, he put in all the hours he could at his Uncle Jack's small construction company.

Meanwhile Margaret, a registered nurse, faced up to the task of raising their fast-growing children. Even if times were hard, there was no relaxing of standards in the Boone home. She and Archie had taken the words of King Solomon to heart: 'Train up a child in the way he should go: and when he is old, he will not depart from it' (Proverbs 22:6). Even as young children, they were expected to exercise self-discipline, particularly in public, and most particularly in church.

Although Pat generally enjoyed church as a young boy, his attention span was understandably short. He was always wriggling around in his seat, trying to see where his friends were. Many a sermon passed while he counted the bricks in the wall or fiddled with his hymn book. This kind of fidgeting did not go down at all well with Margaret. She would not tolerate bad behaviour from her children anywhere, and her discipline was of the hands-on kind. More than once, under the gaze of a curious congregation, a struggling Pat would find himself marched down the aisle and out of the church. In the forecourt his mother would give him a hearty spanking. 'Son, this'll hurt me more than it hurts you … but you've got to learn to be obedient to me and your Daddy and be respectful to the Good Lord when we're in His house on His day!' Pat, fighting back the tears, would then be marched straight back to the family's pew at the front of the church.

Margaret remained convinced that such practical lessons of discipline chipped off the rough edges found in every naturally wayward character. 'If you spare the rod, you spoil the child' was the generally accepted outlook of the day. Looking back now, Pat says he never felt any resentment against his parents for such

10

corporal punishment. 'I believe that "short, sharp shock" type of discipline, with its following conciliatory embrace, was an appropriate part of my loving Christian upbringing. It was also something we carried on with our own children.' Pat laughs as he recalls the last time his mother spanked him. 'I was a strapping, six-foot-tall young man of 17! I'd been squabbling and fighting with my brother Nick. Pulling us apart, big as we were, our dear Mama spanked us with her sewing-machine belt. I can tell you, that belt stung like fire!'

The Christian ethos of the Boone family homestead in Lone Oak Road was burned deep into the memories, motives and values of the young Pat. During his adult life, he was destined to travel countless miles from that starting point, but wherever he went, he found that the down-to-earth piety he had learned from his parents had prepared him well for life's battles.

It was a secure and loving home, and Pat remembers the house being perpetually full of the delicious aroma of cooking as his mother prepared her unique Southern dishes. The timber residence also proved to be a sturdy, sheltering tower on those unavoidable days when weeping and tragedy became a part of life. Such painful times, however, are outnumbered in Pat's memory by the light-hearted days of song and laughter. His obvious love for his 'down-home' childhood and the uplifting values he learned from his parents were clearly reflected in Pat's own life and in the songs he sang. More often than not, his personal choice of repertoire would include those inspirational songs that spoke up for God, country, home, freedom, integrity, family, marriage and solid relationships – the kind of things that, in his view, matter most.

Until their deaths – within weeks of each other – in the spring of 2000, Margaret and Archie remained in the house Pat fondly remembers as his childhood home. Pat is inclined to be emotional about those faraway days. 'My favourite spot in the whole world was that old porch-swing at our house on the outskirts of town.

So many happiest memories are etched into the angles, corners, colours and smells of that old home.'

Archie bought the 10-acre plot and the house in Lone Oak Road in 1940 for a mere $5,500. Back then, it was almost out in the countryside. The Burton Elementary School was later built at the back end of the property – which was wonderful because Pat could simply race through his own back pasture and get to school just on time. Then the John T. Moore High School was built just across the street from the house: by then, the Nashville metropolis had moved out their way and they were no longer on the edge of the open countryside. Today the area is wholly residential, but the old house is still the same, and the 1.5-acre lawn which Pat and Nick used to cut with a clattering hand-pushed mower is still intact. The Nashville tour buses still go by there. His parents loved to wave at the fans from the yard or the porch. Pat would wave too, if he was there sitting on the old swing. In Pat's eyes, the tourists did not realize it, but they were looking at heaven on earth. They were also, of course, looking at a piece of musical history.

Throughout his carefree childhood, surrounded as he was by encouragement both at home and at church, Pat's attention was invariably captivated by the sound of music. It was always his first love. During the winter months, music filled many happy hours. Aged six and seven respectively, Nick and Pat were paraded before their kinsfolk and asked to perform. Their grandparents, JC and Lela Pritchard, had a piano in their living room and urged them on. 'Come on, boys, give us "Sentimental Journey"! Let's hear it!' Pat still remembers the sweet taste of the applause from the assembled relatives – before they all became engrossed in discussing the movie sensation *Gone with the Wind*, which had scooped five Academy Awards in the previous year.

Life was not all music, of course, and there was much else to absorb the young Pat. As his school reports testify, Pat's grades were exceptionally high, hardly ever dipping below the 90 per cent mark. In better weather, glad to be outdoors, Pat abandoned his music-making and headed for the sports field with his friends. Those years nurtured in him an uninhibited, earthy sense of humour – hardly surprising, as he grew up amid the realities of farmyard animal reproduction practices and bodily functions! (There were always animals around the Boone family homestead.) Growing up surrounded by the pleasant green spaces of Tennessee, Pat also revelled in outdoor country life. After school, he and his friends would climb trees or explore the many brooks, ponds and lakes, ready-made playgrounds for adventurous youngsters.

Pat may have developed a strong sense of humour, but he was still open to embarrassment, and – as growing children often find – a parent was the source of the awkwardness. Pat remembers being mortified at having to travel anywhere in his father's pick-up truck. It did nothing for his pride. Exposed to the elements, Pat and his siblings had to suffer the indignity of riding on the back of the pick-up seated on a home-made, hard-timber form. It was the family's only vehicle and, unless it was raining very heavily, Pat was always too embarrassed to allow his father to take him to school in it. Despite the fact that he was nearly always running late, he chose to race across the fields and squeeze under the fence into the school grounds rather than arrive at the front gate in such an 'uncool' manner. It was a memorable day, therefore, when Archie arrived home at the wheel of a two-door black Chevrolet. Pat was 13 then, and relieved that his pick-up days were finally over. Although it had no extras apart from a heater, that shiny black vehicle seemed like the most beautiful car in the world to Pat.

Pat has never been a good time-keeper, always tending to arrive late, and this trait clearly started early. It was not just that he was often late for school. Many a happy day ended with him returning home late, tired and dirty after an adventure with his friends. His mother always demanded a detailed explanation for his lateness – to say nothing of the dirt and the torn clothes. 'My, my, my! Where have you been? Why are you so late? You look a mess! Look at the dirt on your trousers … and you've torn your shirt *again*! Get my needle and thread. I hope you and those other friends of yours have been behaving!' Before the red-faced Pat could splutter out any real reply, his mother would be off again. 'Go and get out of those dirty clothes. Get yourself washed … you can't eat your dinner like that!' The scolding never did lead to an improvement in his time-keeping – and it certainly did not stop him getting into scrapes when he was out exploring with his friends. There was too much to see.

Even at the height of his fame, Pat's love of the outdoors still dominated. He got out to the countryside whenever he could. He particularly cherishes a fishing trip he once took with his Granddaddy Pritchard. By then Pat was well known as a teenage heart-throb. Just sitting by the picturesque riverbank brought some peace and normality back to his life, he recalls. He was not on show, he was just a grandson again, spending time with his grandfather. As the long hours passed, their conversation trickled over a myriad of subjects: politics, fame, money, retirement, homes … nothing too deep, just gentle conversation as the floats hopped on the surface of the stream.

When his grandfather spoke about his own childhood, Pat was amazed to hear about the mischief that this 'old-timer' had got up to as a boy. JC recounted stories of how he and some other boys had sneaked into a farmer's field and gorged themselves on juicy watermelons, how they had rearranged the clothes on a scarecrow, and had smoked tobacco with the hired hands who helped in the fields. He had been a real little rascal, Pat realized. 'Huck Finn would have made a good buddy of yours, Grandpop!' Pat told him. Then he smiled and added, 'Hey, you used to spank us with that big ol' mitt of yours for some of the things we did as kids! It still brings me out in red spots when I think about it. But *you* used to do the same things – *and* worse!'

'Ah, that all changes with marriage, son,' replied JC. 'If your dear grandmother hadn't been around, I'd have been out there with you! I'd have shown you how to get into a melon in double-quick time. Those suckers don't taste better than when they're stolen and eaten in secret…'

CHAPTER 2

GOODNIGHT MAMA,
GOODNIGHT PAPA

Deep inside this country boy, I'll always be the same!
Marijohn Wilkin

THE DREAMY BALLAD 'There's A Goldmine In The Sky' remains one of the most surprising of Pat's hits from the late 1950s. The catchy song originally came to prominence via Bing Crosby in 1938, during the golden era of Hollywood's 'singing cowboys'. Those were the romantic, sunset-reddened days when the white-hatted heroes played by Gene Autry, Roy Rogers, Tex Ritter, Rex Allen and Jimmy Wakeley rode freely across the silver screens of a million cinemas chasing the black-hatted rustlers, cheered on by a multitude of schoolboys – Pat Boone among them. Pat and his friends often played 'cowboys and Indians', and Pat revelled in the nickname of 'The Boone Kid'. When they were not outside enacting their own versions of the drama, the youngsters could often be found at a local movie theatre in Nashville, absorbed in yet another singing cowboy film. For Pat, the open-air heroics, the songs and the popcorn were the perfect combination.

'When I was just a little guy, with my gang of buddies in our cowboy hats, we'd often take off to the Saturday afternoon picture shows. At those matinees we'd ride and shoot along with Gene Autry, Roy Rogers and the others. One of the highlights of those movies for me was the western songs – the guitars and harmony singing just sent chills up my young spine. The first time I heard "Blueberry Hill" and "There's A Goldmine In The Sky" was when Gene Autry sang them in the movies.'

Pat's dreamy version of 'There's A Goldmine In The Sky', recorded on 13 June 1957, nonetheless owed as much to Bing Crosby's crooning as it did to Gene Autry's 'singing cowboy' act for its easy-listening quality. It was a song with a parable-like application, speaking of dreaming big and being rewarded in due time if one endured to the end – an uplifting theme that appealed to the Boone philosophy of life. Years later, Pat was thrilled to have the chance to sing the song as a duet with Roy Rogers on the *Pat Boone TV Show*. 'How many of those kids in that dusty old movie theatre grew up to have the one and only Roy Rogers on his own show?' he gloats now.

On those hot, hazy afternoons during the long summer vacations, Pat and his friends would sneak into the local farmers' fields to imitate Roy Rogers and play 'cowboys and Indians' between the tall and leafy sweetcorn plants. Winding in and out and crouching low to the ground, it was easy to hide. 'The Boone Kid' soon learned to lie very still and listen for the tell-tale rustling of stems to pinpoint a passing 'Indian'. He would wait quietly until the enemy was close enough to be caught with a bellowed 'BANG! BANG!' It never seemed to bother the boys that the Indian would invariably stand up unharmed after the point-blank shot and get right back into the game. Besides, what fun is it if everyone is killed too quickly?

Pat, incidentally, happened to know what it was like to be a real 'cowboy', and heroics on horseback just did not feature in his experience. Rosemary, the Boones' cow, was unfortunately prone to wander and it was often Pat's job to go chasing after her through the neighbourhood, in an attempt to herd her back home. At the same time, he would have to try to make good the havoc she had wrought on laundry lines, flowerbeds and so on.

17

Most unpleasant and demeaning of all, of course, was having to scoop up the deposits that Rosemary had left scattered liberally behind her. It was certainly nothing to sing about.

During Pat's boyhood years, America started to climb out of the economic depression that had persisted for a decade. Just when it seemed as if better times were back again, however, it turned out that graver international stresses were looming ever closer. The storm clouds of a possible world war were hovering over Europe and the Far East, threatening to shatter the New World's fragile peace and growing prosperity. It seemed at first that the USA would remain uninvolved. Certainly, peaceful, pastoral Nashville seemed an eternity away from the troubles of those distant nations, although it was not possible to ignore entirely the warnings of imminent calamity. Nonetheless, for most Americans at the end of the 1930s, including those in sunny Tennessee, their involvement in the new war was not yet personal.

This calm scenario was shattered on Sunday 7 December 1941. In Nashville that morning, with the Church of Christ's worship service over, Margaret was cooking the family's Sunday dinner. She sang as she worked, trying to dispel her uneasy thoughts about the war and what it might mean for her family. The preacher's sermon that morning had offered a twofold message: 'Fear not, but be ready!' They had sung 'Amazing Grace' as the closing hymn, and the words had never seemed more meaningful.

> Amazing grace! How sweet the sound
> That saved a wretch like me;
> I once was lost, but now am found,
> Was blind, but now I see.
>
> John Newton

Archie and his two sons came in laughing from a game they had been playing in the yard, and the mood in the house seemed to lift. Archie went to switch the radio on, promising Margaret he would find some music they could enjoy while the final preparations for lunch were under way. As was typical with those old wireless sets, it took a few minutes to warm up – and when it did, the family's laughter and songs were silenced as they heard the words of an urgent news item that interrupted the relaxing Sunday music. Hawaii's Pearl Harbor had been bombed that morning by Japanese aeroplanes. Shocked to the core, the family listened as the voice of President Roosevelt announced the grim tidings of world war. America was ready at last to use the full power of her manufacturing and military resources in support of the Allies.

That evening, the pastel-painted sanctuary of the church was packed. Many faces not seen for months in the pews were in attendance – and so it continued for the duration of the hostilities. The subject of the war was top of the conversation agenda and the church prayer list. Like many other families, the Boones found that their Christian faith was a continuous, ready supply of strength, comfort and assurance in the face of daily worry and struggle. They were also helped by a strong sense of community fellowship in the neighbourhood. Everyone supported everyone else, and the Boones were always ready to welcome any needy person into their home (although, Pat remembers, there was not much room to spare, what with four children and a shifting population of cats, once as many as 17, some with kittens on the way).

In time, after initial defeats and costly disappointments, the Allies started to accrue victories. People once again dared to hope for peace. Newspaper headlines announced the securing of victory in North Africa, then in Europe, and finally in the Far East. In 1945 came the collapse and surrender of Nazi Germany, followed by the capitulation of Japan after the dropping of the two atomic bombs. After VJ Day, Archie, Margaret and their immediate families headed for church to give thanks for the long-awaited victory and the return of peace. The whole community looked forward to the return of those discharged from military service and the freed prisoners of war.

Even though he was just a young boy during the war years, Pat could not fail to be affected by the dramas and tensions of those days. Looking back, he says he is most grateful to his parents for the constancy of the Christian example they displayed. It could have been a frightening and turbulent time for the children, but from beginning to end Pat felt safe, protected by the steadiness of his family and his parents' determined strength.

Life went on despite the war, of course, and for the youngsters there was plenty of time for fun and friendship. One of Pat's closest boyhood friends was Milford Smith. Together they were an energetic, mischievous duo, guaranteed to be courting trouble in one way or another. Milford's father was a busy insurance man and a devout Christian – although the boys did not see each other at church because the Smiths were Baptists (later joining the Methodist Church) while the Boones were fervent members of the Church of Christ. It did not spoil the boys' friendship in any way, but Pat vividly remembers the differences between the families.

'Our Church of Christ was so sure of its strict doctrinal position that all other church groups were classified as "unsaved"! I remember that the Smith family prayed more than us Boones, and yet we often discussed their so-called errors, debating whether they were "*real* Christians" or not, and whether they'd make it to heaven.' The four Boone children would often walk up the road with their mother to the Smiths' house to play with Milford and his sister Delores. 'Often in mid-afternoon at the Smith home, Mr Smith would get down on his knees before us kids and pray earnestly for both his family and ours! As a child, this always puzzled me as we Boones only tended to pray at church service times or mealtimes.'

Like most children of their age, Milford and Pat often stepped over the line from fun to mischief in their escapades – and sometimes this backfired. They had thought that throwing stones in the local rock quarry was great fun; better still, they discovered, was the excitement of finding discarded bottles by the roadside and smashing them on the asphalt. They had no thought for the amount of splintered glass they were scattering across the highway, but in the end it was not a car that got harmed. One day, while he was gleefully smashing yet another bottle, a piece of glass bounced off the road and cut deeply into the right side of Pat's chin.

The gash was quickly covered with a Band-Aid dressing, but worse was in store. The next day Pat and Milford were boxing and sparring together, when Milford caught Pat a hefty left undercut on the jaw. Margaret observed the blood streaming from the reopened wound on her son's face, and speedily dispatched him to the doctor for emergency stitches. These were administered, as was the custom in those days, without anaesthetic. It was a memorable, if painful, day, and Pat ended up scarred for life. In later years, Pat always gave the same reply whenever he was asked about the scar. 'Oh, that ain't nothin'!' he would say casually. 'I got that in the ring when I was boxing as a kid…'

By the time they were 11, Pat and Milford had moved on to a shared enthusiasm for baseball and often practised their skills by throwing the ball back and forth in the Boones' back yard. One evening, in the rapidly diminishing light, the ball was thrown too far. It landed somewhere in the thick, long grass of the pasture. Pat set off in pursuit. Then came his mother's call from the back steps: 'Suppertime! Come on in! Milford, it's time for you to go on home, son!' Her tone warned against delay. Pat was now on his knees in the long grass, frantically searching for his precious leather baseball. It was a new one, recently given to him by his father. He could not leave it until the next morning. What if it should be damaged by the dew? He was also painfully aware that, with hot food on the table, his mother's patience was quickly becoming exhausted.

Almost in tears, he decided to pray. The scene is vivid in his mind even today. With eyes squeezed tightly shut, he stuttered,

'Oh ... um ... God, this is Pat, Pat Boone. I've lost my new base-ball. Please could you help me find it? I ask this in Jesus' Name. Amen.' He opened his eyes and, through his tears, he saw it! In the tall grass the ball virtually shone white in the moonlight. He grabbed the precious possession and hurried inside. Throughout supper he could not get that answered prayer off his mind. The experience made a deep and lasting impression on him.

The following year, Milford and Pat were team-mates in the eighth-grade baseball team. By then, aged 12, Pat was also becoming increasingly girl-conscious, falling heavily for Joan Askew, a pretty blonde at his school. The daughter of a city attorney, Joan clearly came from a well-to-do family and Pat, living on the 10-acre property stocked with Rosemary the cow, plus chickens and other farmyard animals, started to perceive himself as disadvantaged by what he saw as his farmyard 'country boy' image. Joan was certainly rather cool towards him, although he had once managed to brush her lips with a kiss. Now wholly ashamed to be seen in the company of the cow, Pat started to resist undertaking farm chores. Ultimately, however, he knew he had to take his share of responsibility along with the rest of the family, and he usually did what he was asked, despite his embarrassment.

One day, while he was out herding Rosemary back home after one of her 'great escapes', to his dismay he spied the Askew car heading towards him and his charge. Hoping that he had not been seen by Joan and her father, he dived headfirst into the ditch. Luckily it was dry. Keeping his head down, Pat fervently hoped that the car would just speed past. To his consternation, it screeched to a halt right opposite his hiding place and Joan ran over to the ditch. There she discovered Pat, his raised rear end sticking up, his hands over his head, face down in the dirt. 'Pat, oh Pat! Are you all right?'

Red-faced and dusty, Pat searched desperately for a plausible explanation. 'Oh, hello, Joan ... er ... I'm OK ... I guess. I just tripped! Nice day!' He tried to sound casual, and did his best to ignore Rosemary as the overfriendly cow butted his back with her wet nose. Joan and her father drove away laughing. Pat had the uneasy feeling that the truth of his 'fall' had dawned on them. From then on, Pat was teased at school for his 'country boy' reputation.

The Boone home was comfortable, but not excessively spacious. The two bedrooms housed Pat's parents and two sisters, while Pat and his brother shared a bed on the back porch area. Then, at the age of 12 and seeking some independence, Pat cleared a space in the dusty attic which became his own private bedroom. The attic had no ceiling, just the bare roof timbers and rafters, but the planking on the floor and a fold-up bed was all Pat needed to make himself at home. There were two windows, which he cleaned carefully and which afforded him a view of the side yard and the road.

Pat says that attic bedroom was the place where he learned to pray and where he began to develop a real relationship with God. 'The attic became my trysting place with God. I discovered that He heard my prayers in the humble bedroom in Lone Oak Road. I did my own Bible study, and it was there that I gave my life to Him and asked Him to use me in whatever way He wished. Then, when I was 13, I walked down the church aisle and publicly confessed my faith. Choosing Jesus as Lord was the most momentous decision of my life. At that service, the preacher reminded us of Joshua's words to the nation of Israel: "Choose you this day whom ye will serve … but as for me and my house, we will serve the LORD" (Joshua 24:15). Before family, neighbours and friends, I confessed my need of Christ's forgiveness and was immediately baptized by immersion in water by our minister, Norvell Young.'

Pat's love affair with sacred music, of course, had started well before his commitment to Christ. Like most churches, the congregational singing at Pat's church was spiced up with special music from home-grown choirs, quartets and song leaders. The type of gospel music known as 'soul' began in such churches, although it was later somewhat taken over by the secular music industry. Many churches, particularly those from the evangelical or pentecostal traditions, were characterized by their strong musical emphasis and style. They were, and still are, a significant part of the social fabric of small towns and rural communities in parts of America. They have produced many ambitious singers and musicians (Whitney Houston and Mariah Carey are just two famous examples) who started out on their individual career paths as church singers.

It was not long before the quality of Pat's singing voice was recognized. In the summer of 1948 the preacher suggested to Archie that his son should sing for some of the church services. Archie was proud to hear his son's talent praised, and readily gave permission for the preacher to invite Pat to sing. Pat did not need much persuasion, but his mother raised one big problem: did he have enough smart clothes? Archie immediately proposed a visit to the local department store. Nothing was to stand in the way of his son's moment in the spotlight. The next day, Archie took time out of his busy schedule and went shopping with Pat. Pat was so excited that he even forgot to be embarrassed about having to sit in the rickety old pick-up truck. Despite the tight family budget, Archie bought Pat some Sunday-best trousers, a shirt, a tie and a pair of shoes. 'Wow, did I feel dressed up that day at the store!' recalls Pat. Much to his father's amusement, he paraded proudly up and down the shop in his new finery. 'Peacock!' whispered Archie into the ear of the store clerk.

At the next Sunday morning meeting, Pat sang his heart out with the old Ira Sankey hymn, 'Softly And Tenderly'. It was one of his favourites, a song that Pat had identified with even as a very young child. It was a gentle 'invitation' hymn, urging wanderers to 'come home' to the Heavenly Father. Some years later, in 1957, Pat still cherished the hymn so much that he insisted on including it in his *Hymns We Love* album collection. The public obviously cherished it too – *Hymns We Love* reached number 21 in the national popular music charts, a staggering position for a gospel album. Back in 1948, the preacher was delighted with young Pat's singing, and told Margaret and Archie that they should be proud of their gifted son.

That first success brought immediate rewards for Pat. He revelled in the praise and admiration he received. Despite the encouragement they gave him, however, the Church of Christ held strictly to one belief which might have proved rather restrictive for a budding singer like Pat. Unusually for America's 'Bible Belt', which was renowned for its diversity of Christian musical expression, the Church of Christ forbade the use of any musical instruments in church worship. Pat perforce learned to sing a capella (using voice only) with great skill at a very early age. This discipline required perfect pitching, extra vocal proficiency and flair. Overjoyed at being asked to sing, young Pat barely noticed the lack of instrumentation at the time. 'It was always a joy and privilege, as a young teenager, being asked to go up to the wooden platform and lead the singing in our church. It was my first experience of singing before a crowd.'

Talent shows soon followed. Many were held in the theatre in nearby Belle Meade, and there was a very different atmosphere from the serious attention Pat was used to in church. The youthful audiences lacked concentration, and contestants often battled to be heard above the din of indifference and teen chatter. The theatre manager recognized Pat's potential, however, and would always give him a loud, hyped introduction. 'Ooo-kay! Now, good folks, here's a *great* guy that I tip to be the next Bing Crosby! Give a warm Belle Meade welcome to ... your own ... PAT BOONE!' After many winning versions of songs such as 'It's Only A Paper Moon', Pat developed quite a taste for banana splits, the contest's top prize.

One Christmas shortly after the end of the war, another dimension was added to Pat's musical experiences. Much to the whole family's excitement, Archie bought some phonograph records for

Margaret, including some songs by Bing Crosby, and the children happily sang along to those popular pieces. Many more records were added to the collection as the years passed. Archie would choose carefully, knowing his wife's favourites were the classic crooners like Bing Crosby, Perry Como and Frank Sinatra. Thus began an enthralling pastime for all the household – they never tired of listening to the old 78s. Pat remembers learning an enormous amount about 'modern' singing simply through constant listening and singing along to the records as they spun. More and more, he says, he was sensing a musical calling on his life.

One song that stood out for him over the years was 'Goodnight Mama, Goodnight Papa', a sentimental Red Foley song co-penned by Marijohn Wilkin and Ken Burch. Sophisticated but approachable, Marijohn was a record producer, music arranger, songwriter and artiste, and could aptly be described as one of the mythmakers of Music City USA. Many years later, for the tribute album dedicated to his father-in-law Red Foley, Pat felt he must record Marijohn's emotional song in memory of his boyhood home and happy family times.

Most of Pat's neighbourhood friends attended the large Hillsboro School in Nashville, but Pat chose to go to Lipscomb High School instead. It was a Church of Christ school and he decided that was more appropriate, given the public commitment he had made to his faith. Besides, he could easily cycle to Lipscomb as it was only a couple of miles from home. Pat soon became the captain of the high school baseball team (he boasts of being a good hitter in those days, but admits to a lack of fielding skills!) and made friends with Tommy Pine, a short, stocky, athletic boy who was also in the team. Tommy had a sister called Janie and their father operated a successful plant business at his nursery just outside Nashville.

Pat was often to be found in the company of the pugnacious, energetic Tommy, even though Tommy was one year behind him. The two boys often got into trouble after school hours. Tommy had something of a chip on his shoulder and was always ready for a fist fight, no matter who the opponent might be. 'Tommy got into all kinds of conflicts,' Pat remembers, 'often with much heftier guys than himself!' Together, the boys shared many thrills, some of them heart-stoppingly dangerous. In downtown Nashville one day, they walked along the ledge on top of a six-storey building, peering down at the busy pavement below. Then they dared each other to jump over the decorative sections of the parapet and land on the eight-inch ledge in between. Today Pat says his stomach flips over just to contemplate such crazy antics. 'What were we *thinking* of?'

At the age of 15, Pat was thrilled to get a 'whizzer' – a bicycle with a small motor on the back wheel. It was only a modest, second-hand machine, but it proved useful for the trips he made to baseball games. By then he was playing in the American Legion games during the summer. Sometimes the whizzer was also employed for the occasional errand Margaret asked Pat to run. It had no basket, so its usefulness was limited, but Pat was just glad to be mobile. Tommy's transportation was rather more sophisticated: *he* had a car, a little coupé that his father had provided. It served as the duo's chariot most of the time.

One day, out at the lakes, they stopped at an exciting-looking suspension bridge over a river. The semicircular bridge spans looked worth checking out to those inveterate trouble-seekers. They duly climbed up the 150-foot structure above the fast-flowing water, and got a good view of the submerged rocks beneath. They had no plans to jump into the water from that height, but they did dare each other to walk along the bridge using the metal girders as stepping stones, jumping across the open spaces in between. Going up was difficult enough, but climbing down was much harder, as they had difficulty gauging just how far they should step each time. The safest way, they concluded, was to crawl down on all fours. They did manage to reach the ground without falling, but the fun could easily have backfired with fatal consequences. Pat just shakes his head in disbelief as he tells the story now.

They were also perfectly capable of getting into trouble without the extra buzz of physical danger. On another occasion, Tommy and Pat were downtown and decided to see a movie at the Paramount Theater. They had sufficient funds for the entrance fee, but chose instead to sneak in without paying. Stealing around the back, they scaled a fire escape ladder and tried a door on the first open-air landing. They rattled the bar but discovered that the door was locked, so they went higher. Meanwhile, their noise had alerted an usher inside the building. The boys finally came to an open door which led into the 'black balcony' – Nashville still operated strict segregation laws in those days, and black people were not allowed to sit with white people in the cinemas. Spying some ushers emerging on the landing beneath them, the boys darted into the darkened theatre, disturbing the audience on the balcony midway through a movie. Every eye left the screen and focused on the two conspicuously white youngsters. They had not chosen the best place to hide – they would stand out even if they took a seat and sat quietly.

'Oh, man!' muttered Tommy in the darkness. 'We gotta get out of here!' They darted through the balcony towards the exit stairs, now hotly pursued by two puffing ushers. Racing into the corridor, they hurtled down the staircase, only to encounter two more ushers standing with their hands outstretched. Tommy bumped straight into the first usher, knocking him to the ground, while Pat met the second head on. Evading the grasping hands and thinking that escape was near at hand, Pat and Tommy began to enjoy the fun. They had nearly reached the street when their path was blocked by a robust figure dressed in a three-piece black suit. This was the cinema's manager, and he was clearly enraged. The boys screeched to an untidy halt and were grabbed firmly by the ushers who ran up behind them.

The manager summoned the police and within a minute or so a squad car pulled up outside the cinema. A curious crowd gathered. A policeman seized the boys' arms and marched them unceremoniously up the ramp to the waiting car, where he tried to bundle them into the back seat. Somehow, Tommy managed to break free and darted off down the street. There was no escape for Pat, however. He watched his friend speed away out of sight, then sat humiliated in the car as he was driven to the police station. To make matters worse, he was spied by several fellow students from Lipscomb, who looked on open mouthed as their junior class president was hauled away to jail.

At the police station his fingerprints were taken and he was told to phone his father. It was not a happy call, Pat remembers! Fortunately no charges were brought, but the 'fear of God' was put into Pat that day, as he trembled from head to toe. Tommy escaped scot free, of course, and soon cheered Pat up. When the boys met up afterwards, they relived their adventure over and over again and shared a good deal of laughter about it – although Pat, perhaps, did not entirely forget that Tommy had run away and left him behind.

Some time later, Tommy was at the Boone home for a meal. It was getting late and Tommy was offered a ride home by Archie. He went to bring the car round to the front door, while Tommy hurriedly put on his shoes and tied his laces. Pat urged him to hurry. 'Come on Tommy, I've got the front door open! Daddy's waiting – be quick!' As he said this, he actually latched the screen door closed instead of opening it. Appreciating the need not to keep his friend's father waiting, Tommy ran from the kitchen towards the front door, not noticing that the screen door was still shut. He hit the gauze at full speed, tearing the latch off and ripping the door off its hinges. Rising from the dusty floor, Tommy brushed himself down and eyed his sneering pal. 'I'll get you for that, Boone!' he said. 'You ain't gonna get away with that!'

Pat, as it turned out, suffered a double comeback on his mischief-making. The screen door had to be replaced and Archie gave Pat an appropriate whipping for his behaviour. A few weeks later, Tommy took his own revenge. He and Pat had been working at his father's nursery and it had been a hot, sweaty day. It was time for the youngsters to take a break, and Tommy jumped into the overheated, sticky cab of his father's pick-up truck to drive back to the house. Pat chose to ride the short distance astride the side fender and catch the cooling breeze. Holding on as tightly as he could, Pat did not allow for Tommy 's manoeuvring antics. Instead of turning gently out of the fields and onto the highway, Tommy put his foot down on the throttle, suddenly accelerating and then abruptly stopping. It was enough to throw Pat into the air, landing him in a tumble in a dirty ditch. Tommy leaned out of the cab, laughing loudly. 'Remember that ol' screen door, buddy?' The incident left Pat nursing bruises and cuts for weeks.

The incident at the Paramount Theater did not deter the rebellious duo for long, and they were soon back downtown looking for trouble. *Robin Hood and His Merry Men* was a boring movie as far as they were concerned, and one day they decided to liven it up a bit. Leaving their cinema seats in the darkness, they sneaked backstage to see what havoc they could create. Behind the screen they discovered a set of metal rods that they felt would make wonderful swords. Allying themselves with the roguish Sheriff of Nottingham, they dashed across the bright screen in dramatic black silhouette, brandishing their swords and shouting loudly, 'DOWN WITH THE KING!' Needless to say, the noisy Sheriff's gang were chased backstage, with the 'good guys' of the cinema in hot pursuit. Pat and Tommy got away, though, dashing through the stage door and disappearing into the crowd.

Some time later, one of Pat's other teenage friends purchased an old black hearse that he washed, waxed and polished up into something quite impressive. With the rest of their gang, Tommy and Pat would drive downtown and join in with the nightlife around the theatre district. Outside one of the theatres they would stage a fake fist fight. One punch would lead to another, until the apparently vicious fight would end with a dramatic stabbing. One combatant would fall down on the pavement, covered in tomato ketchup and feigning death. Shocked by the bloody drama, people would stop and stare, and someone would invariably call the police. Then the old black hearse would drive slowly round the corner and halt at the kerbside. Two well-dressed teenagers in black (trying hard to look like adults) would disembark and place the 'deceased' on a stretcher. Once the 'body' was neatly and ceremoniously stowed in the hearse, they would drive off again. All this had to be achieved before a siren announced the arrival of the police. 'Truthfully,' Pat smiles now, 'I doubt if we fooled anyone in the crowds back then with our impromptu piece of street theatre!'

Some of the pranks the gang perpetrated did go too far, however, and the boys were sometimes a nuisance to others at the very least. Pat was often aboard when, on warm afternoons and evenings, the lads would cruise down the main streets in their overcrowded car seeking the kind of fun that really meant mischief. Passing the line-ups at busy bus stops, they would lean out of the car to squirt staining red ketchup and yellow mustard over people's clothes. The general public was not amused, of course, but there was great merriment within the offenders' car.

Throughout this mildly rebellious time in Pat's life, there was a serious side to him too. Pangs of guilt often assailed him. He knew that his behaviour should match the Christian vows he had made, and he did try to talk to Tommy about his faith from time to time. During these years Mack Craig, Pat's high school principal, remained a kind of lighthouse, pointing the Boone ship away from shipwreck and into wholesome, safer waters. Pat remains grateful for Mack's influence. Not that much older than his students, Mack had achieved his status early in his career. Being quite young, he was able to befriend as well as guide his charges, and among those he particularly encouraged were Pat, Dick Beatty, Bobby Mason and Bill Bradshaw. These were all boys in whom Mack perceived leadership qualities, and he did his best to nurture them accordingly. Tommy Pine, Pat felt, was always rather jealous of not being in Mack's 'inner circle'.

Despite good guidance, however, Pat continued to provide fuel for his guilt-trips. One Christmas season, he and Tommy went on a shoplifting spree. There is no doubt, Pat says sadly, that he should have known better. He had no excuse for such behaviour. At the time, however, it seemed a thrilling kick to sneak unpaid-for goods out of some stores. The day's loot included sweaters, shirts, jackets and even a few make-up compacts. These became Christmas gifts for family members and girlfriends. Later, when Pat totted up the value of the goods, it amounted to more than 300 dollars' worth – about 1,500 dollars at today's rates.

The boys got away with the entire heist without detection. During and after Christmas, however, the pain of his guilty conscience plagued Pat without mercy. He found himself deeply embarrassed by every expression of thanks he received for his generous gifts. In desperation, he sought out Mack Craig and confessed to the whole thing. He had let everyone down, he explained. What should he do? He could not exactly return the goods, and he did not have enough money to pay for them.

Mack listened until Pat ran out of steam, then he said, 'Pat, I suggest the best thing for you to do is to get a job after school and pay back everything a bit at a time. I'll go to the store managers and tell them. Give me an itemized list of all your loot and where you stole it from.'

Sobered, Pat did as Mack suggested. Ironically, the job he took on was in one of the shirt stores from which he had stolen. 'I guess my criminal experience made me a rather good watchdog!' he says. 'While I was working there I made sure that no shoplifting took place. I worked three afternoons a week plus Saturdays.' That time spent working was a real sacrifice for Pat, as it took away the free time he had previously filled with sport. The job was no fun and he hated it. He detested standing on his feet all day. It annoyed him to watch people come in with no intention of buying anything, ruffle through the orderly piles of clothes, try some on, then leave them in a mess for him to tidy up. The shop insisted that the stock had to be kept looking fresh and untouched. Despite his frustration, Pat remembers that he stuck at it until all his debts were paid in full. When it was all over, Mack told him that the store managers had been amazed that a student would offer to pay back debts like that. 'That's the power of the Christian gospel being worked out in a changed life!' Mack said.

Pat may have been messing around outside school hours, but he was still an intelligent student. He had discovered the joy of reading at an early age, and kept his love of books through his teenage years. He understood that books opened the door to every kind of learning, and was willing to pay attention to spelling, grammar, expression and 'personality' in the writing. In terms of literary personality, his favourite books in high school were by Mark Twain, a writer he found both entertaining and articulate. He also read and deeply enjoyed *A Tale of Two Cities* and *Oliver Twist* by Charles Dickens, enjoying the challenge of sticking with a long story and really getting to understand the characters.

He managed to avoid the danger of being seen as too much of a 'swot', however, and soon created a cool style for himself that (so he says) had the girls swooning. But fashion can sometimes be a hit-and-miss affair and, despite his normal good taste in clothes, there was the occasional sartorial blunder that Pat could only look back on with regret. One day he was at his usual store after school, searching for something snazzy to wear to make an impression on the girls. After a while he stumbled on the perfect thing. On one rail hung a neatly pressed pair of trousers which he decided he just had to have. The price was a little high for his modest budget, but he figured the extra expense would be worth it when he won over the hottest girls at school the next day. He duly parted with his cash and headed home, where he proudly showed off his new pants to his young brother. Nick just giggled and raised an eyebrow. 'You'll be knocking 'em dead with those, Pat!' he exclaimed, and ran laughing out of the room.

Pat was undeterred and hung the trousers carefully on the door of his wardrobe ready for the next day. What could a kid brother know about fashion, anyway? In the morning Pat made sure that he spilt no milk on his prized new pants and double-checked his reflection in the mirror before he left. Back in the kitchen, his mother and two sisters collapsed in hysterics at the spectacle.

At school, just as he had expected, it was not long before the girls started swooning. Pat noticed that, as he passed them in the corridor, they took one look and dissolved into girlie giggles. He was impressed: the trousers were clearly working. The trouble was, as the day continued, he found that it was not only the girls who were dissolving into giggles. Nearly everyone took one look and gave some sort of reaction – usually laughter. Pat became thoughtful. Perhaps his sleepy Nashville high school was not yet ready for bright green trousers.

It was a very long day. When the bell finally rang to end the afternoon, Pat rushed home and ripped off the offending trousers, vowing never to appear at school in them again. In fact, the only girl ever to see those infamous pants after that was Rosemary, the Boones' faithful cow.

As most people do, Pat treasures the memories of his first romantic encounters. His first steady girlfriend was called Jeanne, and by the time Christmas approached they had been going steady for nearly three months, a record for them both. As the days rolled on, however, Pat felt that the initial sparkle of their relationship had dimmed to a dull wattage. So uninspiring was the romance, indeed, that Pat now had his eye on Kay, another student. Jeanne was also wanting out, as it happened – but, as the song says, 'Breaking up is hard to do.' Then Pat, in his teenage wisdom, came up with the perfect solution. Making use of the special time of year, Pat's plan was to send both girls a gift, but Jeanne's was to be something cheap and Kay's something expensive. Along with the gifts would come cards, a casual one for Jeanne and a special one for Kay.

In the weeks leading up to Christmas, Pat scoured the stores for a smart compact that would impress the lovely Kay. Paying eight dollars for the one he finally chose, he had the store giftwrap it and then wrote his expensive card. Meanwhile, he spent the princely sum of one dollar on a tatty compact for Jeanne. He mailed the gifts and then sat back and waited to see his plan come to fruition: Jeanne, seeing the cheap compact, would end her dwindling affection for him, and Kay, attracted by the expensive gift, would become the latest Boone belle!

The plan failed. In his haste to get his machinations under way, Pat had mailed the gifts and cards to the wrong girls. Needless to say, neither was impressed and both took an instant dislike to young Mr Boone.

CHAPTER 3

IT'S TOO SOON TO KNOW

Does she love me? … It's too soon to know!
Deborah Chessler

FIFTEEN IS A YOUNG AGE to be deciding a future career and yet, across the developed world, many permanent paths are chosen by teenagers who have difficulty choosing their favourite fizzy drink from one week to the next. Pat was just the same. At 15, he was faced with the task of choosing what to do with his life. Although singing was his first love, the uncertain, temperamental nature of show business meant that he had to consider a more conventional path too. Should he be a teacher? He was good at languages and English, but where was the money and glamour in that? Perhaps, if he stored his comic collection for decades to come, he could sell them off and make a huge packet of cash. But then that would hardly help him get a car in the next couple of years… What about journalism? He had been the *Pony Express* reporter at school (his column about making the world a better place, 'Earth is my Beat', was popular), but did he really want to sit behind a desk all day? It would be much more exciting to become an archaeologist: Noah's ark and King Solomon's mines were still waiting to be discovered, after all…

One thing he knew for sure was that his father's profession was not one to which he aspired. In the summer the two Boone boys had jobs at the Boone Construction Company, working for a dollar an hour. As apprentices, both struggled to work harder than all the other boys to prove that they had earned their positions and had not simply been given a free pass by their father, the boss. Pouring concrete, carrying bricks, digging ditches and other such tasks was back-breaking work. Nevertheless, knowing his family's modest means, Pat wanted to pay his way. The aches and pains and sore hands helped him decide that construction work was not a career for him, however. (The construction company was still owned by Archie's Uncle Jack. Some years later, when Jack gave Archie the opportunity to purchase the company, Pat made it financially possible for him to do so. 'Daddy insisted on it being a loan with interest,' says Pat. 'He refused to accept it as a gift. He hated even accepting a loan from me. I counted it a rare privilege, though, being able to help my Dad.')

Pat's real desire was to sing, of course, but it was not seen as a 'proper' job and income was not guaranteed. In the end, despite its unglamorous nature, he decided on teaching and continued his education, majoring on English, Maths and Bible Studies, with the intention of graduating eventually as a fully qualified teacher. Today he can survey the five decades of his show-biz career and see that he has risen almost as far as anyone could go, from his humble, middle-income family to the dazzling heights of Hollywood stardom. In his early teens, however, it seemed preposterous to imagine himself in the superstar category. 'Singing was a growing hobby and a secret ambition for me, but I didn't really expect that I might have a career as a professional singer. So I planned to spend my life in the most worthwhile way I could think of, teaching young people to appreciate learning and to direct their lives in the most beneficial ways possible. To me, "success" is not really just being good at some profession and succeeding in it; it's finding God's individual plan for your life, and utilizing the talents and opportunities He provides. I pursued worthy goals and asked God to direct my steps – and He led me into the career I dreamed of. I could never have arranged it myself!'

The choice of music as a career was certainly outside the experience of the Nashville-based Boone clan. Although musical ability seemed to run deep in the family and some individuals had shown a promising gift, no one had been spurred on to any adventurous public exploits. Pat began to change all that. After his successes at the Belle Meade talent shows, he began to set his sights on bigger goals. All through his early high school years, he won acclaim and prizes in competitions – some in tiny, musty church halls where the highest prize was a pat on the back and a sentence in the local newspaper. More prestigious affairs took place in plush theatres complete with velvet-cushioned chairs and uniformed ushers.

Pat practised constantly for these performances in his attic bedroom, while his family downstairs groaned and rolled their eyes as he burst for the hundredth time into the latest Eddy Arnold weeper or the more sophisticated cabaret mimicry of Frank Sinatra. Standing in front of his mirror, Pat would carefully rehearse his positions and singing style until he felt they were just right. The effort paid off, and prizes and press acclaim for the smart, smiling young singer began to mount steadily. More invitations to perform arrived on the back of his success. Soon Pat was sharing the billing with quality gold-suited guitar-pickers and rhinestoned country wannabes, rather than with violin-strangling, spotty kids from the next block and greasy-haired ventriloquists with moving lips. Eager to learn, Pat also spent time listening carefully to the professional singers on the radio. It was cheaper than singing lessons, after all!

He had his first promotional photograph taken at the age of 15. He sat nervously in front of the professional cameraman, unused to such personal attention and not knowing exactly what was expected of him. 'For heaven's sake,' said the photographer, 'why don't you give me a grin? You ain't gonna be shot! This is a photo shoot, not a firing squad.' Pat was so tensed up that he could barely move his face muscles in response to the joke.

By the time he was 17, he had grown into his role rather more and was no longer frightened of photographers. He amazed the sceptics when he secured his own radio show. *Youth on Parade* was a one-man show with no budget – Pat was both host and singer – but offered priceless value in terms of the experience gained. Few imagined then that this high school student would soon be appearing on countless radio and TV shows across America and abroad.

One huge step towards this subsequent fame came with Pat's participation in a prestigious outdoor event that drew an audience of 10,000 people. The importance of the occasion and the size of the crowd were not what captured his attention, however. Everything else was put in the shade by the sight of a young girl called Shirley. The concert took place in Centennial Park, Nashville and starred Shirley's father Red Foley and Minnie Pearl, with Pat billed as the 'Discovery of the Week'. Shirley was backstage, waiting to watch her father perform, when Pat came off stage after a nerve-racking but successful performance. 'My heart took off double time at the sight of her!' says Pat. (Pat and Shirley had, in fact, first met when Pat was playing city league baseball at the age of 13. He had been introduced to Shirley then by Julia Bradshaw, a mutual friend.)

Back in high school the following week, Pat struggled to keep his mind on the English language class. It was a lost cause. Shirley was sitting at a desk just across the narrow aisle from him. Pat thought she was gorgeous – and admits that her attractiveness was increased for him because her father was a legendary recording star. He found out more about the Foley family in the days that followed. Red Foley's first wife had died giving birth to their daughter Betty. He met his second wife Eva when they both sang on the same radio programme, and some time later they eloped. Shirley was their first child, and they had two more daughters called Julie and Jenny. Shirley was brought up in Peoria, until they moved to Nashville when Red was invited to replace Roy Acuff on the Grand Ole Opry. Sadly, the move soon became marred by the constant illness of Shirley's mother. Eva was eventually diagnosed with a severe heart problem which medication was unable to help.

That day in class, though, Pat was ignorant of all that and was simply interested in attracting Shirley's attention. He noticed that she glanced at him a few times, and was determined to speak to her when the class was over. At the end of the lesson he went to stand by her desk, but she was so busy chatting to her friends that she failed to notice him. Pat was not to be put off so easily, and he sneaked down another aisle to reappear behind her. He peeked over her shoulder and finally had her attention as she swung round. They stared at each other for a moment, then Shirley said, 'Oh, hi Pat!'

Pat remembers his stupid opening line to this day. 'My … um … my English book's been used so often, it's got a few pages missing!' Waving his damaged book as proof, he tried to ignore the smothered giggles of the other girls. His second line was almost as dumb as his first. 'Would you mind if I … um … borrowed your book, Shirley?' Encouraged by her warm smile, he ploughed on. 'Um, are you doing anything this evening?'

Shirley was also clearly trying to ignore her giggling friends, and admitted that she was indeed free that evening. She invited Pat to visit her parents' house. 'Perhaps you'd like to come to the library with me. I've got several books to return.'

Pat found himself offering to carry her books for her, and insisted that the library was not out of his way at all – despite the fact that everyone listening knew that his home was in the opposite direction. 'Ah, the power of love!' he laughs now.

Shirley came to his rescue. 'Pat, if you come to the library you can walk me home from there, *and* you can borrow my English book. I don't live too far away, and you can meet my Pa.'

They walked off to the library together, leaving their amused schoolfriends behind. From that first date came a long-lasting romance that was to lead into marriage just a few years later. Pat lost no time the day after the walk to the library, and invited Shirley to be his date at the school prom that term. Many dates followed. 'We used to meet in the school hallway under the old grandfather clock. We would often sing together in the high school quartet and the modern harmony quintet. We were always singing! Driving home from the movies or a basketball game, we'd just pull off the road somewhere and, well, sing … I clearly remember our very first kiss. It was a beautiful moonlit night and I just sort of edged over to Shirley, slid my arm around her and asked if I could kiss her! She felt I could be a little more romantic and asked me to close the open top of the car.' To mark the occasion, they ended up singing the Lulu Belle and Scotty hit, 'Have I Told You Lately That I Love You?'

From then on, the two were inseparable. Pat frequently visited Shirley at her home, where Red Foley made his daughter's young suitor very welcome, while Shirley bustled about providing freshly baked muffins and home-made lemonade. Pat admits to being totally 'moon-eyed' over Shirley, and he no longer had eyes for other girls. Shirley seemed to be sharing his feelings. She was, however, one of the high school's most popular girls, and Pat remembers that it was a constant struggle to fend off the other boys who were attracted to her like bees round a honeypot.

After leaving high school, Pat continued on at David Lipscomb College, pursuing his plan to become a teacher. Meanwhile, he sang and performed whenever the opportunity arose. Shirley went pretty much everywhere with him. They suited each other very well, having complementary personalities. Pat was the impulsive, sometimes naïve one, while Shirley had a tendency to be more mature and in control of things. She was a bubbly girl, though, and they shared a strong sense of humour, making the most of the time they spent together – whether they were out throwing snowballs, eating popcorn at a movie, listening to the jukebox at a hamburger joint, or driving out into the countryside.

They were both doing well at college, Pat once again involved with the baseball team and the school newspaper, Shirley acting as class secretary and homecoming queen, and both of them singing in the David Lipscomb College Chorus.

Everyone on the community grapevine knew that the Boone boy and the Foley girl were fast becoming close sweethearts. Looking back at the simple pleasures they enjoyed together, Pat considers that their teenage antics were a sort of Nashville version of the *Happy Days* television show! Clouds were gathering, however, and after a long illness, Shirley's mother died. Sad and lonely, Shirley found that Pat was always there to comfort her, and they became, if anything, even closer. Pat began to wonder seriously if Shirley might agree to become his wife.

He was reluctant to speak his mind on the great marriage question just yet, however – they were both very young, after all. Meanwhile, there was much else to occupy his thoughts, particularly on the musical front. As the 1950s progressed, musical tastes were changing radically and Pat, Shirley and their schoolfriends were caught up in the excitement. Guy Mitchell, Teresa Brewer, Eddie Fisher and Perry Como were all the rage. The now familiar term 'rock'n'roll' was yet to be coined by DJ Alan Freed, but the trends were all there in the music the teenagers most enjoyed. What is now called 'rhythm and blues', of course, was known as 'race music' back in the fifties – terminology which Pat remembers with some disbelief today. His own song repertoire was plucked from diverse quarters and cultures, not least from the 'black' circuit. He loved the catchy tunes and strong rhythms.

Country music was another matter, however. While he could have claimed, quite legitimately, to be a 'regular country boy', he had no particular love affair going with country music. Cool high school kids did not admit to liking country music, of that he was sure. Country music was for hillbillies and red-necks. It was certainly not the teenage fashion at his Nashville college in the mid-fifties, despite the proximity of the Grand Ole Opry. Pat was really a typical, middle-class, small-town boy – and the town was none too small, either. Even then, Nashville was much more like a city than a town.

Taking whatever opportunities he could, Pat sang throughout the Nashville area at businessmen's meetings and school assemblies – wherever he was invited to go. His accompanist was a local piano teacher called Ruth Mowery. Pat recalls her helpfulness and competence with great gratitude. 'Any time I'd ask Ruth to play, she'd always oblige, rescheduling her teaching to fit me in. She was wonderful, playing in any key. She also kept up to date with all the hit tunes. I was very grateful for her support.' He continued to practise endlessly up in his attic bedroom, running time and again through his widening repertoire. His brother Nick regularly lost patience. 'Oh, come off it, Pat!' he would moan. 'Can't you give us a rest? That must be the ninety-ninth time you've sung that! You've got us all hearing your songs in our dreams … and they're *nightmares!*' Pat, however, was enjoying himself far too much to take heed of his family's teasing.

Shirley was foremost among those encouraging Pat in his musical endeavours. It was thanks to a suggestion from her that he put in an entry for the annual East Nashville High School Talent Contest. It was always a popular show, and Pat did himself proud. When he had finished crooning his way through his song presentation, the young audience erupted into boisterous applause. He was later cheered back on stage as the winner of the valuable first prize, a trip to New York to audition for Ted Mack's famous, nationally televised *Amateur Hour*. There was a while to wait before his appointment in the Big Apple, but Pat was beside himself with excitement

Shirley was delighted at his success. The couple were now very close, and thoughts about the future surfaced once more. As Pat's plans for his life came under discussion in the Boone household, he tried to make it clear that, as far as he was concerned, Shirley was an essential part of such considerations. Shirley was still battling with grief at her mother's death, and relied on Pat for a great deal of support. Some months after her mother's death, Shirley's father married once again and Shirley found herself in a quandary. Red and his new wife decided, after much thought, that their future lay in Missouri, and they made plans to move there. With Pat and her college education firmly established in Nashville, however, Shirley was unwilling to go with them. Pat's parents looked on with concern. They liked Shirley very much, loved her even, but they felt (and stated in no uncertain terms) that Pat was far too young to be considering settling down, possibly ruining his career chances by burdening himself with a family, and certainly injuring his bank balance. Pat and Shirley were undeterred.

A Christmas Eve party in 1952 found them together as usual. The conversation ranged from England's new queen to America's new president. In the elections a month earlier, Dwight Eisenhower had swept to a convincing Republican victory. With politics out of the way, the party-goers moved on to various silly games, one of which was won by Shirley and Pat. Everyone playfully feted the couple, cracking jokes about their future union. They went home laughing, but Pat had something serious to say. 'Shirley … how about you and me getting together for good? Will you marry me?' Shirley beamed, nodded and planted a warm kiss on his cheek before saying softly, 'Yes!'

They told no one just yet, but carried on trying to see each other as often as they could. Pat was increasingly busy, and admits that when they were apart he missed Shirley very much. 'I found that Shirley was increasingly special to me. We never ceased to enjoy each other's company, so we saw much of each other. My show-business career was taking flight by then, but I didn't want it to interfere in our budding romance. I certainly didn't want to leave her grounded as my career headed skyward!'

Shirley's father readily admitted that he was fond of Pat (who called him 'Mr Red') and approved of this aspiring crooner going steady with his daughter. Pat, in his turn, saw Shirley's parents as the Grand Ole Opry personified and appreciated the warm welcome he received. 'Shirley's parents were sweet folks. They would have had to be, to accept another singer into the family!' Red's first impression of Pat was of 'a serious-minded young fellow, a strict adherent to his religious beliefs, and a boy who lived to sing just for the sake of singing … Pat had a pleasant voice, smooth in harmony – but I guess back then I just didn't recognize the fine quality that was there. I can honestly say that I never suspected that one day Pat would be one of the top names in the business!' Red recalled many pleasant occasions when Pat would call for Shirley and, as they waited for her to get ready, the two singers would wile the time away by harmonizing together over a coffee or orange juice. As time passed, Red saw that Pat and Shirley were becoming very close. Yet the idea of them getting married was far from his mind. He had married early himself, but it did not occur to him that his daughter might want to do the same thing.

For many months, Shirley and Pat remained secretly engaged. Part of the reason for their silence was the attitude of Pat's parents. They were increasingly voicing their concern about his unfinished education and his future career – which, by then, was promising much in terms of radio, television and touring dates but was not yet providing great riches. 'Pat,' they said frequently, 'how on earth could you be obligated to a wife and a potential family when you don't have a proper job? Why not finish your studies first? And you're far too immature to be leading anyone to the altar – you're only 18!' And so it would go on. Pat understood that they meant it all lovingly, but he was resolute, explaining as often as he could that he was starting to pick up good money as a singer, and in any case he would soon be teaching. Nothing was going to make him change his mind about Shirley. Looking back on those months, Pat regrets now that he was so impatient with his parents. They were not really being uncooperative and old-fashioned – although it had seemed so at the time to an 18-year-old who thought he knew what life was all about.

Pat did his best not to dwell on the wrangling at home, and concentrated instead on the exciting opportunities that were beginning to open up for him. Once again, Shirley had an important part to play. As the daughter of the famous Red Foley, she was able to use her influence to obtain Pat an interview with the smooth country crooner star Eddy Arnold. Armed with a couple of simple songs that he had written himself, Pat duly went to Eddy Arnold's office at the appointed time. Shyly, he sang the songs to the great man, accompanying himself on a ukulele. Eddy listened attentively and at the end honestly stated that he thought Pat's singing showed a lot more promise than his songwriting! Indeed, so impressed was he by Pat's vocal talent that he arranged for him to meet Bill Beasley of Republic Records, a small company based in Nashville.

To Pat's delight, Bill decided to record one of his songs, 'Until You Tell Me So', at Owen Bradley's studio in Hillsboro. On a rainy spring day in May 1953, Pat crossed the puddled sidewalk and entered the dimmed Bradley Studio on Nashville's 21st Street. The conversation in the studio was all about Bill Haley and his Comets, who had just that month unleashed a new musical genre with 'Rock Around The Clock'. Studio time was short, however, and producer Bill Beasley soon called for attention to be paid to the job in hand. The recording proved a difficult task. The small studio had a tin roof, and the heavy rain meant that both the band and Pat had to perform extra loudly to drown out the noise.

Two pieces minted that day – Pat's self-penned song, 'Until You Tell Me So', and Charles Adams's 'My Heart Belongs To You' – were played on local radio and proved promising, if moderate, market successes. On the strength of that success, Republic recalled the same team five months later for a four-song session, this time at the Nashville War Memorial Building Studio. With a bigger orchestra and making full use of the vastly superior acoustics, these recordings came out rather better than the first ones.

Meanwhile, following his victory at the East Nashville High School Talent Show, Pat's date with destiny in New York was arranged for 3 July 1953. He flew there on a Dallas Love Field flight, and checked into Room 597 of New York's Astor Hotel. Once he had unpacked, he headed out onto the crowded, noisy streets and found a café where he could sit and watch the bustle outside. It was all a far cry from Nashville. He did not usually suffer too badly with nerves, but this was different. New York was a huge step up from Tennessee, and an appearance on television was a massive leap up from anything he had done before. He would really have to pull out all the stops on the show, hitting every note and clearly pronouncing every syllable.

It was just a short cab ride from the hotel to the studio the next morning. Once inside, he was rushed through make-up and run through his cues. It was all happening very fast. Back home, many people had tuned in to watch, including Pat's family, Shirley, and most of his school colleagues. It was quite an occasion. The strict rules of Ted Mack's *Amateur Hour* stated that only one number could be sung by each contestant. It had been a tricky choice. Should he choose a gospel song or a secular ballad? In the end, Pat skirted the problem by selecting a medley of two well-known songs that covered both the gospel and secular sides. Now there he was, in front of the cameras and a theatre audience of 3,500, singing the jaunty 'Side By Side' alongside the inspirational 'I Believe'. Once he had hit the first few notes successfully, he found that his nerves subsided. He even had the courage to look directly at the TV cameras.

The result was not announced immediately, as time had to be allowed for the TV audience to send in their votes by post. Predictably, the response from Tennessee was outstanding, but other states also voted in their thousands for Pat. Meanwhile, Pat returned south with no inkling of how the voting was going, and later that week travelled to Beardstown, Tennessee, to lead the singing at some modest gospel meetings while Mack Craig preached. Beardstown was well off the beaten track and at that time it was such a small place that nobody even had a telephone. Pat was staying at a farmhouse in the area and on the Friday afternoon, while he was eating, the sound of screeching brakes filled the air as a car entered the farmyard, scattering dust and chickens everywhere. A voice said, 'Is Pat Boone in there?' And when Pat went to investigate, the messenger told him, 'You'd better come with me: somebody's trying to call you from New York City!' The nearest telephone, he added, was some 20 miles away.

Pat and his escort bounced off down the bumpy country roads until they reached the house where a telephone switchboard had been installed. When the connection had been made, Pat picked up the phone and heard the voice of Oscar Schoonmacher from the Ted Mack staff. Oscar told him that he had won the previous week's contest and he was to come to New York to rehearse for the show the next day! It was a bit of a rush, but he made it in time. Ted Mack's *Amateur Hour* was the *Opportunity Knocks* show of its day, and Pat went on to become a three-times winner of the contest, which entitled him to return to New York in the summer of 1954 for the grand final. As well as successful renditions of Frankie Laine's hit 'I Believe', Pat's other winning songs were the romantic ballads 'No Other Love' and 'I'm Walking Behind You'. Although he did not know it at the time, the showman Ted Mack was to play an influential part in the development of Pat's career.

Riding high on the excitement of his New York experiences, Pat felt a new confidence and decided it was past time to make public his love for Shirley and their decision to marry. The first step was to ask Shirley's father for his daughter's hand in marriage. That was how it was done and, despite a feeling of extreme nervousness, Pat was determined to do things properly.

So it was that, late one morning, Pat made his way to the Foley house on Bear Road. Shirley and her father were still seated at the breakfast table and Pat was invited to join them. Holding Shirley's hand tightly under the table, Pat started out on his carefully pre-pared speech. 'Mr Red, you know that I love your Shirley very much … Well, Sir, I'd like to ask your permission – I mean, we'd like to become married.' Then he burst into a nervous grin and subdued a giggle. It had not quite come out as he had hoped, and he had gabbled towards the end. What would Red say?

Shirley's father looked straight at Pat. 'Will you take good care of my girl?' he asked. Very earnestly, Pat assured him that he would, and the matter was settled without further ado.

Pat recalls that, over the years, he and Red never indulged in any 'man-to-man talk'. Perhaps Red felt it was unnecessary. When Pat and Shirley approached him that day for permission to be married, Red admitted to being somewhat surprised, but he was proud that the two youngsters seemed to be approaching their future together in an unusually level-headed manner. Pat convinced his future father-in-law that he was determined to con-tinue with his education, in spite of his developing activities in the entertainment field. Years later, Red would joke about the one piece of advice he did offer to the young couple. 'I sat down with Pat and Shirley and pointed out the many difficulties and liabili-ties they would encounter, especially if they started right out to raise a family. That bit of sage advice was clearly listened to atten-tively by both: in the short period of approximately four years they only had four children!'

Fortified with Red's permission, the couple were eager to go ahead and plan the next stage. No wedding date could be set, however, as Pat's parents continued to resist the whole notion of their son marrying so soon. More arguments about how stupid it was for them to marry followed. There seemed to be no solution. Pat and Shirley discussed the possibility of eloping, but Shirley was initially reluctant to entertain the idea, having set her heart on a big white church wedding. It was impossible to want anything else after the glorious press pictures of the high society wedding on 12 September 1953 of John F. Kennedy to Jacqueline Lee Bouvier in Newport, Rhode Island.

Pat and Shirley had originally wanted to marry the week after they graduated from college. In the end, anxious to put an end to the family arguments, they decided that a *fait accompli* was probably the only way and duly made plans to elope. After all, Shirley said, her father and mother had eloped, so it was not such a bad thing! On 7 November 1953, Pat and Shirley travelled to Springfield, Tennessee, where they were married by their high school principal Mack Craig. 'We drove to a different county on Saturday, got married, then phoned my parents afterwards,' explains Pat. 'We honeymooned until Monday, then we turned up for our studies as usual!'

Reality returned with a bump, as the newlyweds found themselves adjusting to their new life together and the burdens of homeowning (their first home was on Belvedere Drive in Nashville). Pat was often out or away, trying not to let any good singing opportunities slip through his hands. He was constantly on the move, travelling from town to town, and this began to take its emotional toll on the young couple. Meanwhile, Shirley was attending nursing school, and Pat was also endeavouring to keep up with his ongoing studies. He continued to host and sing on *Youth on Parade* for the Nashville radio station WSIX. (Occasionally he also read the news for them!) Shirley always tried to be supportive of Pat's showbusiness aspirations, and even put her own musical ambitions on hold to do so. She also agreed to move away from Nashville. Pat decided to complete his college career at North Texas State Teachers' College, and in order to allow him to do this, the couple had to move to Denton, Texas.

Today Denton is known as the Top of the Golden Triangle, because of its equidistance from Dallas and Fort Worth. The suburbs have swelled along the 35 miles of Interstates 35E and 35W. In 1954, however, Interstate 35 had not yet been built. Denton seemed far removed from Dallas and Fort Worth then, and Oklahoma, just 45 miles to the north, also seemed hours away from the quiet, two-college town. It was to this laid-back community that the young Boones moved shortly after New Year 1954 – already expecting their first child. Shirley was determined that the couple should not be overly influenced by or dependent upon their respective families in the early stages of their marriage, and was happy about the move. Excited by the prospect of a change of scene and a new start, she and Pat packed their meagre possessions into a 1950 Chevy and a U-Haul trailer and made the 700-mile transition to north Texas.

They had learned of Denton and its teaching college through their friends, Russ and Bitsy Dyer, who were already living there. Russ was a roofing contractor, and also operated a chinchilla farm with his wife. Knowing that the question of Pat finishing college was of paramount concern to the young couple, the Dyers had told them about the outstanding English, speech and music departments at the North Texas College. Also, because it was a state school, the tuition was affordable. So was the accommodation. Not long after arriving, the Boones settled into a three-room upstairs apartment, 811 Avenue D, and Pat enrolled for the spring semester.

Texas was suffering a prolonged drought, and Pat and Shirley were rudely introduced to the region's violent wind and dust storms. Black skies with their swirling winds blowing in from the west left their grimy evidence behind in the apartment, despite Shirley's dutiful efforts to keep it clean. 'It seemed that we lived encased in dust. Dust was everywhere – in the sink, in the toothpaste, under the rug!' It did not seem to matter much, and the couple were very happy. They began attending services at the Welch Street Church of Christ which, like their apartment, was within walking distance of the campus. They soon made friends, and also discovered other useful contacts. Cecil Pitt, one of the church members, was half-owner of the Pitt Brothers Grocery, located on the Old Fort Worth Highway. He was impressed with Pat's initiative and hired him to work part-time at the store, scheduling Pat's hours around his college classes. Cecil remembers him as 'a good worker'.

Pat and Shirley had a pool of money they had brought from Nashville – some Pat had saved, and some Shirley had inherited from her mother. Inevitably, however, their supply was dwindling, and Pat's store job did not bring in a great deal, given the restricted hours he had to work. Taking the lead from their friends the Dyers, the Boones decided that their ticket to fortune was investing in chinchillas. They bought a pair that produced a litter of five in short order. The furry family got the royal treatment from the Boones: after all, they were the young couple's ticket to the lifestyle of the rich and famous. Fate, however, had other plans, and in time the chinchillas became surplus to requirements and had to be given away.

When Pat could find the time, he also made trips to Dallas and Fort Worth, hitting the radio and TV stations and trying to find work there. His efforts to be hired by the station KDNT in Denton had already proved futile. With his Nashville radio experience, he thought it would not be too difficult to find a position, but he had no success anywhere.

He was supplementing the income from his store job with engagements to preach at a little country church in Slidell, a small community a few miles to the northeast, but the money he was bringing home still did not amount to much, and the couple were soon to become parents. In desperation, Pat applied for a paper route with the *Forth Worth Star Telegram*. Although he was turned down, the circulation manager referred him to WBAP-TV, the largest station in the area, when Pat explained that he had originally been looking for a singing job. He was overjoyed when WBAP hired him without even an audition for their Friday night show, *The Bewley Barn Dance*. The $44.50 after tax which he earned for that was a truly welcome windfall.

To save money, Pat rode his Victory bicycle whenever possible. He rode from class to class, to the shops, and into the heart of Denton, about a mile from the campus. Besides his ordinary bicycle, Pat had also acquired a unicycle and was quite adept at riding it, according to a classmate called Phil Roberts. In warm weather, Phil would often sit and study on the steps of the Quad, the men's dormitory which was built round a square. Phil remembers looking up from his books to see Pat scudding along on his unicycle, manoeuvring it round the courtyard and even bounding with it up and down the Quad's outside stairs. It caused quite a stir.

One afternoon, bored with his studies, Phil shouted from the steps: 'Hey, Boone, you think you could teach me to ride that thing?'

'Sure, if you're not afraid of falling!'

'Let's give it a whirl, then!' Phil shoved his books aside and followed Pat's instructions. After a few mishaps, he was soon balancing confidently on the unicycle and horsing around with the young man who was just a few months away from becoming the nation's newest singing sensation.

Pat and Shirley had not been in Denton long before they became friends with a church family who would play an important role in their lives for years to come. Troy and Dixie Klein and their children Skipper and Kay lived just a few blocks away from both the church and the campus. Dixie was Den Mother for a Cub Scout troop, most of them Skipper's third-grade classmates from the Sam Houston Elementary School, an old brownish-red brick building directly across from the church. Pat was soon leading singing at the church and occasionally preaching as well. Dixie recognized the positive impact he could have on 'her boys', as she called the Scouts, and approached Pat about working with the group on a Tuesday afternoon after school. Pat was already juggling his time to accommodate classes, studying, working to support Shirley and himself, and being involved in church services and activities. He agreed with some hesitation to take on this extra task, wondering how he was going to tell Shirley that he had yet another thing on his plate – but in the end, he says, it turned out to be enormous fun.

The spring of 1954 found the Cold War at its most frigid, with President Eisenhower ordering a huge increase in weapons spending, yet in Texas there was no hint of any kind of cold as the sun beat down. Pat was certainly discovering a whole new meaning to the word 'hot' as he pedalled uphill to the Kleins' home on Maple Street to attend his first Cub Scout meeting.

Dixie's 'boys' were waiting eagerly to meet him (news of the unicycle had spread fast), and Pat was pleased to find that he got on well with the youngsters from the start. The first thing they were to tackle was how to tie knots. Within minutes Pat was part of a circle in the back garden, handing out lengths of rope to the boys, among them Skipper Klein, Don Cole, Morris McCormick, Ray Sadler, Mike Gammon, Terry Smith, Wickie Wier and Billy and John Cundiff. These same youngsters would soon be glued to their TV sets, cheering on their Den Chief as he sang in New York talent contests during the summer. For the time being, however, they were concentrating on the more prosaic intricacies of square knots and slip knots.

The session was deemed a success, and Pat became a regular participator at the Scout meetings. Shirley sometimes came too, and chatted to Dixie while Pat worked with the boys. This led to a marvellous story which the Boones still tell to this day. After one of Shirley's visits to the Klein house, young Terry Smith went home with some news for his family. Sitting at the supper table, still wearing his blue and yellow Cub uniform, he announced abruptly, 'Shirley Boone's gonna have a *baby*!'

Terry's mother Gertrude gazed at her son (who, incidentally, would grow up to have a musical career of his own as a country songwriter, his song 'Far Side Banks Of Jordan' becoming a blue-grass standard and a Johnny Cash classic). Third-graders in 1954 were not supposed to know much about such things, and they were certainly not supposed to speak about them. Gertrude narrowed her eyes. 'And just how would you know that?'

'I just know!'

'What do you mean you just know? *How* do you just know?'

Terry squirmed on his chair, lowered his eyes and responded, 'Well, I just know. I guess I *should* know! Shirley was wearing her *eternity clothes*!'

As the baby's birth drew nearer, Pat was glad to continue his appearances on WBAP's *Bewley Barn Dance*. Dixie and Troy sometimes accompanied him to the Fort Worth studio, and one day Pat gave their son Skipper and his friend Don Cole from the Scout troop a chance to experience some of the TV excitement. WBAP had given Pat a solo spot on the *Barn Dance* as a result of his Nashville connections – they assumed he was a 'hillbilly' singer. Despite preferring to avoid the country tag, Pat knew some country songs and decided to act the part. In blue jeans and a country-style shirt, he made his debut singing 'Navajo Trail'. Skipper and Don sat behind him on the bales of hay that decorated the set, and apparently loved every minute of it.

Pat's 'country' act must have convinced the producers, because he was soon hosting the show, also creating a Saturday afternoon teenage music and talent show called *Foremost Teen Times*. The TV sponsor for the show was Foremost Dairies – leading Pat to muse that there was clearly no escape from cows! The success of the *Barn Dance* also prompted WBAP officials to ask Pat to host a one-hour radio show. He readily accepted the invitation, even though the added responsibilities did not increase the $44.50 paycheque. Foremost Dairies did sweeten the weekly take-home benefits, however, by offering Pat a gallon of ice-cream and two cartons of cottage cheese, for which, he maintains, he was appropriately grateful.

CHAPTER 4

IF DREAMS CAME TRUE

If dreams came true, I'd dream you everything.
Robert Allen and Al Stillman

MANY PEOPLE OVER THE years asked Red Foley if he was in any way responsible for his son-in-law's rapid rise to fame, but he always stated adamantly that he was not. The only thing he ever did for Pat, he said, was to write a letter to Arthur Godfrey, host of the popular New York *Talent Scouts* show. How instrumental his letter was in getting Pat on the show no one will ever know, however.

Pat had already gained some TV experience on the Ted Mack shows, but they were geared towards amateurs, while the Arthur Godfrey show was for those already elevated to professional levels. It was a major nationwide network TV show, and to appear on it was a much valued prize. One week in 1954, the ever-hopeful Pat made the lengthy trip up north from Texas to audition for Arthur Godfrey. Being on national TV was a nerve-racking undertaking, despite his previous experience, and this time the stakes were higher. It was all very different from a live performance on a concert stage. Had he picked the right material to sing? Should he have dressed differently? Should he tone down his Southern accent? Should he try to sing in a more sophisticated style? Eventually, on a sudden wave of self-confidence, Pat decided that the best thing to do was to stick with what he knew. He should just do what he normally did, and be himself.

Backstage, he waited anxiously for his moment, working through in his mind where he should stand and when he would glance at the cameras. Finally the stagehand piloted him into the glare of the lights and Pat glanced over to Arthur Godfrey for his cue. He sang 'Answer Me, O My Love' with no trace of nerves, and before he knew it, he was singing the final note. The crowd exploded into applause, and their enthusiasm won him the competition. Years later, he cherishes his memories of that event, clearly recalling the enormous satisfaction which the performance gave him.

Having won the contest, Pat's immediate task was to make the most of his prize – the opportunity to perform on coast-to-coast network television every morning of the week following the show. Arthur not only hosted the *Talent Scouts* show, but also a five-days-a-week morning show and a Wednesday-night variety show. Back then, Arthur was the USA's king of television.

Pushing money into a grubby payphone outside the studio on a busy New York street, Pat had to raise his voice so that Shirley could hear him. 'How'd I look on the little screen? I guess I won't be coming home this week!' He asked her to call the university and explain why he would be missing some lectures, then the conversation turned to monetary matters: Pat needed to use some of their precious cash to stock up on clothes to wear for the show. Lacking foresight, he had not packed sufficient clothes for the week. He had not, realistically, expected to win.

His first-place finish on the Godfrey show disqualified him from the Ted Mack finals because he could no longer be considered an amateur. Pat was more than happy at the progress this signified, and it certainly did not bother the folks back in Denton. Pat's college and church acquaintances, the Dyers, the Kleins and the Cub Scouts, had all been huddling round their TVs to watch the outcome of the *Talent Scouts* competition. When the winner was announced there was much whooping and hollering among the Scouts, and phones began ringing all over the normally quiet college town, spreading the news of Pat's victory. Disqualification from the Ted Mack finals seemed a small price to pay for such glorious success.

The Godfrey shows were watched by thousands of impressionable teenagers in those days, and Pat Boone rapidly became a nationwide phenomenon. Chris Bujnovsky was just one of the young people who followed Pat's regular performances on the Godfrey morning shows. One day she would become President of the National Pat Boone Fan Club. Chris recalls those TV appearances as if they were yesterday. 'As I watched Pat I admired his fine style of singing and his personality as an individual … the sparkle in his eyes, and the way he kept Mr Godfrey posted on the studies back home!' The young singer was making an indelible impression on his audience.

Those days in New York were immensely exciting, yet the week of morning broadcasts seemed to be over in a flash and it was soon time to leave the Big Apple for Denton and a return to the summer-session teacher-training courses. On his way home, however, Pat stopped in Nashville to visit his family, and it was during that visit that he made another vital step forward in his career.

Randy Wood was the owner of a record store and an independent recording label in Gallatin, Tennessee. He had founded Dot Records in 1951 and had already been instrumental in helping several new artists break into the market. Always on the lookout for promising new talent, he had watched Pat's appearances on the Mack and Godfrey shows with keen interest.

Randy's background is a worthwhile story in itself. In 1945, having completed his army service, he invested in an electrical appliance store in Gallatin, 30 miles outside Nashville's city limits. He diversified into repairs, and then added a small record section as a sideline. Randy's boast was that he handled the 'widest musical spectrum of the public's audio preferences'. His selling did not live up to his promotional hype, however, and he learned his commercial lessons the hard way. Nobody seemed to want to buy the classical stock he carried, but customers were hungry for rhythm and blues. Where were they hearing this kind of music? Finally, he discovered that it was being played on the radio station WLAC, broadcasting from Nashville. Randy met the DJ responsible for the hugely popular show and suggested starting up a mail-order service, selling the records he played.

With a meagre stock as his initial investment, Randy set about advertising his wares. He paid 30 dollars for a half-minute advertising slot for six nights on the WLAC radio station, but when he received no orders after the first week he telephoned the station to cancel the advert. The following Monday morning, however, he was overwhelmed to find his mailbox bulging with 150 letters, all containing money orders. From that modest start, Randy's Record Shop went on to become renowned as the world's largest mail-order record store, carrying more than 20,000 titles. On its mailing list was the proud claim to be able to obtain 'any record you want'.

By the early fifties, Randy was also the part-owner of a daytime local radio station. Programmes went off the air at sundown, and Randy saw the potential of having an empty studio each evening. Losing no time, he began to make recordings there. His first venture was a ragtime piano recording of the Bing Crosby and Bob Wills western swing standard 'San Antonio Rose', by a young man named Johnny Maddox. Working in Randy's store packing records, in his spare time Johnny performed ragtime piano to earn a little more money. Clearly, Randy had picked out a winner. Johnny Maddox surprised everyone when he went on to have a big hit with his 'Crazy Otto Medley'.

Randy's next signings were Billy Vaughn and three of his friends from Western State College, Bowling Green, Kentucky.

The quartet called themselves The Hilltoppers after the basketball team. Soon after that, Randy expanded into bluegrass territory with the old-time country artist Mac Wiseman (the song ''Tis Sweet To Be Remembered' was a Mac Wiseman hit that Pat later covered in a more sophisticated style). Randy's Dot label was now on a roll, and further rhythm and blues hits followed with the Griffin Brothers. As well as making recordings at the little radio station, Randy also made full use of the concept of location or field recording. One of these live recordings was by the rhythm and blues artist Rusty Bryant, with Randy arranging to record his big hit 'All Night Long' in 1953 in a club in Columbus, Ohio. It was an excellent way of gaining good profits from little investment.

Randy's enviable reputation was in stark contrast to many show-business entrepreneurs of the time, who were reported to be influenced to varying degrees by their involvement in organized crime. By contrast, Randy was noted for his integrity. During the 'payola' scandal of 1959 (when there was an uproar about bribes being paid to DJs for preferential treatment of particular recordings) he offered to have his company's finance books audited by the authorities. 'Neither I nor my company has anything to hide under our skirts!' he announced.

In 1954, having followed Pat's success on the Ted Mack and Arthur Godfrey shows in New York, Randy discussed Pat's potential with Hugh Cherry, a DJ friend of his from Music City. Then he rang the Boone home in Nashville and spoke to Pat's parents. Could Pat drive up to Gallatin so they could talk? Despite the promise that the meeting held, Pat was eager to get back to Denton. Shirley's due date was just days away and he did not want to miss the birth. On second thoughts, however, he decided to take an extra day and meet with the young record executive.

It was well worth it. Over a hamburger at the café next to his record store, Randy wasted little time getting to the point. 'Pat, I'd like you to record for Dot. I think we can get things going for you!' he said. With a baby due very soon, Pat did not take long to consider the offer, and accepted with enthusiasm. Randy promised to call him as soon as he had found the right song for his first record.

Pat had already achieved modest success with his early recordings for the Republic label, and those debut records had led to appearances on TV and radio. Randy was promising much more. It was just a verbal agreement, an undertaking given during a chat in a café, but Pat could not wait to get back to Denton to share the news with Shirley. Meanwhile, Randy waited for the right song to come along for Pat to record. He had to wait for many months, until February 1955, to make good his promise, but such patience paid off. Randy was quick to recognize Pat's star potential and signed an exclusive recording deal with him (he was well aware that larger industry labels would be watching the smaller outfits for promising artists they could lure away). Within a very short time, Pat became Dot's best loved and most successful artist. He also became a close friend and confidant of Randy Wood. In the summer of 1954, however, that was all some months in the future, and for a time show business took a back seat to Pat's studies and his wife and new baby.

On 6 July 1954, President Eisenhower confirmed that he would deny Senator McCarthy an investigation into alleged communist sympathies within the CIA. Unconcerned by such complex affairs of state, Pat and Shirley spent the day swimming with friends in Lake Dallas. Before dawn the next day, Shirley nudged Pat awake and whispered, 'It's time!' The baby was coming two weeks early. Within a few hours Cheryl Lynn Boone, the first of their four daughters, was born at Denton Hospital. Pat spent the morning at the hospital with Shirley, but once he was assured that the baby and his wife were both fine, the new father headed off to attend his classes. He could not afford to miss any more.

After a brief respite during the summer break, Pat's hectic schedule began again with the start of the fall semester – he attended classes, studied at home, worked at the grocery store, preached in Slidell, participated in other church activities and helped with the Scouts. One weekend he and Dixie arranged an overnight camping trip for the boys. Dixie's parents, Tip and Mamie Hall, owned a farm west of Denton with plenty of open space. The weekend camp on the farm was designed to give the boys an opportunity to spend a longer time together and to earn points for the pins they were working on. The pins were awarded at city-wide Scout banquets, and were worn proudly on the Cub uniforms.

Late on Friday afternoon, the troop gathered at the Klein home and piled into the waiting cars. At the Hall farm, Pat led the boys in search of a campsite. He remembers catching the boys' excitement as they searched for the best place. In the distance loomed Pilot Knob, a flat-topped hill that is one of Denton's landmarks. According to legend, there is stolen gold buried somewhere on the hill, but countless searches over the years have produced nothing but blistered hands. Nonetheless, the idea of finding gold was fully absorbing the Scouts when Pat broke into their fantasies with the suggestion that they look for firewood instead – otherwise there would be no supper. After the meal they sat round the glowing fire telling ghost stories and singing songs, and vied with each other to act coolly when mysterious noises sounded out in the darkness.

It was an unforgettable experience, both for the boys and the adults. Pat took advantage of the longer, more relaxed time they had together to tell the Scouts something about his own Christian beliefs. Even at the weekday meetings, he tried never to miss an opportunity to speak to them about what was right and wrong. Dixie also arranged for the pack to visit the Welch Street Church occasionally. There the boys were able to see their Den Chief leading the song service and speaking to the congregation. Pat says he always hoped it would make some kind of an impression on them. The boys certainly seemed to listen carefully to what he had to say.

Thanks to Pat's involvement, the Cub Scouts not only learned some moral lessons, they also received first-hand experience of how to handle a baby. Whenever Shirley came with Pat to Dixie's Scout meetings, she brought Cherry with her. The boys seemed fascinated by the baby, and Shirley and Dixie sensed this interest and capitalized on it. They gave the boys some basic instructions on picking up and holding an infant and allowed the boys to take turns rocking Cherry. Pat was struck by their looks of wonder as they held the baby as gently as they might a fragile vase. It certainly made a change from normal Scout activities!

It was a busy and satisfying life, but there was not much money to go round, and little spare time. Pat and Shirley were only able to see a movie if they were offered free passes when Pat sang at a campus talent show which also happened to include a film. The wheels that turned the music industry seemed worlds away from the daily grind in Denton. One day, however, a phone call came through that suddenly brought that world very much closer again.

Dixie had arranged a series of suppers to be hosted in rotation by the parents of her Cub Scouts and that evening, in February 1955, it was the turn of Terry Smith's family. Terry's mother Gertrude was busy in the kitchen, trying to get the food ready while she kept the Scouts from stealing cookies, when the phone in the dining room rang. Dixie answered it for her, then scurried straight past Gertrude and shouted through the back door: 'Pat, telephone!'

Pat was puzzled. 'Who'd be calling me here?'

'I forget his name, but it's something about music. I think he wants you to sing somewhere!'

Pat hurried to the phone. Soon, to the astonishment of everyone within earshot, he started singing into the receiver. In years to come Gertrude enjoyed telling the story of how the famous Pat Boone, with preparations for supper going on all around him and with young Scouts darting back and forth, had auditioned over her dining-room telephone. Eight months had passed since his conversation with Randy Wood, and Pat had just about written him off as another of the all-talk, no-action characters so common in the music business. Yet here he was on the phone, saying excitedly, 'Pat, I've found it! I've found you the hit I've been looking for. Take a listen to this.' The song was 'Two Hearts, Two Kisses, Make One Love', a rhythm and blues hit, but Randy wanted to record it in the new rock'n'roll style that was sweeping the nation. From the tender-sounding title, Pat's first thought was that the song would be something soft that would suit his crooning style of voice – a Como-style ballad. When Randy played it to him in its original rhythm and blues version by Otis Williams and the Charms, he says he was 'flabbergasted'. It was not what he had expected at all. 'I'm sending you a ticket to Chicago,' Randy told Pat. 'Meet me there, and we'll cut this thing!'

Pat's first Dot session took place soon afterwards, on a cold March day at the United Recording Studios in windy Chicago. Pat admits that he was dumbfounded by Randy's choice for his debut songs, 'Two Hearts, Two Kisses' and 'Tra La La' (written by Dave Bartholomew and Thomas Ridgely). 'Two Hearts' was already a huge rhythm and blues success, and Pat wondered how much more mileage there could realistically be in the song. He was willing to go with Randy's idea, however, and at the studio, under the guidance of respected sound engineer Bill Putnam, Pat chanted the song over and over until his voice was raspy – ideal for the style and sound they were aiming for.

The session over, Pat returned to his classes while Wood rushed back to Gallatin. The recording was not an immediate hit. As Pat had predicted, it suffered from severe competition in the crowded market place. Versions by well-known names such as Doris Day, the Ames Brothers and Frank Sinatra kept Pat's sales much lower than would have been expected if he had had the course to himself. Undeterred, Randy decided that it was time to take the bull by the horns and pitch the new recording to as many radio stations and distributors as possible. Pat duly embarked on a mammoth tour, visiting 18 cities in 18 days. It was a gruelling trip, but it did pay off: commercial interest in his record was definitely stirring at last. Any remaining gloom was quickly dispelled when the Boone version of 'Two Hearts, Two Kisses, Make One Love' entered the American Top 20 on 2 April 1955. Even Randy was surprised at the way the hit snowballed. Keen to optimize this success, Randy rapidly arranged more recording sessions for Pat. That was the beginning of a rewarding relationship between the Dot label and Pat Boone which lasted for 13 golden years.

Life was suddenly even more hectic than it had been before. Faced with growing national success, Pat struggled to keep up with his course work and make the increasing numbers of show dates. Shirley, expecting a second baby, had her hands full taking care of Cherry, helping Pat all she could, and in general holding the fort at home. For his part, Randy was spending hours on the phone promoting Pat and looking for a follow-up to 'Two Hearts, Two Kisses'.

For all the joy that Pat's early success brought, it was not an altogether easy period for the young couple. Most of the time, Pat was simply not at home. There was not enough time for everything, and personal tensions inevitably built up. The problem is a common one in the entertainment industry: how do you make a young marriage work in a positive way, despite the long absences of one half of the couple? Pat and Shirley were determined to hold everything together and worked very hard at it. When Pat was away, he made sure to phone Shirley every day, despite the expense of the long-distance calls. It did not make her any less lonely, but at least it made for some kind of contact between them.

Pat returned to the studio in Chicago on a bright spring day in May 1955. Randy had chosen a follow-up song, 'Ain't That A Shame' by Fats Domino, and Pat was there to record it, together with two other songs – the ballad 'Angel Eyes', written by Jimmy Cassin and Freddy James, and Red Foley's country dance favourite, 'Tennessee Saturday Night', penned by Billy Hughes. Pat's initial reaction to the catchy Domino number was that, as a would-be English teacher, he could not possibly sing the ungrammatical 'ain't'. Changing it to 'isn't' just did not sound right, however, so Pat put his pride in his pocket and sang the song as it was originally intended. 'Ain't That A Shame' became his first big hit. The song must have had some kind of effect on the academic world, too, because the word 'ain't' was added to English dictionaries soon afterwards!

'Ain't That A Shame' reached the dizzy heights of number one in the USA charts, and a few months later it rose to number seven across the Atlantic in the UK. Some years later, Fats Domino was on stage in New Orleans when Pat happened to be in the audience. Fats spied him and pulled him up onto the stage, much to the audience's delight. The big man then held up his plump hands, which sported several large diamond rings. Pointing to the largest one, Fats addressed the audience. 'You folks! See this ring? Well, this man, Pat Boone, bought me the ring with this song!' Sitting down at his piano, he proceeded to sing. 'You made – BOMP BOMP – me cry – BOMP...' It was the opening Pat had used for his recording of Fats Domino's 'Ain't That A Shame'. To the crowd's delight, the two went on to sing the song together as a duet.

With two bona fide hits to his name, Pat found that bigger opportunities were coming his way. One of these was an invitation to appear on Perry Como's popular TV show. Some of the nationwide audience for that show were reportedly surprised to find that the rhythm-and-blues-singing Pat Boone was not a black artist, which goes to show how clearly separated things still were in musical terms in those days. The Como appearance was also notable for being the first time a national audience had seen Pat wearing white shoes, which later became his trademark.

Three months after the Como date, in late summer 1955, Pat was back in the Chicago studio minting four more tracks, including 'Now I Know', written by the increasingly influential orchestrator Billy Vaughn. More hastily organized sessions followed in the next two months. By the time winter came, Pat Boone and Randy's musicians, headed by Billy, were very familiar faces at the United Studios in Chicago. Pat found that these studio visits offered welcome respites in his heavy touring schedule. The change of pace to studio work, though still busy, was refreshingly different and lifted his spirits.

The band met up again in December to record three memorable songs for release in the new year: 'I'll Be Home', written by Ferdinand Washington and Stan Lewis, 'Tutti Frutti', written by Richard Penniman, D. LaBostrie and Joe Lubin, and Billy Vaughn's 'Hoboken Baby'. The mid-fifties saw the height of the Cold War, and the Western Allies still had compulsory military conscription. The hopeful sentiments of 'I'll Be Home' caught the prevailing mood, and it became a standard radio request all round the world. In contrast, the outrageous 'Tutti Frutti' would always be associated with Little Richard, the stage name of one its writers, Richard Penniman. The Boone version was a toned-down adaptation which appealed to the more conservative tastes of 'middle America' and gave the song a much wider audience.

'Back in those early rock'n'roll days,' says Pat, 'I got many of my songs from the field of "black music". This crossover from black to white was somewhat revolutionary in a South which was still socially segregated. Many Afro-American artists in those days were impressive showmen and phenomenal vocalists. I was one of the first white acts to record so many songs from that field.' History documents that this 'crossover' policy paid huge dividends. In rapid succession came 'At My Front Door' (1955), a cover of The Eldorados; 'I'll Be Home' (1956), a cover of The Flamingos; 'Tutti Frutti' and 'Long Tall Sally' (1956), both covers of Little Richard; 'I Almost Lost My Mind' (1956), a cover of Ivory Joe Hunter; and a cover of Jo Turner's 'Chains of Love' (1956).

Meanwhile, Pat's star continued to rise. Sometime during the summer of 1955, Arthur Godfrey suggested that his daily show should bring Pat back for several appearances as an example of a successful ex-*Talent Scouts* winner. After his final guest spot, Arthur called Pat aside. 'Any time you're in New York,' he said, 'I want you to be on my show. I mean that! You don't have to call ahead – just drop in.' Pat was gratified. He saw it as a meaningful sign of acceptance from the wider industry.

By the end of the summer of 1955, with two chart records under his belt, a performance schedule that was becoming increasingly more demanding, and Arthur Godfrey's offer promising more exposure to the national audience, Pat decided it was time to make a move. The short year and a half that he and Shirley had spent in Denton had brought changes in their lives almost too dramatic and swift to track. They discussed their options and prayed about them. Pat felt he needed to be 'closer to the action', and Shirley was anxious to get the move over before their second baby arrived. Pat was determined not to give up on his education and made enquiries about changing to a different college. When the change was deemed to be feasible, the Boones set their sights on New York. They gave their chinchillas – clearly now *not* the key to their future – to the Dyers; they said goodbye to the Kleins (who would later manage the restaurant Pat built half way between Denton's two colleges); they met with the Cub Scout pack for a final get-together. Then they packed their belongings and moved north.

New York was a busy, bustling shock after the gentler pace of life in Denton, but it was undeniably exhilarating. Pat enrolled at Columbia University to continue his studies, and made the most of the chance to appear regularly on Arthur Godfrey's show. The Boones' second daughter Lindy was born at French Hospital in New York City on 11 October 1955. Soon after that, the expanding family moved to a newly built house in Leonia, New Jersey.

They spent some of their happiest years there. Pat's career was blossoming, fuelled by his regular spots on the *Godfrey Show*, and repeated hit records helped to bring the money in, while Pat somehow still managed to attend college and obtain good grades.

Arthur Godfrey had taken a liking to Pat, and seemed to display a certain intuition about the young Boone couple when he asked Pat live on TV one day if there was to be the patter of any more tiny feet in his household. Blushing, Pat said he thought not. Some time later, however, Shirley and Pat were astounded to discover that they were expecting another child. The news was duly announced to the Arthur Godfrey audience, who burst into rapturous applause. Pat was a strong favourite with them by then. Their third daughter, Deborah Ann Boone, was born on 22 September 1956 in Hackensack, New Jersey.

Meanwhile, Pat was gaining new fans every day. His first fan club had been started back in 1953, and a national fan club was formed in 1955, based in Nashville. Pat received hundreds of fan letters every day. In 1956, young Chris Bujnovsky joined the club and was just one among many young people to be thrilled by the discovery that she could help support her favourite singer. 'I could buy and request Pat's records through the fan club system, and could help raise his profile by writing to various magazines requesting features on the Boones. All in all, I tried making him known more widely in every respectable way I could think of!'

Pat's success was remarkable – something to admire whether you were a fan or not. His association with the Dot label was to earn him a staggering total of 23 Top 20 successes in the USA and 19 in the UK. From 1955 to 1959, he was one of only two male solo artists (Elvis was the other) to remain in the USA Top 100 for over four consecutive years without a break. His recording artistry was evident even in those earliest, rather experimental mintings. Highly acclaimed too was the orchestral wizardry of Billy Vaughn as he enhanced Pat's smooth vocals. It seemed that every song Pat released from the mid-fifties to the early sixties became an instant hit around the globe. Throughout those years, he managed to negotiate successfully the tricky musical terrain of song choices during subtle shifts in the notoriously fickle public taste. There was, however, always a clear thread of consistency in his professional work, a singular ability that stood out over time. He and his producer shared a valuable gifting, an ability to discern quality songs that reflected their knowledge of both the art form and the market place.

As the decade progressed, Pat's plentiful recordings became immensely popular in the developing teenage market, earning numerous awards and nominations, a clear affirmation of the high esteem in which he was held by the industry and music devotees alike. Soon more great opportunities opened up for him, including a nationally networked TV series, more hit songs and even Hollywood movies. The idea of an unpretentious career in school teaching was relegated to the back-burner. Yet, despite all the early glamour and hype, the people closest to him would testify to the fact that Pat remained essentially the regular, everyday kind of person that his parents had always wanted him to be. He kept his close family ties, retaining good relationships with his brother and two sisters.

Nowadays, Pat finds it hard to believe that the first of his big-selling hits appeared way back in the Cold War fifties. Internationally, teenage pop music was just coming into vogue, challenging the comfortable status quo of the music scene. Of course, Pat was not the only aspiring singer to be pulled into the evolving phenomenon of rock'n'roll. There were many so-called 'white guys and gals from the South' who would have become died-in-the-wool country singers, had it not been for the advent of rock'n'roll. The list includes Elvis Presley, Roy Orbison, Brenda Lee, Don Gibson, Conway Twitty, Carl Perkins, Buddy Holly, Wanda Jackson and many others. The explosive success of rock-'n'roll opened the stable doors for an unstoppable stampede. Pat made the most of that aura of success. He holds the record – never broken – of being in the USA Hit Single Chart for 220 consecutive weeks between 1955 and 1959.

He was in a unique position. In many people's eyes, he was not 'rural' enough to be a country singer, but was far too 'nice' and strait-laced to be a rock'n'roller. Yet his recordings, diverse in style and tempo and including conservative pop and country material, were often featured on dedicated rock'n'roll shows. Agents booked him for all sorts of engagements, teaming him up with an enormous variety of pop, country and rock acts on major concert tours, some worldwide. Despite the apparent clash of identities, Pat went where he was asked and absorbed it all. Offstage, he identified very well with his youthful peers in the rock'n'roll brigade. He had a genuine empathy with many of his singing peers, remaining friends with the few who survived those dizzy days. Some of the performers, such as Buddy Holly, Carl Perkins, Cliff Richard and George Hamilton IV were essentially gentle people to whom Pat related extremely well. They were poles apart from the rebel image most people expected of rock'n'rollers. Both George IV and Pat, for example, maintained lasting marriages with their home-town sweethearts. Interestingly too, in later years, colleagues such as Cliff Richard and George IV would go on to become well-respected advocates of the Christian faith in many parts of the world.

There seemed to be no end to the opportunites before him, and Pat was having the time of his life. Early in March 1956, he was once more ensconced in the United Studios in Chicago. His bouncy cover version of Little Richard's energetic 'Long Tall Sally' certainly captured the carefree spirit of that fresh spring day. The whole studio seemed to enjoy the fun, Pat remembers. Then they moved on to the next song on the recording list, and Pat was able to demonstrate his versatility in the bluesy, Ivory Joe Hunter song 'I Almost Lost My Mind'. As he concluded the recording, Pat was in high spirits and could not resist some mocking self-praise. 'How about that, boys? Pretty good, eh? Especially coming from a WASP-ish guy like me!'

71

Four months later, in the July heatwave of 1956, Pat was back in the studio again. The band was running through the parts for 'Friendly Persuasion', a song from the Civil War movie of the same name . 'Friendly Persuasion' was a beautiful, dreamy ballad. It conjured up a tranquil mood, the antithesis of what was happening in the real world, where the Suez Crisis was reaching boiling point. In the weeks that followed, Pat's recording of 'Friendly Persuasion' would enjoy heavy sales, having once again appealed to the popular mood. Written by the versatile Dimitri Tiomkin and Paul Francis Webster in simple Quaker style, everyone in the studio agreed that the audio take that day exhibited top quality artistry with a lasting appeal.

It was the only song recorded that day, but work resumed a few weeks later with a change of musical direction when 'Chains Of Love' was minted for the flip side of the 'Friendly Persuasion' single. Not such a familiar piece, this composition was more bluesy in style. From there they moved on to record 'Harbour Lights', by British writers Jimmy Kennedy and Hugh Williams, a standard hit among others to be included on Pat's next album release. His repertoire choice on that hot, late-July session was astute, diverse and challenging, and surprisingly few of the songs were obviously rock'n'roll numbers. Nevertheless, the bounce and general 'sellability' of his sound was a conscious effort to impact what was then known as 'the Hit Parade'. From the country field came 'Chattanooga Shoeshine Boy', clearly a choice gleaned from his father-in-law. 'That Lucky Old Sun', a philosophical song, had done well for Frankie Laine and seemed capable of doubling as a spiritual. Cole Porter's 'Begin The Beguine' was a popular dance-time number from a few decades earlier.

The next studio session, on 11 November 1956, took place amidst mounting international tension that was impossible to ignore. Under American pressure, British Prime Minister Anthony Eden agreed to pull troops out of Suez only if a UN force took over. Simultaneously, the UN was demanding the withdrawal of

Russian armies from Hungary. The cool studio seemed like a good place to escape, as Pat concentrated on making a recording for the credits of the Ingrid Bergman movie *Anastasia*. Pat had been chosen because of his 'Friendly Persuasion' success, and his recording of the theme song 'Anastasia' (again by Dimitri Tiomkin) also resulted in high sales. The flip side of that single was 'Don't Forbid Me', loved by Pat for its low bass parts. Pat observes today, 'I guess I'm a frustrated bass singer! I love to sing low – I'd do well deputizing for guys like J.D. Sumner, George Younce or Ray Walker of the Jordanaires!'

The pace was relentless, and Pat was back in the studio on 24 November, once again with a change of style and theme for his renditions of Bill Haley's hit, 'Rock Around The Clock' and Tennessee Ernie Ford's hit 'Shot Gun Boogie'. These were closely followed by two gems which were destined to become part of what might be called Pat's timeless classics: 'It's Too Soon To Know' and 'Love Letters In The Sand'. Pat is particularly fond of the former. '"It's Too Soon To Know" was a great song that seeped into my artistic soul and is one of the songs that I am truly proud of, the kind I'd like to be remembered for.' 'Love Letters In The Sand', recorded three times by Pat and always a favourite with Randy Wood, was originally a pop hit in 1931 for the Ted Black Orchestra and later also for Bing Crosby. Pat recalls with a smile the experience of miming the song for some Hollywood movie bosses. 'For my *Bernadine* movie, the Twentieth Century Fox studio folks decided they wanted another song and asked me to lip-sync "Love Letters In The Sand". I did, and the DJs flipped over the song, but I could never figure out what folks saw in it!'

The dizzy heights of worldwide success came to Pat very suddenly, giving him very little time to prepare himself for the onslaught. Yet, as he explains, it was a fulfilling time, even if it meant endless work and long separations from Shirley and his young family. 'I find it impossible to adequately explain the deep pleasure I felt when I received a warm reception by fans and peers,' he says. 'It was such a wonderful fulfilment for me as an artist. My boyhood dreams were all coming true!' Over the years, despite being swept along on the white-water rapids of a successful show-biz career, and experiencing the ever-present enticements of corrupting fame, Pat kept his feet solidly on the ground. Personally, he remained his own man and emerged, even in success, still sober-minded, self-effacing, God-fearing and committed to his family. Amidst so much fickleness and superficiality, he always came across as wise, witty and versatile, as well as possessing an admirable talent. Some critics inevitably declared that he seemed too good to be true, but Middle America loved him. He is convinced that the Christian family values imparted by his parents strengthened him well for those heady days – and for the future when adversity threatened to overwhelm him.

By the autumn of 1956, still under the commercial direction of Randy Wood, Pat had emerged as Middle America's number-one teenage heart-throb. His rock'n'roll was selling well, and he was equally at home utilizing his velvet-smooth voice on sentimental ballads. Despite the teenage tag, his appeal stretched far beyond his own generation, offering strong competition to the Crosby-Como-Sinatra crooning style. Pat's movie songs ('Friendly Persuasion', 'Anastasia', 'Love Letters In The Sand' and 'April Love') were top standard ballads of their day. All were featured in Hollywood box-office successes, the latter two in movies which starred Pat himself.

Much of his success could be attributed to the constant airplay his records received from America's top DJs, including Dick Clark, whose *American Bandstand* was a hit show on network TV on weekday afternoons after school time. Pat enjoyed many guest appearances over the years on Dick's show. Often lovingly referred to as 'America's Oldest Teenager', Dick was an individual that Pat always regarded with respect. *American Bandstand* was a prized venue, a happy meeting point for a host of great names such as Connie Francis, Wanda Jackson, Frankie Avalon, Bobby Rydell and many other celebrities from those exciting days.

In 1957, delighted with Pat's ongoing success, Randy started to look around for further sellable talent. He did not have to look far. Pat's younger brother Nick was already making a name for himself locally by then, and Randy was quick to sign up this other handsome, vocally talented Boone. Nick's break into the entertainment world had come when he appeared at the 'Discovery of the Week' concert (sponsored by the Nashville *Tennessean* newspaper) held in Centennial Park. This led him to take part in further concerts around the local area. Since he was still at school, however, he did not consider a singing career as a serious option. He did, however, appreciate being paid for his appearances! Randy had offered Nick a recording contract then, but Nick had turned it down because he wanted to obtain his degree first. Once he had graduated, however, it was a different matter, and on 29 August 1957 Nick found himself in a studio session in Hollywood, recording 'Plaything' and 'The Honey Song' under the pseudonym of 'Nick Todd'. Randy and his personal manager Jack Spina had decided that it would be too confusing to have two singing Boones around!

There followed a plethora of stage appearances for Nick, the first on the *Ed Sullivan TV Show* in September 1957, followed by a guest appearance on his big brother Pat's own TV show in October, and then it was on to Toronto for the Canadian *Hit Parade*. Patti Page's *The Big Record* beckoned in November, and the famed *Bob Hope Show* in December. More records followed as Nick's career progressed. He achieved several modest hits with cover versions of songs generally made famous by better-known artists. For example, 'At The Hop', a hit by Danny and the Juniors, was a Nick Boone cover for Dot. That, however, was as far as it went, or as far as he chose to go. Nowadays Nick's singing is mainly done in his local church. For years, he was the worship leader of a church in Memphis. He also headed up a church welfare programme called Agape that placed orphans for adoption and was involved in helping meet the needs of unmarried mothers and emotionally disturbed people in his local area. Today he is executive director of the Madison Children's Home and the Domestic Violence Program in Nashville.

Meanwhile, Pat's hit songs were blasting up the international charts, and fresh opportunities continued to pour into his manager's office. Not all were welcome. Suddenly, he found himself being shoved and tugged in all directions, not always along routes he wanted to follow. Still young, he was tempted on all sides by offers to increase his fame and fortune. He might so easily have lost his way, but somehow managed to hold on to his principles. One offer that came in was a lavish proposal for him to star in a series of TV shows sponsored by Chesterfield Cigarettes. Pat refused. His agent was aghast. What was he thinking of? He did not have to smoke himself, he just had to get on there and do his songs. Pat was unmoved, explaining that he would not take part as the purpose of the show's sponsorship was to encourage young people to smoke, and he did not want to play a part in that. It was not a message he wanted to send out.

The lucrative offer was duly turned down. His manager was annoyed and many business associates thought him insane. Two months later, his hardworking agent returned to Pat, this time beaming outwardly, but inwardly unsure of his reception. 'Pat, you can still be the youngest singing host with his own TV series,' he said. 'We've found you a new sponsor … it's a drinks company.' To Pat it seemed that history was repeating itself. He shook his head and turned down that offer as firmly as he had the first.

Amazingly, several weeks later, his persistent agent returned. This time, he clearly could not contain his excitement. 'Tell me, Pat,' he said, 'how old are you?'

'I'm 22 … Why?'

'Well, Pat, you're *still* going to be the youngest singer to have his own TV show – unless you've got anything against Chevrolet?'

'No *man*, I don't! I drive one!'

So finally, in 1956, ABC TV signed the young Pat Boone for his first personally hosted TV series. It was entitled *The Pat Boone Chevy Showroom* and the series made him a household name, the youngest performer with his own network show. It was to be the start of hundreds of major TV appearances throughout his long career.

People often asked Pat why he always wore those white buckskin shoes. There was really no specific reason, he says, other than that all the other college kids were wearing them at the time! He may have been the first to wear them on TV, however, and they quickly became his trademark. Indeed, if ever he appeared in shoes other than white bucks, the audience was visibly disappointed – and told him so. 'After seeing how disappointed my fans were in the early days when I didn't wear those white shoes,' he comments, 'I began to think I should oblige them! Besides, I like them anyway – they go with anything. And I guess I feel more like Pat Boone when I look down and see those familiar white bucks…'

Superstar guests, such as Nat King Cole, Andy Williams, Johnny Mathis and others, became plentiful as the series shot up the ratings chart. Very soon the new singing star on ABC TV became hugely popular across North America. Cliff Richard remembers with gratitude the early exposure Pat's show gave his own career. 'I certainly enjoyed working with Pat. He really made me feel at home as a guest, although I was a little nervous because it was my first TV appearance in America. I was impressed by Pat both on and off stage, and became convinced he was one the greatest artists of our time.'

Pat's fondness for live TV performances had its pros and cons, however. Usually he revelled in the charged atmosphere where unpredictability brought an added excitement to each session – yet it also opened the way for things to go horribly wrong. One notable disaster struck when the show included the Irving Berlin classic 'Lazy'. To complement the song, a lavish set had been constructed, consisting of a lake and some trees. Pat was lying on the bank of this 'lake' ready to sing. Irving Berlin had been contacted and invited to watch the broadcast, as his song was to be featured. Unfortunately, 30 seconds before the red light came on to signify that the programme was being broadcast to the nation, the teleprompter got stuck. Pat had not memorized all the lyrics because they were due to be there for him to see on the teleprompter. He had little choice but to think on his feet, so he started to sing, making up his own words to Mr Berlin's classic composition. It was not a success. Pat later recorded a whole album of Berlin songs, *Pat Boone Sings Irving Berlin*, which contained a one-line note from Irving for the sleeve notes. Needless to say, however, 'Lazy' was not one of the songs included.

Live broadcasts were full of risks. Pat recalls one memorable occasion when the sound failed and the big boom microphone, brought in to replace the broken one, swung round and knocked the whole studio set flying, leaving him stranded alone on stage, with no mike and no props. Pat was forced to continue the show for some minutes using sign language, while the sound man scrambled to get the equipment working again. When a functioning microphone was finally put in front of him, Pat got his own back by silently mouthing the words, horrifying the already sweating technician.

TV made Pat's face famous across North America, but even then there was room for mistaken identity. In September 1956, he was entertaining at a State Fair in Springfield, Massachusetts. Meanwhile, back in New Jersey, Shirley was expecting their third child, and in case Pat could not get home in time, his close friend Don Henley promised to take Shirley to hospital if it became necessary. When the time came, Don did as he had promised and accompanied Shirley to the hospital for what turned out to be a difficult delivery. The doctor who came to greet them shook Don's hand warmly and exclaimed, 'It's a great pleasure to meet you, Mr Boone! I'm one of your biggest fans. I've watched you on TV many times, and I enjoy your show very much.' Don was not quite sure what to say, and in any case was more concerned about Shirley than about correcting the doctor. It was not until after Debby was born that Pat was able to set matters straight with the doctor.

Pat loves to recount the follow-up to this little incident. 'When our fourth baby was due in January 1958, I took Shirley to hospital myself. The same doctor came up to me, grinned, shook my hand warmly and assured me he was still a regular viewer of my shows and was certainly aware of my identity!' The Boones' fourth child, Laura Gene, arrived on 30 January 1958, and Pat comments further that all he could think of at the time was that he was still very young, and he was already outnumbered at home five to one by females.

In New York the Boones attended the Manhattan Church of Christ, where Pat took on the responsibility of song leader. It may seem strange that he could continue to sing at church while attaining so much chart success and becoming internationally known as a TV and movie star, but the Boones enjoyed the fellowship at the church and continued to make the 45-minute drive from their home as often as they could, believing strongly in the importance of their relationship with God, in spite of the hectic pace of life. Pat remained concerned to be supportive of the Church of Christ doctrinal and cultural teachings, too. 'I turned down several movie roles and changed song lyrics to accommodate the Church of Christ teachings,' he says. 'I wanted to be a good Church of Christ boy!'

One journalist, commenting about the anti-dancing teaching of the Church of Christ, wanted to know Pat's feelings about the teenagers who danced to his records. 'Look,' Pat told him, 'I record these songs as music. I can't be responsible for what happens to them afterwards. What kids do is up to them!' When his comment appeared in a column, it was made to look as if Pat was actively discouraging teenagers from dancing to his records. This was picked up by many DJs across the USA, who promptly quit playing his songs. Pat became very wary of granting interviews.

Meanwhile, Pat was also experiencing private problems. It was impossible to avoid entirely the obvious difficulties of being an absentee husband and father. Pat recognized that an entertainer's life would never offer him a consistent or reliable existence. It was a case of fantastic feast and frustrating famine. Without continued promotion, travel and public performances, an entertainer's career soon stagnates. Both Pat and Shirley accepted the fact that frequent and prolonged absences were an unavoidable part of the career deal, but it caused heartache nonetheless. Among other potential problems were the not infrequent advances made to him by co-stars, young wannabe performers and even older married women who thought it would be some kind of feather in their caps to brag about a liaison with the young singer. Pat took to heart the problems he saw all around him in show business, as less stable colleagues succumbed to the temptations of drink, drugs and women. He remains grateful that he was never sucked down into such depths, but admits that it was not always easy to keep his head above water.

He did his best to do the sensible thing, however, and was still sufficiently motivated to finish off his education, despite the demands of his growing fame. He finally graduated in June 1958, *magna cum laude*, from Columbia University, having majored in Speech and English. His success owed much to Shirley's help and encouragement – indeed, he feels her name should be written alongside his on the degree certificate. He now had his qualification at last, but any teaching aspirations he might have harboured inevitably faded as exciting show-biz doors continued to open up for him. There was not much time for reflection as Pat was swept along on the wave of success.

The heady pace was beginning to take its toll as he commuted between the ABC TV studios in New York and the latest family home in Teaneck, New Jersey. Perhaps under the stress of the endless whirl of activity, Pat momentarily lost his judgement one afternoon and regressed to the days of his schoolboy pranks. He chose an unorthodox way of letting off steam, which ended up with him being suspected of causing a bomb explosion. Pat's office at 6 West 57th Street was just around the corner from Tiffany's. On one of his trips through Virginia, he had purchased a large quantity of fireworks and that afternoon, just for fun, he dropped a large, lit firework from his office window high above the busy street. The firework exploded with a deafening bang that echoed around the skyscrapers, causing a great deal of panic in the passers-by. The police who came to investigate the apparent bomb threat against Tiffany's took a dim view of Pat's experiment, and his 'heart-throb' status did not protect him from a sharp reprimand. It was not, he says, one of his finer moments.

CHAPTER 5

FRIENDLY PERSUASION

Thee I love, more than the meadows so green and
  still,
More than the mulberries on the tree!
    Paul Francis Webster and Dimitri Tiomkin

BY THE END OF 1956 Pat was achieving the kind of fame and following from which legends arise. His velvet voice, backed by Billy Vaughn's ear-catching arrangements, gave him a distinctive quality that stood out from other performers. He believes he owes Billy a great deal, and their collaboration was a particularly special one. Billy was a good bit older than Pat, having been born in April 1919 in Glasgow, Kentucky. As a teenager, Billy joined a barbershop singing group at Western State College in Kentucky. The inexperienced group made a recording of their singing in the Van Meter Auditorium, which happened to be heard by Randy Wood. He persuaded them to rename the group The Hilltoppers, and Dot Records released the song. Billy's recording career was long-lasting and included many hit singles. His trademark twin saxophones were used in many of his arrangements, creating the distinctive 'Billy Vaughn sound'. It was thanks to Randy Wood that he and Pat were brought to work together, and Billy was certainly instrumental in Pat's success, making an invaluable contribution to the musical quality of his recordings.

During those early years, Pat was marketed not merely as a 'teen rock'n'roller' but also as a sophisticated song stylist in the Como, Crosby and Sinatra mode. Ironically, as the popularity of rock'n'roll spread like wildfire, his concerts also heralded acclaim in another genre. Pat was seen as part and parcel of the 'new' breed of singers, and was swept up in the tide. He did not object. 'I was being designated as a rock singer and therefore I had to play up to those teenage expectations, as well as trying to concentrate on the more serious market! I'll admit that my eyes were set on long-term career success in both fields. After all, I saw country singers by the score jumping ship and scrambling onto the rock-'n'roll pleasure boat. Why shouldn't I benefit too?'

When it came to likes and dislikes for particular songs, however, Pat was always very opinionated. He was not prepared to be happy with just anything that was put in front of him. Billy Vaughn reckoned that Pat had an unusually fine ear for choosing the best songs to record, and Pat is happy to explain what drove his decisions. 'Sometimes I'd get irritated with people telling me what was a "good song" and what wasn't! I've always been a holder of firm views. Even during my short career back in the fifties, I'd seen big changes in pop music, many of which I applauded. What I wanted was always to be in the *forefront* of what was happening – an influential artist is one who acts as a catalyst of change.'

Looking back now, it is plain that Pat's lengthy career has seen a wonderful parade of differing styles and made use of the most diverse songwriters. On the secular side, his choices have covered a range of sources, including Cole Porter, Hank Williams, Irving Berlin, Stuart Hamblen, Bill Haley, Red Foley and Johnny Mercer. On the sacred side, he has sung a wide repertoire which encompasses Bill Gaither, Fanny Crosby, Larry Norman, Ira Sankey, Andrae Crouch, Charlie Landsborough and Wes Davis. The list is endless. He has always tried to make a point, he says, of choosing songwriters capable of advancing beyond the usual restricted, often banal output. 'I'm glad to say that today there are still refreshingly novel and innovative performers, worthy of the status of the truly great artists of the past.'

In the late 1990s, *Rolling Stone* magazine recognized Pat's historic importance in the chronicles of pop history in a front-cover feature. The article explained that his grounding had been in country and gospel music and in the crooners of his youth, as well as the so-called 'golden rock'n'roll years'. Artistic maturing came via a range of teachers and mentors, including Red Foley, Eddy Arnold and Perry Como. He witnessed the 'rebel rockers' pilfering some of the core songs from the fields of country and gospel music – yet in turn he admitted that the 'old guard' also stole some of the rockers' fresh sounds and techniques. There is room for both the old boys and the new boys on the block, in his opinion.

'As we enter a new millennium,' he says, 'fads and customs have clearly altered many times since I started, of that there is no doubt. The music sector has seen earth-shaking changes in movies, stage shows, records, radio, TV and now videos. I like to think that "yours truly" has tenderly championed each progressive transformation for good. I'm convinced that the popular music of this century will be a kaleidoscope of fresh colours and innovative sounds that will enfold the traditional *and* the modern age.'

After the publication of the *Rolling Stone* article, Pat sent an ice-packed crate of 50 cartons of fresh milk to the magazine's editorial offices in San Francisco, with his greetings. When it arrived, the white nectar was dutifully unpacked and distributed among the bemused staff. The story goes that they all sat at their office desks and solemnly toasted the achievements and integrity of 'good ol' Pat Boone'!

Like many teenagers, Pat had initially been strongly influenced by the big-band ballad music his parents listened to. He had originally tried to copy the style of those old-time performers, too, envisaging himself on a lighted stage just like them. All that changed with the advent of the more energetic rock'n'roll, and much of the older style of performance disappeared into the shadows. Pat was happy to join in with the innovations. 'Good Rockin' Tonight', originally a rhythm and blues hit for Wyonie Harris in 1948, was always considered by Pat to be the perfect rock'n'roll standard. It was one of Randy Wood's favourites too, and entered the charts for Pat in January 1959.

Pat continued to follow his penchant for recording cover versions of songs from the Afro-American field. Nevertheless, while his recordings of these were increasingly played on 'conservative' radio stations and widened the market for the genre, his efforts did cause a certain amount of resentment among some of the original artists – to say nothing of more than a few self-righteous critics. Little Richard in particular was said to be exceptionally angry when Pat covered two of his hits, 'Tutti Frutti' and 'Long Tall Sally'. He even voiced his anger in public during an autobiographical movie entitled *Hail! Hail! Rock and Roll!* 'When Pat Boone cut my record,' he said, 'I was real mad. I wanted to get him because he was stopping my progress!'

Pat did not agree with Little Richard's perceptions. 'Before I covered the songs, Little Richard was washing dishes in a bus station in Macon, Georgia, because his records weren't selling!' Interestingly enough, a more friendly Little Richard later told Pat that his covers of 'Tutti Frutti' and 'Long Tall Sally' were indeed partly responsible for getting him out of that bus station and on his way to international fame.

As far as Pat is concerned, far from preventing such music from becoming more popular, he and a few other white rock'n'roll singers were partially responsible for enlarging the popularity of the genre. Back then, Pat in particular was perceived as the 'acceptable' voice of rock'n'roll. Eventually, his efforts led to the opening of lucrative doors for the original artists, who finally received the exposure and recognition they deserved. Ask anyone today who sang 'Ain't That A Shame', and they will say 'Fats

Domino'; ask anyone today who sang 'Tutti Frutti', and they will tell you 'Little Richard' – few remember that it was Pat Boone who effectively paved the way. There is room in the market place for both, however, and Pat does not feel he has stolen their limelight, or that they have stolen his.

Despite the sneers of some critics, Pat remained a determined advocate of cross-pollination between 'black' and 'white' music. In any case, as he points out, the crossover worked both ways. Fats Domino made extensive use of the Hank Williams songbook, and his big hit 'Blueberry Hill' had long been associated with Gene Autry and other western singers. Ray Charles's smash hit 'I Can't Stop Loving You' was penned by Don Gibson. Whitney Houston's blockbuster 'I'll Always Love You' was originally written for Porter Wagoner by Dolly Parton. Even a rudimentary perusal of the repertoire of the likes of Chuck Berry and Little Richard himself will turn up examples of cross-pollination from the country and gospel fields.

Whatever controversy might have raged, Pat certainly never lost his admiration for the talents of the immoderate Little Richard. He was an outrageous anomaly in the 1950s. Men just did not perm their hair in those days! And he loved travelling round in super-sleek limousines, driven by a chauffeur in black suit, bow tie and white gloves. Little Richard would emerge at the stage door with an ermine cape draped round his shoulders and a crown on his head. It certainly attracted attention. 'Years before Elvis,' Pat remembers, 'he behaved as if he really was the "King of Rock'n'Roll".' An undoubted legend, Little Richard was perhaps the most vividly eccentric icon of the early rock'n'roll years, becoming something of a cult hero to aficionados – well before the phenomenon of Elvis, let alone the Beatles. His colourful repertoire came to be both adopted and adapted by many of the greats who followed him, including Elvis, Carl Perkins and Pat himself. Songs like 'Tutti Frutti' and 'Rip it Up' were standards in those formative years.

During the final season of Pat's *Chevy Showroom* TV show in the summer of 1959, the producers made the unusual decision to do four of the shows from Europe. Making the most of the opportunity, Pat and Shirley left the four children with their grandparents in Nashville and travelled to Paris together. It was the honeymoon they had never had. Staying at the George V Hotel, they enjoyed candlelit dinners in Maxim's Restaurant and visited tourist attractions such as Notre Dame Cathedral and the Eiffel Tower between recordings for the TV shows.

Their next stop after Paris was the picturesque Austrian city of Salzburg, famous as the birthplace of Mozart. Surrounded by the majestic Alps, the setting for *The Sound of Music*, the city made the perfect backdrop for the show. Pat sang with the Salzburg Boys' Choir and even danced a waltz to the music of Strauss's 'The Blue Danube'.

Moving on to Vienna, they experienced one of the most memorable moments of the tour, and it had nothing to do with the TV show. For many years Pat and Shirley had supported the Foster Parents' Plan (whereby couples in America 'adopted' a child or children in another country and helped ease the family situation with financial contributions). They had adopted an Austrian foster son named Franz and were finally able to meet him and his mother. She was able to keep Franz with support from the Plan.

In Venice, their final destination, the couple enjoyed drifting along the canals in a gondola, and also took the chance to visit another foster child, Giuseppi from Florence. He spoke no English and they spoke no Italian, but Pat was touched by the loving communication they managed despite the lack of a common language. It was, he says, a very precious time. Eventually their time was up and they boarded a train to travel on through Italy, soaking up the atmosphere and countryside before sailing home on the luxury liner the *Queen Mary*.

By this time, Pat was being classified as one of 'the greatest crooners of all time'. The golden age of the classic crooners (among them Bing Crosby, Frank Sinatra, Perry Como and Nashville's own Eddy Arnold) was reaching a peak when *The Pat Boone Chevy Showroom* hit the TV screens. Among all the crooning greats, Pat exhibited a distinctive sophistication and professionalism. The famed Grand Ole Opry radio broadcasts from Pat's home town could boast of country crooners such as Ray Price, George Morgan, Jim Reeves and Red Foley. Pat's style famously married the best of the north and the south. The impressionable youngster who once thirstily drank in all the influences around him was now a ground-breaking role model in his own right. It gave him enormous satisfaction to know that he was realizing his dream. Many great crooners of the day sought his friendship – and a guest spot on his TV show – but Pat would be the first to acknowledge the great debt he owed to them.

Pat's admiration for Bing Crosby, nurtured at an early age, ran deep. He was, he says, the biggest of his vocal influences. He loved Bing's style so much that he tried to model himself on the great man, as did many others, including Perry Como. When Pat did his first movie, *Bernadine*, he tried to imagine himself as a teenage Bing. 'For my money, Bing was the true father of crooning. He defined the term more than anyone else. When I was a boy, my parents played his music every day. It's no wonder that it had such a profound effect on me! It always flattered me when people compared me with Bing.'

Bing's real name was Harry Lillis Crosby, and he was born in Tacoma, Washington, on 2 May 1904. He grew up in Spokane, and at the age of seven earned the nickname which stuck like glue for the remainder of his life. He was an avid reader of the comic strip *The Bingville Bugle*, and his friends nicknamed him 'Bingo from Bingville', which ended up as just plain 'Bing'. Thereafter, he was rarely called anything else.

In 1920 Bing formed a band for school functions, in which he played drums and sang. Later, in the face of fierce parental opposition, he and his friend Al Rinker set off to make their musical fortunes in California. In 1931, three years before Pat's birth, after small success singing vocals in the Gus Arnheim Orchestra, Bing finally landed his own CBS radio show. That same year saw the minting of Bing's now classic songs 'Stardust', 'I Surrender' and 'Where The Blue Of The Night Meets The Gold Of The Day'. Many years later, Pat considered it a privilege to record these Crosby classics himself. Bing's lengthy career included a number of memorable Hollywood movies, including *High Society* (with Grace Kelly and Frank Sinatra), the seasonal favourite *Holiday Inn* and the famous *Road To...* series (with comedian Bob Hope).

Bing had a smooth style all his own, and it impressed a great many people. Pat was one of them, and remembers enjoying a round of golf with his hero in the 1960s, during which he waited patiently to pose a pressing question. Finally the opportunity came. 'Hey, Bing,' he ventured, 'every John Doe in the country thinks he's a Bing and practises that "ba, ba, ba, ba boom" in the shower! Where did that come from?' With a twinkle in his eye, Bing replied, 'Well, Pat, to tell you the truth, one time I kind of forgot the words to a song and I substituted "ba, ba, ba, ba boom"! I guess it came in handy here and there, down the years...'

A short time after Pat began his TV show, he was delighted to receive a fan letter from none other than the great Mr Crosby. 'It was a letter that came out of the blue, but it has always had a place in my heart,' he says. The letter read:

Dear Pat
I've read in the trade press that you're doing a TV show ... I've been following your career ... I'm rooting for you!
    If I was advising you I'd leave you with these words from the late, great George M. Cohen: 'Never stay on too long!'

Gratis, Bing.

When Bing died in 1977, Pat felt that he had lost both a friend and a supporter.

Pat was also in awe of the legendary man born Francis Albert Sinatra. Sinatra himself was an avid admirer of the slightly older Bing Crosby. As a skinny 17-year-old, Frank and his girlfriend Nancy Barbato (whom he later married) travelled from their native Hoboken to Jersey City to see Bing appear on stage. Inspired, Frank decided there and then that he wanted to be a successful singer too. Sinatra's musical break came in 1936 when he won an amateur talent competition as part of a foursome called The Hoboken Four. He was signed up by the Harry James Orchestra, moving on later to join Tommy Dorsey's band, where his solo career really began to take off. He soon had an immense following. Frank's superb vocal skills and good looks brought him success among a wide audience, with stylish songs such as 'Fly Me To The Moon', 'My Kind Of Town', 'Strangers In The Night' and, of course, 'My Way'. His acting ability was evident in musicals such as *On the Town* (with Gene Kelly), *Guys and Dolls* (with Marlon Brando and Jean Simmons), and the more serious *From Here to Eternity* (with Burt Lancaster and Deborah Kerr).

At the start of Pat's career, Frank was heard to declare his admiration for the new boy on the block. 'Take my word for it,' he commented, 'this Boone boy will be one of the biggest names in show business within the next few years.' Frank died in 1999, but Pat still recalls the time when someone told him that whenever Frank wore white shoes, he would laughingly tell his friends that they were his 'Boone booties'!

Another influential crooner from a rather different background was the unforgettable Nat King Cole. Born on 17 March 1917 in Montgomery, Alabama, to a clergyman and his wife, he spent most of his difficult childhood in Chicago. There Nat made his first appearance on stage, performing in his brother Eddie's orchestra. A gifted pianist, he always said that his earliest influence was the 'King of the Ivories', Earl (Fatha) Hines. Pat says, 'He was the Louis Armstrong of piano players. And he had a great band – great musicians. Nat told me that he admired him so much. He'd still say that Earl was his greatest influence.' In 1939 Nat formed a mainly instrumental trio (later known as the Nat Cole Trio) consisting of himself on piano, Oscar Moore on guitar and Wesley Price on cello. 'Gradually,' Pat recounts, 'Nat found himself singing more and more solos, and when his career really began to take off the group remained with him as his backing group.' It soon became clear, however, that a different kind of orchestral backing was needed to bring out the beauty of Nat's smooth, mellow voice. The resulting sound produced many classic hits, such as 'When I Fall In Love' and 'The Christmas Song'.

The 'King' part of Nat's name took hold after a man placed a crown on his head one night during a performance at the Los Angeles Century Club. Pat held Nat in great esteem. 'Nat deserved that celebrated name! Soon he became a king of his music genre, with hits such as "Unforgettable", "Smile" and "Mona Lisa". I can hardly tell you how the news of his untimely death in 1965 stunned me and the entire music world. His songs live on, though!'

The crooner Perry Como became one of Pat's closest show-biz friends in the mid-fifties, when Perry's TV show was hitting its highest ratings. He was born in Canonsburg, Pennsylvania, in 1912 and started work as a self-employed barber, although he had a driving ambition to sing his way to the top. He was a deep thinker, and at the height of his success he commented, 'I now have what money can buy. But what money can't buy, I've always had.' What Pat appreciated most about the great song stylist (who became his daughter Debby's godfather) was his humble insight and his even-temperedness. 'Perry communicated in a spontaneous, amiable, relaxed style, with much modesty. He had a crucial input into my emerging performance style. In 1956, when my version of "Tutti Frutti" was charting, I was thrilled to receive a summons from the master TV host. He wanted me to be a special guest on his prime-time network TV show on NBC. The

Boone family, like most folks at that time, were big fans of the cel-ebrated Como show. It was a regular viewing slot for families across the country.'

When Pat met the superstar in the rehearsal hall, he was aston-ished at his genuine informality, devoid of any hype. Perry came straight up to him, right hand extended. 'Hi, I'm Perry Como … You sure are kicking up some good action with your fine records, Pat. Thanks for finding time to grace us with your presence on our little ol' TV show!' Pat stammered something about 'Without a Song' being his favourite from Mr Como's repertoire, and Perry nodded understanding, agreeing that it was a popular song. 'But nowadays,' he went on, 'I've got some competition from kids such as you. You're crowding us oldies off the jukebox, Mr Boone!' This teasing introduction was the start of a real friendship, and Pat remains humbled by and grateful for the advice and support the great man gave him.

Another show-biz friend of Pat's, closer to his own age, was Andy Williams, born on 3 December 1929 in the small farming community of Wall Lake, Iowa. Music was a permanent feature in the Williams house, and at the tender age of nine, Andy and his three brothers formed their own musical group. The Williams Brothers even managed to get on their local radio station, WHO in Des Moines. The family moved several times, but it was in Chicago in 1939 that the Brothers became staff artists with the radio station WLS, and later with WLW in Cincinnati. When the family moved to California in 1943, the Williams Brothers became regulars on local LA stations singing background vocals, including 'Swinging On A Star' with Bing Crosby, a song which went on to become a 1944 Academy Award winner.

After a spell touring nightclubs with Kay Starr, the brothers went their separate ways and in 1955, when Pat was hitting the charts consistently, Andy Williams became a featured vocalist on the Steve Allen *Tonight* show. His first hits on the Cadence label consisted mainly of cover versions of rock'n'roll songs, as he followed a similar career pattern to Pat. The two were also remarkably similar in that both were great admirers of the mature crooners of that time. In time, Andy left Cadence for CBS, and went on to record the ballad material that was to become his trademark – 'Almost There', 'My Cherie Amour', 'Days Of Wine And Roses' and many others. The two young singers got on very well, and shared a sense of humour too. When Andy appeared on Pat's *Chevy Showroom*, he pretended to have no interest at all in Pat's singing, sitting in the audience among the crowd of enchanted teenagers yawning and reading a book. Ironically, Andy's greatest hit song, 'Moon River', was offered to Pat before it was so successfully minted by Andy. 'Moon River' was certainly one that got away, and Pat admits to a rare misjudgement of its commercial potential. He was later to make it an album cut on his 'movie themes' collection.

One other colleague from those days stands out from the crowd. Anthony Dominic Benedetto is better known by the anglicized name of Tony Bennett. Starting his long and distinguished career at the very young age of seven, he gained his initial success before World War II. Like Pat, his career received a huge boost from Arthur Godfrey's TV talent show; then, in 1951, 'Because Of You' (written by Arthur Hammerstein and Dudley Wilkinson) made him a star. In 1953, when Pat was just launching out, Bennett scored his third million-seller with 'Rags To Riches', a song written by the Broadway team of Richard Adler and Jerry Ross. Four years later, he hit again with 'Till'. Pat willingly declares, 'It was a great song, perfectly suited to Tony's voice timbre and texture.' At the height of the Kennedy years, Tony added another million-seller to his tally – 'I Left My Heart In San Francisco'. 'That,' comments Pat, 'is the song that best captures the charm of that beautiful city. It came at a time when the Beatles invasion was adversely affecting the crooning trade, but Tony scored highly with "San Francisco". It amazed us all!' Like Pat, Tony is one of the very few great crooners to survive into the third millennium still singing successfully.

No one can deny that Pat's career has been successful. Of the top 40 recording artists of the rock'n'roll era, Pat is counted among the top three. Sixty of his songs have been in the USA charts, 15 of them hitting the Top 10. Pat has sold more than 45 million records, has 13 gold discs, two gold albums and two platinum records denoting 3 million sales (eventually exceeding 4.5 million sales). Many of his early hits were recorded in Chicago's United Studios, including 'Ain't That A Shame', 'I'll Be Home', 'Long Tall Sally' and 'I Almost Lost My Mind'. Clearly United had proved itself to have a good track record as far as Boone recordings went. It therefore came as something of a surprise to the watching media commentators when Randy Wood moved his studio contract work to California in the warm month of July 1956.

For Pat, there followed a busy few years of commuting between New York and Los Angeles for recording sessions. In an added bonus, however, Hollywood movies began to provide much profitable exposure for the now familiar Boone vocals. In 1956, as has already been mentioned, the Gary Cooper film *Friendly Persuasion* provided Pat with yet another chart hit. The success of that particular song was all the more surprising, coming as it did amidst the louder rock'n'roll songs of the day. The lyrics of 'Friendly Persuasion' were rather quaint, reflecting the film's story line which revolved around a Quaker family during the American Civil War. Gary Cooper starred as the father and Dorothy McGuire as the mother. Musical director Dimitri Tiomkin wrote the theme song especially for the film and auditioned several singers, including Harry Belafonte and Pat Boone. Pat won the day and was chosen by Dimitri to record 'Friendly Persuasion' to the lush accompaniment of a large Hollywood studio orchestra. It was a tense experience, Pat admits, but the session earned him his fourth million-seller, and the song went to number five in the national charts. It also led to him being chosen to sing the theme song to another Tiomkin film that year – *Anastasia*, starring

Ingrid Bergman, the story of the woman who claimed to be a daughter of the last Czar of Russia.

All in all, 1956 was a hectic and exciting year for Pat. Now a highly successful singer, he found himself being fêted by the Hollywood film studios. All seemed gratifyingly eager to sign up this good-looking young man who had apparently found the secret of how to achieve hit song after hit song. Before the year was out, Pat had signed a million-dollar contract with Twentieth Century Fox, as well as securing his own high-profile TV series. Although the prized Hollywood contract was undoubtedly something not to be missed, it did carry a price tag. It meant yet another house relocation and more family disruption – although they did not move to California until 1959, which meant that Pat spent even less time at home in the intervening years due to his commitments away from New York State.

Looking back, Pat feels that perhaps he should not have been so foolhardy and it might have been better had he not rushed so quickly into everything. It was wrong of him, he says, to expect Shirley and his four young daughters to follow him to LA regardless, just because of the demands of a movie contract. He could have been more thoughtful. 'To Shirley's merit, she stood by me through all those difficult decisions,' he says. 'As a result, I genuinely appreciate her forbearing stance, because it must have been distressing at times. Nowadays, our decisions are more carefully thought about!'

In 1957 the Hollywood connection began to pay off and Pat enjoyed considerable success in his debut movie *Bernadine*, and with his record of the same name. Many more chart hits were to follow as his movie career progressed. The musical *Bernadine* was a teenage love story starring Terry Moore, Janet Gaynor and Dean Jagger as well as Pat, and it provided him with two hits. 'Bernadine', which was specially written for Pat by the renowned songwriter Johnny Mercer, rose to number 14 in the national charts. On the B-side was the memorable 'Love Letters In The

Sand', which was only included in the movie as an afterthought when the directors decided that they needed to make more of their new young star.

'Love Letters' was not a new song, having previously been recorded by the crooners Rudy Vallee and Bing Crosby. Pat first recorded it after Randy Wood recognized the song's continuing potential as a hit. They recorded a second version for inclusion in the film soundtrack, then they recorded it a third time, intending to use it for a 45rpm release. On listening to all three recordings, however, Randy decided that Pat's original version was the one best suited for release, a choice which proved to be the right one. 'Love Letters In The Sand' went on to become Pat's best-selling single ever, staying at number one for five weeks in the national charts and for 23 weeks on the bestsellers chart.

Bernadine was followed almost immediately by Pat's second movie, *April Love*, a remake of an old movie called *Home in Indiana*. He classes this as his favourite out of all his films – probably because he felt perfectly comfortable with his character, Nick Adams, a city boy turned country boy.

It was not all plain sailing, however. Pat had barely set foot on the sound stages of the great Hollywood Studios before it was widely reported in the popular media that the new movie star was not willing to do any love scenes, let alone sex scenes, in his films. It was rumoured that he had refused a starring role opposite Marilyn Monroe because it would have involved kissing. It was certainly true that, right from the beginning, he refused to do any nude scenes, but his views on the subject in general were rather more balanced than the media reports indicated. It was not, however, something he had thought through early on in his movie career, and he remembers vividly the first time he was asked to kiss an actress on set.

It was during the making of his second film, *April Love*. The cameras were ready to roll, and Pat was preparing to finish up a musical scene with his co-star Shirley Jones. Suddenly, the voice of the director boomed out. 'Now, when this song ends, Pat,' he called, 'lean over and kiss Shirley!'

Taken by surprise, Pat coloured up, aware that all eyes were on him. 'On the mouth?' he asked. (He concedes now that this question was somewhat dumb!)

'Er, yes, Pat – on the mouth, of course, son!' There was an air of irritation as well as amusement in the director's tone.

Pat was uncertain, however. 'Well, sir, there's no kiss in the script!'

'No, that may be so, but I just think it would be a nice way to end this scene.' The director was losing patience.

Stalling for time, and aware that it was nearly the end of the day, Pat decided to make a suggestion. 'You know, sir, I'm married to Shirley and neither of us have ever discussed the idea of me doing any love scenes. Can we wait until tomorrow? I'd like, at least, to alert my wife if this is what I'm going to do!'

The director, frustrated, but recognizing that Pat was not to be moved, agreed to return to the scene the next day, and Pat duly went home to explain the situation to a bemused Shirley. Shirley's response was practical: 'Well, *try* not to enjoy it too much, Buddy – that Shirley Jones is a good looker!'

Back on set the next day, armed with a clear conscience, Pat was ready to do his duty. Instead, he found himself ushered into the office of Buddy Adverd, the President of Fox. He was livid. The story, with embellishments, had already hit the headlines: 'Pat Boone refuses to kiss Shirley Jones!' According to the papers, he had 'refused to kiss his leading lady for religious reasons'.

Pat was astonished at the fuss that ensued. 'I hadn't refused – I'd simply said, "Can I go home and talk to my wife?" From that little twisted tale a huge international news controversy was created. I began to get telegrams from all over the world, urging me to stick to my guns and not to give in. I hadn't made any kind of stand, but after that I was sort of shackled into it! In the end I didn't kiss Shirley Jones in *April Love*, but I did get to kiss

Christine Carere on the cheek in the next film. I then gave Diane Baker a real smacker in *Journey to the Centre of the Earth*... After that I kissed many a leading lady, including Ann-Margret, Debbie Reynolds and Barbara Eden. You could say I started getting a bit more steamed up, but I honestly did nothing at all extreme on screen at any time!'

Pat's 'lily-white' reputation became ideal fodder for talk-show hosts and comedians looking for a quick gag. Dean Martin, for example, would regularly work the subject into his comedy routine. One of his favourite jokes made the most of the contrasts between the hard-drinking Dean and the clean-living Pat. 'Oh, that Pat Boone,' Dean would say, 'he's so religious! I shook hands with that boy the other day and my whole right side sobered up!' The two men were friends off stage, and Pat was saddened when Dean began to suffer from appalling stomach ulcers and was forced to stop his drinking. Pat recalls his late pal with great fondness. Dean had another favourite gag about making a movie on the life of Pat Boone, which he was going to call *The Milk Dud* (a Milk Dud was a popular American candy bar at the time). 'One day,' Pat recalls, 'Dean and I were playing golf and took a break to have a sandwich in the clubhouse. As a joke I had the waiter bring him over a bottle of milk, wrapped in a towel, "compliments of Pat Boone". Dean stood up, toasted everybody in the bar with the milk, and sat down roaring with laughter!'

April Love provided Pat with yet another number-one hit, this time composed by the Academy Award-winning songwriters Paul Francis Webster and Sammy Fain. 'April Love' was a fine piece, and became Pat's theme song for his stage act. 'I love the way the introduction builds,' he says. Initially, however, Pat was not overly keen on the song, as he thought it too simplistic and sweet, and rather lacking in excitement. He was also acutely aware that the top-selling records at that time (by artists such as Elvis, the Everly Brothers and Buddy Holly) had a much more commercial rock sound. '"April Love" just didn't fit into that category at all, and I was doubtful if the song would make it in the charts against such strong competition. I persuaded my orchestrator, Billy Vaughn, to change the opening bars to give it a much more dramatic beginning. I wanted to make the listener know that something was about to happen!' Released on 45rpm in November 1957, 'April Love' had reached number one in the charts by 23 December, fighting off competition from Danny and the Juniors' 'At The Hop' (at number two), Elvis's 'Jailhouse Rock/Treat Me Nice' (at number three), Bill Justis's 'Raunchy' (at number four) and Sam Cooke's 'You Send Me' (at number five). 'April Love' became Pat's ninth million-selling disc. The week it hit the number one spot, incidentally, was the week Elvis Presley was called up for army service.

In every century there are people who surpass all expectation and become icons of the age, and surely Elvis Presley was one of the foremost icons of the twentieth century. Pat was shaken to the core by the news of Elvis's sudden death in 1977. 'Like most other people, I can remember when and where I heard the news. Two decades earlier, Elvis and I had been just two of a mixed multitude who revolutionized pop music. Rockabilly music took America by storm and broke out worldwide, shaking the establishment. The new sound was so different from anything that had gone before it – it was shockingly gaudy!'

Pat vividly recalls his early impressions of Elvis, his only real opponent at the time for the top prize. 'Elvis was a Southern boy by birth and spirit. I remember that his musical preferences ranged from the peppy music of his Afro-American "rhythm and blues" neighbours to the white Southern gospel sounds of the Blackwood Brothers. He also loved to do the rustic ballads of the Grand Ole Opry stars. His style was really a melting pot of influences.'

Young Pat's first appearance alongside an even younger Elvis was in 1955, when they were both invited to appear on a show arranged by DJ Bill Randle in Cleveland, Ohio. Sitting alongside Pat on their car journey from the airport, an excited Bill mentioned that he had a young kid with the unusual name of 'Elvis Presley' from Memphis, Tennessee, on the bill before Pat. 'Take my word for it, man!' he said. 'In my opinion, this kid's gonna be a big star. You mark my words!'

In fact, Pat was already familiar with Elvis's sound, as he had heard his rockabilly songs being played on the jukeboxes in Dallas, but at the time he considered him to be more country than rock-'n'roll. The Elvis phenomenon was already beginning to take shape, however. When Bill introduced Pat to the young man, a small entourage of admirers surrounded 'the Memphis Cat'. 'This entourage was just a foretaste of what was to become the norm in Elvis's glittering career,' explains Pat. 'Whenever most folks met Elvis, the entourage was always there! I was surprised to find him to be just a shy country boy, ill at ease in unfamiliar surroundings.'

Elvis was still in the process of consolidating his career at that time, and appeared to be star-struck at meeting Pat, already a successful hit-maker. Pat was convinced that Elvis would dry up on stage – he certainly seemed far too nervous and inarticulate. As the time for the performance drew near, Pat was increasingly worried that his new friend's act would prove to be a show-biz disaster. 'How wrong could I be?' he laughs now. 'Elvis stepped onto the stage of that large school auditorium and sang a couple of songs in his own unique style, no trace of nerves. I couldn't help smiling at his use of a rhythmic leg twitch [copied from James Weatherington, bass in the Statesmen Quartet]. It became such a hot talking point among conservative folk! Even then, it was obvious that this young man had something unique which audiences responded to. The rest, as they say, is history.'

Pat's *Chevy Showroom* TV series guaranteed huge audiences wherever he performed, not only in his home territory in the South but in the North too. It seemed that everyone appreciated his clean-cut 'All-American Boy' persona. Elvis's flamboyant appearance was an outrageous contrast to such a 'normal' image, and Pat found it hard to imagine what a superstar this young teenager was destined to become in hardly any time at all. Meanwhile, Pat's success continued, with his records now regularly hitting the Top 10. 'I had my early hits first, but for many years after that, Elvis and I chased each other up and down the charts. It seems to me that, although people may not have realized it, we appealed to the public in a complementary way –you might say the negative and positive aspects of human nature. In many instances, it was the same people who bought both Elvis songs and Boone songs, despite the differences in lifestyle. It seemed that I wanted to keep the rules and win, and he wanted to break the rules and win! Yet looking back now, Elvis seems quite straitlaced and conservative compared to the celebrities of today.'

In 1957, Pat beat Elvis to the title of Male Singer of the Year, and still retains the record of spending the highest number of consecutive weeks in the national charts from 1955 to mid-1959. 'In the late fifties it seemed that my music was a constant feature on the pop-rock radio stations. Back then, secretly, I didn't feel as though I could identify fully with rock'n'roll, but it's clear with hindsight that I *was* very much part of that special era. It's trendy now for critics to pretend I never existed – but the Boone sound was an essential part of that rock'n'roll era, whether you're willing to credit it or not.'

From personal experience, Pat found Elvis to be something of a contradiction. His public reputation was out of step with the private reality that Pat knew. Some of the establishment's old guard and parts of the media seemed determined to highlight only the worst aspects of the star's persona, but that was not all there was to see, Pat maintains. 'They branded him and his music a threat to the morals of young America. As a performer, Elvis had an undoubted magnetism in his stage act that set audiences alight. His slick, jet-black hair, sideburns and flashy dress sense were all somewhat divergent from the standards of the day, raising conservative eyebrows and sending young girls hysterical. Artistically, he revolutionized a whole generation. The art form was changed for ever. Yet, for all his wild rebel image, I know that he adored his parents, and was courteous to everyone, especially women and elderly people. He didn't try to duck out of his obligations and dutifully undertook his spell in the military – reaching the rank of sergeant. Elvis always revered the gospel music scene too. Sacred songs were ingrained into his character, and that love never left him.'

Much was made in the media of the differences between Elvis and Pat Boone, and magazine editors seemed particularly intrigued by their different views on marriage. Pat's overtly moral stance was at odds with Elvis's more worldly view on the subject. Indeed, when he was asked once if he would marry soon, Elvis replied, 'Why should I buy a cow when I can get milk through the fence?' Nonetheless, this 'magazine talk' was not the whole truth, as Pat well knew. With their Southern backgrounds and church upbringing, he and Elvis had more in common than many people thought. Sometimes, when Elvis visited Pat and Shirley's LA home, they would fall to talking about their roots. They shared a similar sense of humour, and on more than one occasion Pat says he detected a wistful look on Elvis's face as he surveyed the Boones' happy home and children. Perhaps, after all, he felt the need for something similar of his own.

As the years passed, Pat broadened his repertoire, choosing to concentrate not solely on rock'n'roll but varying the styles to include movie themes, country, gospel, teen ballads and the odd novelty song such as 'Speedy Gonzales'. In 1964, however, the rock'n'roll itch returned and Pat persuaded Randy Wood to assemble an album of rock'n'roll under the title *Boss Beat*. Included on the album were 'The Loco-Motion', 'Mashed Potato', 'Hey Baby', 'Kansas City' and Chuck Berry's 'Memphis'. With considerable foresight, Pat also included a song by a new British band called the Beatles, entitled 'I Want To Hold Your Hand'.

Warmed by the album's reception, Pat conceived another idea – a tribute album to his friend Elvis. He recorded the Presley songs in a lighter-than-usual style, using some of the best musicians on the West Coast. Unfortunately, Elvis's fans were not too enamoured by someone else trying to sing their hero's songs – and Boone fans were less than keen too. Pat had originally wanted to call the album *Pat Sings Elvis*, but apparently Colonel Parker, Elvis's legendary manager, did not take too kindly to that suggestion. If Pat Boone insisted on using the title, he was reported to have said, then Dot would be obliged to pay a royalty to Elvis for the use of his name! Randy was livid and threatened to call off the whole project, but Pat talked him round and the album project progressed under the title *Pat Boone Sings Guess Who?* On the front cover was a picture of an out-of-character Pat dressed in a gold lamé suit, strumming a guitar in an Elvis-like pose.

Not everyone saw the joke. Many conservatives were upset by the album cover, and Elvis fans were unimpressed by the completely different approach Pat had taken to his friend's well-known songs (including 'Teddy Bear', 'Hound Dog', 'All Shook Up', 'Love Me Tender' and 'Blue Suede Shoes'). Using mainly jazz artists, the Boone sound for these famous pieces was more like that of a swing combo than the rock'n'roll style of Elvis's regular backing musicians. Pat's 'Hound Dog', for instance, was given a completely different feel by the inclusion – of all things – of a harpsichord, accompanying Pat's voice singing in measured tones. Midway through, however, the mood suddenly changed to a jumping rock'n'roll solo, admittedly still on the harpsichord. The song then slowed down again, resuming its measured pace, with Pat's voice calmly narrating the lyrics. Anything less like Elvis's version was hard to imagine! 'Love Me Tender' was given a soft, almost Latin beat, whilst the Carl Perkins classic 'Blue Suede Shoes' was done Count Basie style, omitting the word 'liquor' from the original wording and substituting it with less strong wording: 'You can drink my cider from an old fruit jar.' Pat even managed to personalize the lyrics by substituting 'white buck shoes' for the usual 'blue suede shoes'!

It was a fun session and produced an unusually innovative release, completely different from any other tribute album dedicated to Elvis. There were many over the years, but Pat's unconventional, comic approach remained unequalled. One is left to ponder whether Elvis himself approved of the venture, however! Perhaps surprisingly, the album certainly tickled Colonel Parker's funny-bone, successfully winning his approval. Some time later, he invited Pat to become a card-carrying member of his very exclusive Showmen's Club. Pat was highly amused. 'I think it's probably one of the only times that anybody ever got around the Colonel, and he paid me a tribute accordingly!'

Although both men were increasingly busy, Elvis and Pat became close confidants over time, often visiting each other's homes. Years later, Ray Walker (from Elvis's vocal quartet, the Jordanaires) spoke about the developing camaraderie between Elvis and Pat. 'For a while in Bel Air, Elvis loved to play knock-out football – not just tackle but knock-out – with Pat Boone. They played roughly and toughly, and Elvis said he found out the hard way that Pat was no cissy! They were both good friends to each other.'

Not long before he died, Pat recalls his friend divulging to him his great fear of flying. 'Elvis was really a white-knuckle flyer. The last time I saw him was in Memphis Airport as I was waiting for my plane to Las Vegas a few months before he died. Elvis arrived at the airport in a large limo, looking very overweight and puffy. Such was his fear of flying that he had to take some kind of powder to settle his stomach. I saw that the remains of the dose were still caked around his mouth as we hugged and talked.' Pat did not know that it would be his last chance to chat to his friend, but that meeting – although nothing of great note was said beyond a friendly exchange of news – now has a special place in his memory.

CHAPTER 6

GOOD ROCKIN' TONIGHT

I heard the news.
There's good rockin' tonight!

Roy Brown

In between filming sessions for his first Hollywood movies, Pat found time for some hard work in the recording studio too. In one session on 11 February 1957, still under the wise direction of Randy Wood, Pat was called upon to reinterpret one of his favourite love songs. 'It's Too Soon To Know' was re-recorded that day with a mellow string accompaniment. He had originally obtained the song via the Orioles' hit version of 1948. Before the session ended, 'Love Letters In The Sand' was also revisited, this time at a faster tempo. At about that time, a young country singer named George Jones was having success with a bouncy number called 'Why Baby Why'. A song with the same title and sentiments was accordingly scheduled to be minted during that busy session. It was a fun song, and Pat suggested that it be accompanied by some sharp hand-clapping. Randy agreed, saying that if the listeners did not end up clapping their hands too, they would at least secretly be tapping their toes.

'Peace In The Valley' was a complete change of mood. Originally this biblical song was published by Ben Speer of the Speer Family, under the mistaken impression that it was already in the public domain. Years later, he gave the song to the Blackwoods to record and it went on to become a classic. The Blackwood version was a favourite of Elvis Presley, and under his influence the song traversed the globe. The song's writer, Thomas M. Dorsey, was born in 1899 and raised in the poverty of a rural Georgia that still resented the freedom from slavery granted to his parents following the Civil War. When he left his boyhood home, he rubbed musical shoulders with some of the legendary blues and jazz artists of his day, including Bessie Smith. Later, as the pastor of a Chicago church, he penned the famous songs 'Take My Hand Precious Lord' and 'Peace In The Valley'. 'Take My Hand' was written after the death of his wife and newborn baby, and the lyrics form a very moving prayer. Pat made recordings of both songs, and they were standard features in many singers' repertoires.

From the serious tones of 'Peace In The Valley', the packed recording session moved straight on to the happy-go-lucky entertainment of 'Great Googa Mooga'. It really was a musical journey through the ups and downs of life. The last song of the heavy day was the comforting 'He'll Understand And Say Well Done', from the pen of Lucy Campbell.

Pat was back in the recording studio five weeks later for a two-day session towards the end of March, again covering a wide range of styles and moods. 'Technique', a Johnny Mercer original, was an unusual number to kick off with – done in a Harry Belafonte calypso style. This was followed by a complete change of mood as they recorded yet another version of 'Love Letters In The Sand'. The next day, the session concentrated on two popular compositions from Red Foley's songbook, 'Steal Away' (by Hank Williams) and 'Just A Closer Walk With Thee'. After the narrative song 'Steal Away' ended, Pat burst out, 'What a sad song! Those lyrics, "I ain't got long to stay here" – they touch the emotions, don't they?' One of his favourite subject matters for songs was the expectation of heaven, but this song seemed to have tapped a sombre nerve, and he remembers that it affected the whole crew that day.

Spirits were restored with a break for coffee, however, and then it was time for another change of mood. Johnny Mercer's movie song 'Bernadine' was not something you could stay serious with for long, and everyone appreciated its bright, breezy tone. Pat considers it a privilege that someone of the calibre of Johnny Mercer was prepared to write a song just for him to sing in his first movie, and he worked very hard to do the great lyricist justice. At the end of that day's recording, others in the studio assured him that he had succeeded.

Variety was the spice of life for Pat, and he absorbed influences from many genres – and in turn passed on a certain amount of influence himself. Although he never fully subscribed to the country music scene, as an adult he never turned his nose up at it either. Indeed, he revelled in the excitement of Music City which, after all, was his home town. The so-called 'Nashville Sound' was developing in those days, and Pat Boone played a part in it, however unrecognized. The velvety Boone voice was a major seller well before Jim Reeves' deep voice had matured, for example. Country Jim initially struggled to win 'pop' recognition, but eventually made it to the heights of stardom as a silky vocalist, and one wonders just how much he borrowed from the Boone sound. His early releases were novelty songs such as 'Bimbo' and 'Mexican Joe', but these raw ditties were a far cry from the smoothness of his later hit 'He'll Have To Go', which was very much more in the smooth-velvet style of Pat Boone (in fact, Pat had originally turned the song down, but did not begrudge Jim his success with it).

Pat's very first performances and recording sessions were undertaken in and around Music City and, although his recordings during the mid-to-late fifties were made in other big cities, his part in the formation of the 'Nashville Sound' should not be underestimated. Even in the sophisticated Chicago and Los Angeles studios, Pat's Nashville influences were always prominent in his repertoire, which included Eddy Arnold's 'Anytime', Red

Foley's 'Tennessee Saturday Night', Ernest Tubb's 'Walking The Floor Over You', Pee Wee King's and Redd Stewart's 'Tennessee Waltz', Ned Miller's 'From A Jack To A King', Mac Wiseman's 'Tis Sweet To Be Remembered' and Hank Williams's 'Cold, Cold Heart'. The list goes on. Added to this obviously country repertoire was his full use of the Southern gospel songbooks – 'Just A Closer Walk With Thee', 'Beyond The Sunset', 'Peace In The Valley', his million-selling 'A Wonderful Time Up There' and many more. His best albums from the 1960s, such as *Look Ahead*, displayed his Nashville roots to the full, although his own personalized Nashville Sound was late in maturing. It really only came of age in the 1970s.

Top of the list of Pat's country music heroes was the legendary Red Foley, who was a big presence in Nashville throughout Pat's childhood. Red had a deep, mellow voice that lacked the nasal tones of many of his contemporaries and earned him the title of 'The Bing Crosby of the Hillbillies'. Pat admired his talent, and the fact that he passed his singing skills on to his daughter. 'My father-in-law's contribution to country music was justly celebrated in 1967, a year before his premature death, when he was inducted into the Country Music Hall of Fame in Nashville. My wife Shirley inherited much of her father's talent. For a while she sang with the Anita Kerr Singers, who later became backing singers for scores of big names such as Jim Reeves, Perry Como, Hank Snow, Eddy Arnold and George Beverly Shea. Shirley's association with the group ended a short while after our marriage, however, when we moved away from Nashville.' Many years later, Pat made it up to the Anita Kerr Singers when he used them as back-up vocalists on his innovative *Look Ahead* album.

Red Foley was born on 17 June 1910 in Blue Lick, Berea, Kentucky. His father, who ran the town's general store, was a fiddle-player and paternal encouragement was to have far-reaching effects on Red. As a youngster, Red discovered that he had a natural ability on the harmonica. Eager to encourage his

108

son's musical gift, Mr Foley Senior bought him a basic guitar, which took some sacrifice because the family were not well off. By the age of seven, Red was playing his guitar confidently and singing well-loved folk tunes. Ten years later, he was persuaded by his mother to enter a local talent competition. Red bowled the audience over, won the competition, and was on his way. In 1930 he joined a hillbilly band of local renown known as the Cumberland Ridge Runners. Two years later, while he was a student at the Georgetown College, Kentucky, he was brought to the attention of a talent scout from WLS, a radio station in Chicago. In 1933 he was invited to perform on the nationally popular showcase, the *WLS National Barn Dance*, which boasted great stars such as Gene Autry, Lulu Belle and Scotty Wiseman. In the same year, Red signed a valuable contract with Conqueror Records.

During the early years of World War II, Red returned to Chicago to co-star with the great comedian Red Skelton in a nationally networked radio show sponsored by Avalon Cigarettes. He signed a new contract with Decca Records and increased his fame overseas with his transcribed discs for Armed Forces Radio, aired all over the world. He was a masterful entertainer with a vibrant and versatile vocal style. Indeed, Pat's early singing idol, Bing Crosby, once paid tribute to Red as 'the best all-round singer in the business'. In 1944, Red had his first hit song in the country charts, entitled 'Smoke On The Water'. It was a jingoistic and sabre-rattling song, and it went on to reach number seven in the US pop charts as well as hitting number one in the country charts.

In 1946, when Pat was just 12 years old and a schoolboy in Nashville, Red was summoned to become a regular member of the Grand Ole Opry, a membership reserved only for the elite of the country music fraternity. He became the focal point of the whole set-up, taking over the spot Roy Acuff had occupied for years. He also acted as the Opry's master of ceremonies and was even the straight man for country comedians Rod Brasfield and Minnie Pearl. Pat remembered how Red was well known for his big-hearted nature. 'Red helped many young artists to showcase their talents, including guitar virtuoso Chet Atkins. Our family always tuned the radio to the weekly Opry broadcast!' Red was also busy recording material himself, and Decca producer Paul Cohen hit on the idea of recording Ernest Tubb and Red Foley singing several duets, including Hank Williams's 'Steal Away', minted in 1950, which was a runaway success.

On the back of such success, several TV stations tried to sign Red up for a series. Pat recalls that Springfield's KWTO TV station eventually captured him. 'KWTO gave Red an offer he couldn't refuse, so he moved from Nashville to Springfield to be the host of a promising new format of the *Ozark Jubilee* show. It was the first prime-time, country music TV show in history. I made several appearances on it myself later on, and felt very proud to be guesting with my father-in-law!'

With over 40 Top 10 hits in the country charts, six of which reached number one, Red Foley's songs were well known to Pat. In 1950, Red recorded his million-selling 'Chattanooga Shoe Shine Boy', which successfully crossed over into the pop charts. By the early fifties, gospel music also played a large part in Red's career, bringing him several million-sellers that endeared him to many of the South's Christian believers, including the Boone household. Some years later, Pat covered several of his father-in-law's gospel hits – 'Peace In The Valley', 'He'll Understand And Say Well Done', 'Just A Closer Walk With Thee' and the plaintive 'Steal Away' – on his first gospel EP album, recorded in 1957.

Perhaps Red's greatest song-writing legacy was the sentimental ballad 'Old Shep'. The sad song was also recorded by country giant Hank Snow and later became a hit of sorts for the up-and-coming Elvis. Pat remembers the story that inspired the ballad. 'As a youngster, Mr Red had a particular affection for his German Shepherd dog named Hoover. The two were inseparable, but then tragedy struck. The dog was apparently deliberately poisoned by an unfriendly neighbour and died. The sadness felt by the young Red comes across clearly in the lyrics and melody of this poignant song.'

In September 1968, Red was on tour with Hank Williams Junior in a travelling Opry show through Indiana. On the 19th the troupe was in Fort Wayne for an evening show, and afterwards Red retired to his motel bedroom, pleading exhaustion. He was last seen talking to Hank Junior. During the night, Red suffered a massive heart attack and died in his sleep. Hank later wrote and recorded a unique tribute narration, entitled 'I Was With Red Foley (The Night He Passed Away)'.

Pat held his father-in-law in high esteem, and treasures the musical and personal memories he has of Red Foley. Although their careers followed quite distinctive paths, he always longed for the chance to record more Foley material, ever on the lookout for ways to introduce new life to the repertoire. Many years after Red's death, he had his chance. On 14 April 1983, producer Billy Lineman welcomed a seasoned team of musicians to the Hilltop Studio in Madison, not far from the Boone homestead which still housed Pat's parents. Out of the spring sunshine, armed for two days of dedicated session work, paraded the instrumentalists Jimmy Capps, Ray Edenton, Johnny Gimble, Buddy Harman, Jeff Newman and Jerry Whitehurst. They were closely followed by the world-renowned Jordanaires quartet and Pat himself. New life was about to be brought to a dozen songs from the old Red Foley songbook.

It was a labour of love for Pat, and he counts those two days as very special indeed. At the end of the session the team had recorded all the material for the tribute album *I Remember Red*, which came out first on the Laserlight label and then on Pat's Gold label. It contained many of Mr Red's most unforgettable songs, including 'Just A Closer Walk With Thee', 'Tennessee Saturday Night', 'Chattanooga Shoe Shine Boy' and, of course, 'Old Shep'.

Throughout the 1950s, Pat's huge audiences just seemed to go on growing, and he attracted a notable following. One regular Boone fan was an unknown teenager serving out his national service in the Air Force. Originally from a poor, rural background in Arkansas, Johnny Cash became a devoted fan of the smooth-voiced balladeer. Decades later, the ageing country superstar was quick to point out how much spiritual direction he had received via the musical radio messages of Pat Boone back in those difficult times. Pat himself has enormous respect for the 'Man in Black', and the feeling is clearly returned, as is obvious from the touching letter Johnny wrote to Pat in the early 1970s.

Dear Pat,

...I was converted on my knees at the altar in a little town in Arkansas when I was 12 years old. I grew up in the church, working, doing my part in my little world ... I started in the music industry when I was 23, in 1955. You were already an inspiration for me, though I didn't meet you until 1960. At that time you weren't singing much gospel, however you had recorded 'A Wonderful Time Up There', which I had been singing since I was a kid. When we met in 1960 at the Steel Pier in Atlantic City, New Jersey, you were finishing a concert and I was about to go on stage. I was ... already stringing myself out on amphetamines and alcohol and I can remember, to this day, how you looked: clear-eyed, clean-cut, I even remember the white sport shirt you had on. How I envied your appearance, for I knew how bad I looked. Though I was to be on amphetamines, barbiturates, alcohol and other drugs for six more years, that meeting with you then had an impact on me spiritually ... though I was abusing myself physically, mentally and spiritually, I was still a 'child of God' ... To me, Pat Boone was the man who sang 'A Wonderful Time Up There' and nothing else mattered, record-wise. You took me back, not only to my childhood, but also back to that day in 1955 when I signed my first recording contract. On that day I made a pledge … that at least ten per cent of whatever I record in my life will be gospel or evangelical in nature. (A pledge I have kept to this day.) In 1967, I won, through God, the victory over drugs, through human anchors that He sent me … Then, I was beginning to gather spiritual strength again. Three years later I went on network TV with my own weekly show. It was during my television run that I privately and publicly re-affirmed my faith, and re-committed my life to Christ.

It was a high time for me, and a time in which many shocking changes came about. Many of my old friends vanished … Many people doubted my sincerity, which didn't bother me in the least. I was beginning to realise that I was in a position of influence, my mail was full of letters from parents telling me how their children loved me, and that they held me up as an example. Adults, by the hundreds, wrote to me for advice on drugs and alcohol problems.

During this time, I saw you on a talk show discussing your commitment to Christ, a little later discussing your concert work, and I got a great revelation: a Christian performer, entertainer, cannot turn in a totally secular performance on stage. If Christ is in you, those people in that audience, whether Pat Boone sings a gospel song or not, are going to see and feel the presence of Jesus Christ in His Pat Boone form! So you've really helped me grow, Pat. I thank God that I've finally got to know you better … I've learned so much from you…

Your friend, Johnny Cash

P.S. Ain't we gonna have a wonderful time up there!?

Johnny Cash was born in 1932 in Arkansas, where he had a tough upbringing on an impoverished rural smallholding. Tragedy struck the family with the death of his older brother Jack, and

Johnny was forced into long hours of back-breaking work in the cotton fields to help support the family. He loved music, however, and took any opportunity to sneak within earshot of a radio so that he could listen to the broadcasts of country and gospel music. Pat recalls Johnny telling him how he had thrilled to the sound of the Grand Ole Opry songs, but nothing had touched his heart like the sacred music of Jimmie Davis, the Blackwood Brothers, the Chuck Wagon Gang and Sister Rosetta Tharp. Gospel was his preferred inspirational choice and provided him with much comfort.

At the age of 18, Johnny was conscripted to an Air Force posting in Germany, where he rose to the rank of staff sergeant. At this time, as he readily admits, he was greatly affected by Pat's example – a strong Christian in a very secular environment. When he left the USAF in 1955, Johnny's prime ambition was to pursue a professional singing career. He tested for a record company boss in Memphis, telling him that he was gospel singer, but that was frowned upon and he was encouraged to try out some country songs as well as his self-penned gospel song 'Belshazzar'. As a result, he attained a record deal with the now legendary Sun Records label and soon found himself rubbing shoulders with other greats of the era, including Elvis, Charlie Rich, Conway Twitty, Roy Orbison, Jerry Lee Lewis, Carl Perkins and eventually Pat himself, although they did not meet until 1960.

Pat says he was always impressed by his friend's striking appearance. 'Johnny's stage garments were principally black. He told us all that his dark clothing was characteristic of the sad, social objectives he campaigned for. His songs also often mirrored his own inner struggles. The first time I ever met Johnny was in 1960. It was at a time when he was having many physical and personal problems. We were on a plane together. He was gaunt and didn't look at all healthy. He looked distracted when we met and talked briefly, but I felt he was friendly with me. The plane stopped somewhere and some of us got out to stretch our legs.

114

Johnny never got back on! We had to take off without him. Of course, I know now – and he did confirm that this was the case – that during that time he was very messed up pharmaceutically. I was so pleased and relieved for him when he got straightened out and became a deeply committed Christian.'

Johnny Cash's confidence in God motivated him to compose many great gospel songs, one of these being 'Over The Next Hill', which was first sung by Pat. Pat clearly recalls the way it came about. 'I was in Charlotte with Arthur Smith doing an album of country-gospel classics, using great musicians who had worked with some of the legends of the Southern gospel genre. It was something of a departure for me because I'd been doing so much pop, movie and rock'n'roll music, and now I wanted to get back to my gospel roots. Johnny heard that I was doing the album and called me. He told me he had a couple of new songs he wanted me to hear. He hadn't recorded them himself yet, but he offered to let me do them first if I was interested. He played me "Over The Next Hill" and it touched me deeply. It had all the depth and raw truth of those classics I was busy recording. I told Johnny straight away that I'd be honoured to do the very first recording, and so we did it. It *was* a real honour.'

As a result of his Nashville connections, Pat has come to know some of the greats of country music down the years. George Hamilton IV has been one peer of particular note. The two singers' paths crossed very early on. Both received kickstarts to their careers through appearances on the Arthur Godfrey TV shows. The astute Mr Godfrey clearly saw similar qualities in the two Southern gentlemen.

George IV remembers how, in the mid-1950s, he and Pat became fair game for the Nashville country music community, including the featured female singer on the *Jimmy Dean Show*. Tough-talking, hard-living newcomer Patsy Cline had her sights set on Grand Ole Opry stardom. She pulled no punches in her attitude to her fellow performers. One day, with work over, the TV cast were milling round the foyer before heading home, and Patsy took the opportunity to tease George, the shy singer with the 'college' appearance. 'Hey, George!' she said in her penetrating voice. 'Does ya Ma know y'r still wet behind the ears? Ya don't look like a hillbilly to me! Y'r more like the college goody-goody – the Pat Boone of country music!' George says that Patsy's attitude was typical of the Nashville view of Pat (and himself). The teasing masked a genuine concern for him – his niceness, they felt, was unsuited to the rough and tumble of show business. Sometimes in hurtful ways, they were really just trying to toughen him up.

Like Pat, George is still singing successfully today, and he is known around the world as the 'Ambassador of Country Music'. In July 2000 he was elected to the North Carolina Hall of Fame. Modest and courteous both on and off stage, George also holds the same priorities as Pat, remaining fully devoted to his wife, family and his Christian faith. Both men over the years have been taken to the hearts of Middle America and other communities worldwide, including the UK. George has represented the interests of Music City USA in many parts of the globe with great distinction, and has worked with Dr Billy Graham on his evangelistic missions.

'Over the last 50 years, no one has enjoyed a more enviable reputation in international country and gospel music than George,' says Pat. 'George is a modern-day troubadour. You might say he has planted musical seeds of happiness and love wherever he has gone!'

Given the faith they shared, George Hamilton would no doubt have approved of the venture Pat embarked on in the summer of 1957. On 3 June he returned to the Radio Recorders Studio on Santa Monica Boulevard, Hollywood, for a lengthy 10-day session during which he planned to record a whole album of classic hymns. The session began with 'The Old Rugged Cross', often called America's favourite hymn, written in 1913 by the Rev. George Bennard of Albion, Michigan. It was to be just one of a dozen popular hymns included on Pat's *Hymns We Love* album, which astonished everybody not only by reaching the secular charts but also by achieving Gold Record status. Dot produced the record with a striking sleeve. Behind Pat's portrait was the impression of a stained-glass window, designed by a graphic artist, and it was certainly eye-catching.

Other established favourites on the album included 'In The Garden', penned by C. Austin Miles as an Easter contemplation describing Mary Magdalene's encounter with the risen Christ; 'Whispering Hope', written by Philadelphia music publisher and teacher Septimus Winner under the pseudonym Alice Hawthorn; and 'Beyond The Sunset', a sacred ballad inspired by the comments of a blind man who described a beautiful sunset – despite his lack of sight – to the songwriters Virgil and Blanche Brock. It was popularized by a hit version in 1950 by the country duo Elton Britt and Rosalie Allen, and was later covered by Red Foley.

Pat also recorded 'It Is No Secret', written by Red Foley's friend Stuart Hamblen. The song was first minted by Decca in a version by Bill Kenny of the Inkspots, and it went on to become a much-recorded favourite. Hailing from Texas, singer Stuart Hamblen became very popular on the West Coast during the golden age of the Hollywood cowboy. Movie stars such as Gene Autry, Roy Rogers, Tex Ritter and Rex Allen were his close buddies. Many of Stuart's love songs, including 'Remember Me, I'm The One Who Loves You' (which Pat also recorded) became established standards in the 1930s and '40s.

At the end of the 1940s, Stuart responded to the preaching of a young evangelist named Billy Graham and abandoned his rather wayward lifestyle. Inspired by his conversion to Christianity, he penned a number of evergreen sacred songs, many of which Pat recorded – 'I Wanna Be There', 'But For The Grace Of God', 'Until Then', 'He Bought My Soul At Calvary' and 'My Religion's Not Old

Fashioned'. It was the western movie star John Wayne who gave Stuart the idea for 'It Is No Secret', after he heard of the fuss Stuart's conversion had caused. Many top-class acts have since recorded from the Hamblen songbook, ranging from Sir Cliff Richard to Mahalia Jackson. 'It's significant to note,' Pat points out, 'that high-ranking gospel songwriters Bill and Gloria Gaither once devoted an entire album to Hamblen material. Seldom if ever does one find songwriting legends of their status saluting *another* songwriting legend in that way!' (Also, on a personal note, I am happy to say that Cliff Barrows and George Hamilton IV have both recorded my own tribute to Stuart Hamblen, entitled 'The Open Secret' and released by Word Records of England.)

During those packed sessions in the first two weeks of June 1957, Pat also recorded the ever-popular 'My God Is Real', written by Kenneth Morris. There was a Nashville connection even here, as the song was popular at the time thanks to Wally Fowler's promotion of it at his Nashville All-Night Sing concerts in Music City's Ryman Auditorium. 'I hope we never lose those inspirational witnessing songs,' comments Pat. 'I love telling others through song what the good Lord has done for me!'

Then it was back to real country music territory for a recording of 'From A Jack To A King', a catchy ditty that was later to be a hit for its creator Ned Miller. The Boone version recorded in 1957 had all the ingredients necessary for a hit, but somehow it suffered from lack of exposure at the time. 'Remember You're Mine', however, suffered no such lack and gave Pat his eighth million-seller. It was a demanding song – requiring an octave jump at one stage, which takes some skill to achieve with ease. Randy Wood was more than happy with the results, and his confidence was repaid when the song shot to number one in the charts. Pat still associates the ballad with pretty Barbara Mandrell, since he first heard it when she was in a show down South as a young girl. He was 'knocked out' by her talent, he remembers, and loved the song from then on.

The second week of August 1957 saw Pat changing styles yet again, as he returned to the recording studio for four days to work on the interpretation of pieces from Irving Berlin's songbook. The style of Berlin's music was undoubtedly suited to Pat's silky voice, and Randy wanted to capitalize on this with an entire album of Berlin songs. In 1956, Pat had recorded Berlin's 'With You' on his *Howdy!* debut album. Now this was followed by a whole album entitled *Pat Boone Sings Irving Berlin*. It featured gems such as 'Always', 'Remember' and 'The Girl That I Marry'. Milt Rogers used gentle and opulent orchestration to full effect, perfectly enhancing the Boone vocals. Several of the songs had previously been recorded by Pat's hero Bing Crosby, including 'Be Careful With My Heart' and 'How Deep Is The Ocean'.

Irving Berlin came to the USA as a young immigrant with the name of Israel Baline. Leaving the family home at 14, the young boy made a living as a singing waiter in Pelham Café in New York's Chinatown. He could not read music or play any instrument, and he would sing his new melodies to the resident pianist, who wrote the music down for him. The story goes that Irving acquired his new name after a spelling error on the sheet music for his first song, 'Marie From Sunny Italy'. He did not correct the mistake, and the name stuck. Irving eventually learnt to read music and play the piano, and went on to write many classics. His first hit was the ragtime number 'Alexander's Ragtime Band', and it brought him fame and fortune.

His first marriage to singer Dorothy Goetz was tragically short-lived, as she succumbed to typhoid on their honeymoon in Cuba and died five months later. Immersing himself in his work, Berlin began to write for the stage, producing his first Broadway show, *Watch Your Step*, in 1914. A spell in the military produced an army revue entitled *Yip Yip Yaphank*. Included in the score was the song that was to bring him national recognition, becoming the nation's unofficial second national anthem: 'God Bless America'.

Irving married for the second time in 1926 and set off for Hollywood. There he wrote the score for the 1935 film *Top Hat*, starring Fred Astaire and Ginger Rogers. Other musicals followed, including *Annie Get Your Gun* and *Holiday Inn*, which saw the birth of perhaps the greatest winter-season song of all time, 'White Christmas'. It must be one of the most recorded songs of all time, but many people believe that Pat Boone's smooth version, first minted in 1957, wins hands down.

A month after the recording sessions for the Berlin album, Pat returned to the Christmas theme – an odd experience, he remembers, because Hollywood was still baking under a Californian heatwave at the end of September. Having spent some time perfecting the sound for Pat's movie song 'April Love', the studio musicians turned their attention to more traditional fare for his forthcoming seasonal album. As with the classic hymns, the old favourites were judged to be sure-fire winners for Christmas, and that day they recorded an entertaining version of 'Jingle Bells' and a more soothing 'Silent Night'.

CHAPTER 7

REMEMBER YOU'RE MINE

Be faithful, darling, while you're away,
for when it's summer a heart can stray!
Karl Mann and Bernie Lowe

RANDY WOOD WAS KEEN to make the most of Pat's chart
successes and Hollywood exposure, and the packed programme
of recording sessions continued after the Christmas break. Pat
and his musicians duly crowded back into the studio on 9 January
1958 to record 'It's Too Soon To Know'. (The joke in the studio
that day was that it was definitely too soon to know whether
anyone would stick to their New Year resolutions.) Pat's hugely
successful version of 'A Wonderful Time Up There' was also
recorded that morning. The foot-tapping boogie had a radical
rock'n'roll beat and bold lyrics:

Listen everybody, I'm talking to you:
Jesus is the only one to carry you through!

Widespread acceptance of 'Christian songs with a beat' did not
truly come about until the late 1960s, and Pat recalls how some of
the more conservative churches were initially very suspicious of
him and his 'popular' sound. At least, there were raised eyebrows
among the adults. The teenagers loved the rock'n'roll gospel

songs, clapping and jigging their feet whenever Pat sang in church. 'A Wonderful Time Up There' was penned by the legendary and innovative Leroy Abernathy. Also known as 'Gospel Boogie', it was one of the few gospel songs ever to attack the pop charts with any real impact – a remarkable achievement which Mr Abernathy, born in 1913, actually lived to see. Although controversial for its day, 'A Wonderful Time Up There' proved to be Pat's tenth million-seller, remaining in the USA charts for 19 weeks and peaking at number four.

Randy was in charge again for the next recording session, this time in Hollywood's Masters Recorders studio, North Fairfax, Los Angeles on 28 March (incidentally the day after *Bridge over the River Kwai* took three Oscars). It was to be another busy day, as Pat had eight songs in prospect, including 'Sugar Moon'. Danny Wolfe had written the song especially for Pat, and he loved the sweet, crooning sound of it. Three further love songs were minted in the same studio in April, including 'If Dreams Come True'. This was followed by a May session which laid down some top-quality standards, among them the poetic 'September Song' (by Kurt Weill and Maxwell Anderson) and 'Autumn Leaves' (by Joseph Kosma, Jacques Prevert and Johnny Mercer), Al Jolson's 'Anniversary Song' and Hoagy Carmichael's 'Stardust'. The pace was varied with W.C. Handy's 'St Louis Blues', Fats Domino's hit 'Blueberry Hill' and last, but by no means least, Eddy Arnold's 'That's How Much I Love You', co-penned by Wally Fowler.

Along with Bing Crosby, Tennesseean Eddy Arnold was one of Pat's boyhood heroes. Born at the end of World War I, Eddy was one of the most senior of Chet Atkins's RCA team, along with Hank Snow. 'At a time when Hank Williams's gutsy honky-tonk style ruled the roost,' Pat explains, 'Eddy, wearing suits and ties, was determined to upgrade the image of country music. He evolved into a crooner of great class – the South's match for the Northern crooners like Sinatra, Como, Bennett and Crosby – and was a worthy inductee into the Country Music Hall of Fame. His stage costumes, relaxed attitude and poise greatly influenced me in my own stage presentation. I favoured smart suits and ties over all those rhinestones!'

Pat's popular *Stardust* album, put together in 1958, contained just the kind of material in which Eddy Arnold also excelled – romantic, sentimental songs and evergreen ballads with a full, orchestrated backing provided by Billy Vaughn. The title song and enduring favourites such as 'Deep Purple', 'Heartaches' and the Hank Williams hit 'Cold, Cold Heart' were all quality 'Tin Pan Alley' repertoire.

Pat remembers hearing Hank Williams regularly on radio broadcasts in Nashville when he was growing up. 'That skinny country superstar's impression on mainstream music has never been exceeded by any other country singer,' he says admiringly. 'It's an amazing fact when you remember that Hank's entire career spanned a mere six years.' Pat was to record many of the Hillbilly Shakespeare's songs, all destined to become standards. 'Jambalaya', and 'Kawliga' were just two of Hank's outstanding catalogue of self-penned songs. 'You might say Hank was the first rockabilly,' says Pat. 'He cleverly fused rhythm and blues with rural music. His stage talent was unique, but he was also one of the most engaging songwriters ever. Few tunesmiths had his extraordinary ability to touch human emotions.'

Hailing from the obscure town of Georgiana, Alabama, Hank Williams signed an exclusive recording contract with MGM in 1947, and packed a great deal into his truncated career before he died suddenly in 1953. His very first recording was the rock'n'roll-style hit 'Move It On Over'. From that time on, in addition to love ballads, novelty numbers and blues laments, Hank also recorded country hymns and story ballads, many of which would later receive the Boone touch. An examination of the credits on Pat's sacred and secular recordings reveals just how much of Hank's poetic material he sang over the course of his career, including the favourites 'I Saw The Light' and 'Are You Walkin' and a-Talkin'

With The Lord'. Songwriter Fred Rose gave Hank 'Wait For The Light To Shine', a song Pat recorded with the First Nashville Jesus Band. 'Much of Hank Williams's repertoire displayed an almost missionary zeal. He poured his heart into his gospel compositions. It's said that he had a "deep hunger for God". Not only his gospel repertoire revealed this, but also his secular songs.'

More sacred songs were recorded in the same studio in June, and Pat was still on top vocal form, despite the relentless pace of work that year. During that session he added his own special feel to Frankie Laine's inspirational 'I Believe', and to a timeless setting of 'The Lord's Prayer'. He also recorded an unusual secular love song entitled 'Her Hand In Mine', which was a rewrite of the classic Southern gospel gem 'His Hand In Mine', originally penned by Mosie Lister (an early member of Hovie Lister's Statesmen Quartet) and later made famous by Elvis.

Pat's first recording of the song 'For My Good Fortune' (in the version penned by Otis Blackwell and Bobby Stevenson) was made on 11 August 1958, but the tape was lost somehow after the session and the song had to be re-recorded 10 days later, shoehorned into what was already a packed schedule. There is some confusion today whether 'For My Good Fortune' was written as a gospel song or as a secular love song. James Blackwood of the Blackwood Brothers said that they first heard 'For My Good Fortune' as a gospel song, performed by a black pop singer whose name they could not recall. It was published, oddly enough, by the Blackwood Music company of New York, who were actually unrelated to the Blackwood Brothers. Pat, however, performed the song as a love lyric. James Blackwood had not been aware of Pat's recording of 'For My Good Fortune' until I happened to mention it to him when this book was being written, and the origins of the secular version of the song remain a puzzle to him!

Pat was one of Hollywood's main attractions in 1958, and was busy making his third film, *Mardi Gras*. This was a musical set in New Orleans, and 'I'll Remember Tonight', a song from the movie, charted for 11 weeks, reaching number 34. Pat remembers with gratitude the encouragement he received from Lionel Newman, who did the orchestral scoring for *Mardi Gras*. 'Lionel really boosted my confidence! He said he'd never known another singer other than Bing Crosby who could walk in front of an orchestra and sing *anything*. His belief in me made me feel that I was no longer a new kid at school, but rather that I really could make it in the Hollywood movie business.'

September was a particularly heavy month of recording commitments for Pat that included 'Mardi Gras March' and a batch of songs penned by Sammy Fain and Paul Francis Webster. This was followed by a couple of Christmas favourites, including a reprise of 'Jingle Bells' and Gene Autry's 'Here Comes Santa Claus'. The Christmas season started in earnest for Pat on 10 October, however, when he was given the task of minting 10 Christmas songs in one session. Standing at the mike looking at the running order for the day – including 'Rudolph', 'Hark The Herald Angels Sing' and 'Joy To The World' – Pat was amused by the fact that it was still only October. 'May I be the first to wish you all a very merry Christmas this year?' he announced to the assembled musicians. Laughter echoed around the crowded studio, and it turned into an unseasonally festive and entertaining session.

With the Thanksgiving holiday fast approaching, Pat found time in his busy schedule to head back to New York's Capital Studios on 46th Street for a long-awaited duet recording session with Shirley, conducted by Mort Lindsey. They were both very excited about this chance to work together. Shirley had more or less given up her own singing career to follow Pat and look after their children, so this was undoubtedly a special occasion. 'This is going to be an important session, Mort,' said Pat as they set things up in the studio. 'We've picked out some great material, so let's see if we can do it justice – otherwise we'll have my wife chasing our backs!'

Shirley pulled a face at her husband. 'Remember, Pat,' she responded, 'there's nothing like a woman's touch. King Solomon said that "the price of a virtuous woman is far above rubies and her husband doth safely trust in her"!'

The good-humoured, sparky session kicked off with 'My Happiness', a sentimental love song. Then came the harmonious 'Now Is The Hour', which started its life in New Zealand. Sung by the likes of Bing Crosby and Gracie Fields, it had been a wartime favourite, capturing the sentiments of families parted by the hostilities. 'Now Is The Hour' was followed by the tongue-in-cheek 'Side By Side' and 'You Can't Be True, Dear', a popular Tennessee Ernie Ford and Kay Star duet. Shirley and Pat both enjoyed the rare treat of harmonizing together and were sorry when the session ended, although they finished on a high with Red Foley's big hit 'Midnight', penned by Boudleaux Bryant and Chet Atkins.

Pat completed his recording commitments for the year on the bright, crisp morning of 12 December. He remembers arriving at the studio preoccupied with the thought that he had found no time yet for any Christmas shopping. Life had simply been too busy, and now time was running out! His first duty, however, was to concentrate on the task in hand, which was to record 'Wait For Me, Mary', an engaging song about a military serviceman's farewell to his beloved. After that came two peppy rock songs, Roy Brown's 'Good Rockin' Tonight' and Jesse Stone's 'Money Honey'. Then it was time for a change of tempo and mood, as Pat showed off his crooning skills in the sweet ballad 'With The Wind And The Rain In Her Hair'.

Pat left the studio to snatch an hour for some hurried shopping, and was looking forward to a few slower-paced days over Christmas with his young family. He had packed the year brimful with concerts, recordings and film work. It had been exciting and worthwhile, but life seemed to be whirling ever faster. Could he keep up?

There was not much time to rest, however, and more heavy recording sessions were scheduled for January and February 1959.

The people at Dot were continually pressing for fresh Boone material. New York was the venue for the early 1959 sessions, and Pat returned to work refreshed by the Christmas and New Year holiday. He was willing to record almost anything that looked like a strong song, and had some energy left over for some fun. First on the list for the day was a country song, and a studio full of bemused musicians looked on as Pat strutted around like a knock-kneed chicken, announcing the hillbilly song in Minnie Pearl-style mimicry. 'How-dee, friends! Let's git down to some real good pickin' an' grinnin'!' The normally soft-spoken Billy Vaughn got into the spirit of things too, letting out a high-pitched yell as he bustled about arranging positions for staff and equipment in the studio. The ice was broken and everyone launched with enthusiasm into Texas Troubador Ernest Tubb's 'Walking The Floor Over You'.

Next came 'You Belong To Me', a sentimental song from Pee Wee King, another huge name in country music. Pee Wee was the co-writer with Redd Stewart of the famous 'Tennessee Waltz', another song later given the Boone touch. Next came a trio of love songs: 'True Love', a contemporary hit duet for Grace Kelly and Bing Crosby; 'Anytime', one of Eddy Arnold's million-sellers; and 'Secret Love', a never-to-be-forgotten hit for Doris Day from her *Calamity Jane* western movie.

After the New York recordings, trips to Hollywood's United Recorders studios became regular occurrences throughout 1959. In March, for example, a few weeks after hearing the shocking news of the deaths of Buddy Holly and Richie Valens in a plane crash in Iowa, Pat began work on re-recording some of his own hit songs. He recorded covers of Buddy Holly songs over subsequent years. It was a desperately sad task, he remembers, but felt like a fitting tribute from one singer to another.

The public, it seemed, were gaining a definite appetite for the Pat and Shirley duet sound, and Shirley was enticed back into the studio on 3 April. She took little persuading. That day, to the accompaniment of Billy Vaughn's sophisticated country-and-western-style arrangement, they waxed Bob Nolan's best-known hit, 'Tumbling Tumbleweeds'. Bob, a founding member of the cowboy group called The Sons of the Pioneers, was also the composer of the classic 'Cool Water'. The nine-song session continued with the popular pieces 'Let Me Call You Sweetheart' and '*Vaya Con Dios*', again duets performed to the same Vaughn styling.

A month later Pat recorded 'Twixt Twelve And Twenty', a title obviously associated with his best-selling book, published the previous year. On the strength of Pat's popularity in the teenage market, the publisher Prentice Hall had suggested that Pat bring out a book for young people. It was to contain easy-to-read advice on life, love and morality. Their initial suggestion for a title was *Pat Talks to Teens*, but Pat was unimpressed by that and eventually they settled for *Twixt Twelve and Twenty*. It went right to the top of the *New York Times* bestseller list, where it remained for two years. By 1959 Pat was receiving thousands of letters every week from teenagers seeking counsel and advice.

Back in the Hollywood studio on 31 July, Pat was in top form with 'Didn't It Rain' and 'Remember Me, I'm The One Who Loves You'. Frankie Laine, the dramatic ballad stylist from San Diego, had enjoyed a big hit with 'Didn't It Rain', a spiritual-style song about Noah and the Flood. The Dot folk had great plans for the Boone version, and the peppy item did indeed work well as an album track, as did Pat's fresh airing of Stuart Hamblen's 'Remember Me'.

That summer also saw Pat appearing on his final *Chevy Showroom*, before he and his family relocated at last to Hollywood. It was quite a wrench, he says, and the show brought tears to many eyes. The whole Boone family appeared on the show to say goodbye, and they sang 'May The Good Lord Bless And Keep You' while Pat's four little girls were wheeled off the stage in a box marked 'To Disneyland'.

It was not that easy to find a suitable house in California. Pat and Shirley found that they had rather different priorities for their new home, and in any case the property prices in the Beverly Hills, Brentwood and Bel Air areas were phenomenal. Shirley's wish-list was for more bedrooms and bathrooms and a big kitchen. Pat, on the other hand, was more interested in there being enough room to throw a football, hold a barbecue and perhaps even to keep a few chickens and a cow (he had forgiven Rosemary for those awkward moments in his youth). In the end, however, they found something to please everyone. Their new house in the centre of Beverly Hills had enough bedrooms and bathrooms to satisfy Shirley, while Pat had an acre and a half of land to enjoy, plus a swimming pool and a basketball hoop already installed on an outside wall.

Shirley had fun decorating the house while Pat was away on tour, and in 1960 the family settled down once more to as normal a life as they could manage. They joined the local Church of Christ, and soon found themselves teaching Sunday School and attending every church meeting there was. They had no money worries, thanks to Pat's success, and the four girls enjoyed a large, fully equipped outdoor playground of their own and attended the very best elementary school in southern California.

Not everything was good, however, and early LA times proved to be very rocky indeed for Shirley and Pat as a couple. Pat was putting more and more time into his career pursuits. There were copious bookings coming in, valuable openings which had to be snapped up or lost. He was often absent for weeks at a time – it was simply not worth to-ing and fro-ing between closely packed dates in other parts of the country. Shirley was busy at home, of course, but she had hoped that the move to California would mean that she saw more of Pat, not less. It was not working out as she had wished, however, and there was so little time to talk that the two seemed to be operating in separate spheres. The situation was distressing for both of them, but there seemed to be no immediate solution and they simply soldiered on as best they could.

Meanwhile, Pat was having to fit filming commitments into an already packed tour diary. In 1959, now well experienced in movie-making, he was given a starring role as a Scotsman opposite James Mason in Jules Verne's adventure story *Journey to the Centre of the Earth*. The soundtrack for this action movie was an instrumental one, but the ever-enterprising Pat offered a version with lyrics as an alternative. To his disappointment, however, it was not included in the film, having been deemed unsuitable. This did not prevent Pat from recording it for his *Journey to the Centre of the Earth* EP (which also featured his rendition of 'My Love Is Like A Red, Red Rose', whose words were originally penned by the Scottish poet Robbie Burns).

Journey to the Centre of the Earth was one of Twentieth Century Fox's all-time top-grossing enterprises, and Pat revelled in the whole experience of its filming. It was a particular privilege, he says, to work with the British actor James Mason. He was an actor of distinction, a 'real professional'. Pat would be the first to point out that James was in an entirely different league from himself when it came to acting ability, and he came to respect the great actor's precise, well worked-out style. Pat also describes his surprise when he heard James humming and singing to himself between takes. 'I noticed that he hummed aloud a good bit, and I even heard him singing sometimes in his trailer. It seemed to me that he was doing it not to enjoy the music, but to keep his voice mellow and tuned up. And boy, did it work!'

It was a memorable film in many ways, and Pat still chuckles over his recollections. One scene stands out particularly vividly for him. The actress Arlene Dahl, who appeared to see herself as too fragile to do anything very strenuous, was nevertheless called upon to take part in a particularly demanding scene (it was an action movie, after all). In case of accidents, she insisted on having a nurse standing by. The scene involved the intrepid Victorian explorers mounting a wooden raft on the sea at the centre of the earth. Backstage staff were 'walking' the raft around from underneath while the actors balanced precariously on top, screaming out their lines above the noise of a great storm with buckets of water cascading over them to give the impression of huge waves and pouring rain. It was far from easy, says Pat, and Miss Dahl did not enjoy the perilous experience at all. 'Help! Help!' she cried suddenly. 'Stop! I'm feeling seasick!'

This temperamental display did not go down well with the experienced James Mason. Over the noise of the 'storm' came the familiar English tones. 'Shut up, woman!' he shouted impatiently. 'Shut up! If you keep that up, we'll have to do this scene many more times – we'd all like to get it over with and go home!' As the speaking parts were not being recorded at the same time as the visuals due to the complicated nature of the scene, James felt quite safe shouting as he did. Pat and the other actor, a big Icelander, laughed themselves silly. According to Pat, it is possible, if you look carefully at the finished movie, to see the actors yelling while no voice is heard. They can also plainly be seen turning their heads away to laugh.

Pat was once asked to write about his impressions of the great actor by the James Mason Appreciation Society, and in his article for the fan club magazine he stated:

My lasting impression of James Mason is that of a sturdy English workman with almost a farmer's hands, a man of basically simple tastes but an actor's sensibilities and extreme dedication to his craft. He always exuded a gentlemanly strength and courtesy, and I think that will probably assure his place in the history of films even more than the variety of roles he played. I would have loved to have had the honour of working with him again.

More recording sessions were on the cards for the autumn of 1959, and on 24 September Pat came out of the hot Californian sun to mint another Christmas collection. He recorded 12 carols in one day and remembers having to stop himself humming the tunes outside the studio. 'What kind of man sings Christmas carols while wearing Bermuda shorts and sunglasses?'

Another lengthy session began on 25 November, this time backed up by a majestic brass-band sound orchestrated by Jerry Fielding. First up were several masterpieces from the Ira Sankey era, and Pat relished this chance to 'get back to basics', as he put it. He was always happy to sing the classic hymns. 'My singing career spanned a whole spectrum of subject matters and styles. Yet I'm most satisfied being able to sing songs about Christ. I make no apology for injecting Christianity into my music. I like to expand folks' horizons!' The public seemed to like it too, and Pat's sacred recordings were invariably successful.

That session's chosen songs from the Victorian era were only a sample of the hundreds that Pat regularly performed. He admired the Pennsylvanian Ira Sankey's work in particular. 'Ira David Sankey popularized a new concept of gospel song. It was designed to awaken the apathetic and guide the honest seeker. It also inspired many singers in his own and later generations to perform such music professionally. In Ira's day, it was something new to perform these powerful revival songs in public. His influence spread far and wide, and his hymns were much loved by rich and poor alike. Most churches embraced the Sankey songs to some degree.' By the time Pat was recording, Sankey songs such as 'I Love To Tell The Story', and 'God Be With You Till We Meet Again' were well-loved classics, and Pat went on to fill a number of albums with Sankey's work.

Pat's next film did not appear until 1961. It was the entertaining *All Hands on Deck* with the rubber-faced comedy actor Buddy Hackett. Disappointingly, however, the catchy title track failed to reach the charts, despite having been written by top tunesmiths Jay Livingston and Ray Evans (Ray had penned 'Mona Lisa' for Nat King Cole). It was an unexpected failure for Pat, whose impact on the world pop scene had been unmissable while he enjoyed an apparently never-ending series of sure-fire hits. He was a huge name through the mid and late fifties, and his success did continue, although times were changing, and he had no further million-selling singles after 1962.

His work rate remained as high as ever, and he continued to explore a variety of sounds. His 1963 album *The Touch of Your Lips*, for example, was orchestrated by the outstanding big-band arranger Gordon Jenkins. The Missouri-born Jenkins was well known for his work as pianist/arranger for the likes of Benny Goodman, Danny Kaye, Louis Armstrong and others. For Pat he used lush strings to complement the mellow Boone voice on standards such as 'In The Heat Of The Day' and the Bing Crosby hit 'Just One More Chance'. He died in 1984 at the age of 74.

Any gloom Pat might have felt about the under-performance of his movie single 'All Hands On Deck' was soon dispelled in 1961 by the success of his version of 'Moody River'. The song had previously been a country hit for Chase Webster, and when Randy Wood heard it again one day, he was struck by the thought that it would make a perfect pop single for Pat. The recording session for it was a memorable one for several reasons, as Pat recalls. 'We recorded the song in a very high key because Randy wanted me to sound really in pain. It was *hard*, trying to sing so very high! I then went from the studio to a friend's house to pick up Shirley, who had been waiting for a little while. We were just walking out of the door when I was halted in my tracks by the radio, which was tuned to a Top 40 station. What I heard was the intro to my new record, "Moody River" ... or was it Chase Webster's version? I turned up the volume just in time to hear my own vocals begin and the DJ say over the music, "And now our brand-new hit of the week: Pat Boone's 'Moody River'!" There I was, not yet home from the studio, and already I was pick of the week on a major Top 40 radio station. I couldn't believe my ears!'

What had happened was that Randy believed in the single so much that he had an immediate acetate made from the master and carried it straight to the local radio station. He met the programme director and offered him the chance to be the first to spin the disc on air, telling him with some enthusiasm that he was convinced it was going to be a massive hit. The programme director was naturally delighted with the idea of gaining such a huge scoop for his station and put it on the air immediately. The song went to number one in the charts on 19 June 1961 – ahead of Ricky Nelson, Gary U.S. Bonds, Ben E. King and Dee Dee Clark – and went on to become yet another million-seller for Pat.

As Pat's popularity grew in his USA market, he was also increasingly in demand to tour abroad. Overseas, millions of fans were eager to see him perform, and one of the places most keen to welcome him was the Philippines. It was there that he was destined to hear the comedy song that nobody thought he should record, 'Speedy Gonzales'. Appearing at the Aranetta Coliseum in 1961, he enjoyed capacity shows for 10 days, entertaining around a quarter of a million people. Such was his star status that he did not dare venture very far from the stadium or his hotel unless he had a bevy of security men shielding him. Without their protection, he was afraid he would very quickly be mobbed by the hoards of screaming fans.

Late one night, tired of being so shut in, Pat decided to risk being recognized and headed for an 'after hours' club. It seemed customary at the venue for anyone present to have a turn singing a solo if they wanted, and he remembers a TV director standing up and singing – very competently – a quirky song that sent the whole audience wild. Intrigued by the catchy melody and the funny lyrics, Pat asked the singer afterwards what the song was and who had written it. It had been a hit song for an American called David Dante, the man told him.

Pat had never heard of it. Nevertheless, highly entertained by the song, he kept singing it over and over again in his mind. It was one of those songs that he just could not shake loose. He took a copy of the sheet music home with him and, sensing its hit potential, he tried to convince the people at Dot that he should record it. His arguments were to no avail: they could not envisage the sophisticated balladeer coming across at all well with such a flippant, comedy song. Undaunted, Pat persisted until finally – no doubt just to get him off their backs, he says now – the powers-that-be relented and let him record it.

Using the powerful voice of Robin Ward for the high parts and comedian Mel Blanc (the voice of Bugs Bunny and his cartoon friends) for the cheeky 'Speedy' voice, the song was duly recorded in what Pat remembers as being a very high-spirited session. Robin's voice opened the novelty song with the memorable strains of 'La la la, la-la la-la la' – the bit that seizes attention and which everybody remembers. Elton John once confessed to Pat that he had used that 'riff' on his 'Crocodile Rock' recording. 'Speedy Gonzales' confounded the doubters by becoming a phenomenal success, proving Pat's forecast by going not only gold but platinum in 1962. Even now, the silly song is a very popular request from Pat's fans during his stage performances. He usually has to improvise somewhat, however, with a band member taking the part of Robin Ward while Pat himself does a very creditable imitation of Mel Blanc's voice!

As with the late fifties, the early sixties saw Pat running to keep up with a very pressurized booking diary. Continuous travelling became a way of life – and everywhere took longer to get to than is the case in these days of high-speed road and air transport. Pat lost count of the number of days and hours he spent meandering along America's city-to-city and state-to-state highways. He maintains that it was all more than worthwhile, however, and he enjoyed his encounters with community audiences the length and breadth of the country, as well as the bigger, glitzier occasions. He sang live wherever he could, both at home and abroad, and also kept up a crippling agenda of TV appearances and recording schedules. At the height of his popularity he could do no wrong. Audiences lapped up whatever he offered them and he walked off with countless awards, his face and distinctive sound well known across the globe.

The heady days at the top had to come to an end sometime, however, and by the late sixties the popularity of the Boone sound had started to dwindle, the result of inevitable shifts in public taste – a plight common to many of his peers, including the great Elvis Presley and those long-lived classic crooners. Socially, a new, more radical era had dawned. On many fronts, accepted conventions were being brought tumbling down, largely in the wake of unrest following the USA's military role in southeast Asia. For many, it was a testing time of rethinking and the upheaval meant that the very foundations of Western culture were shaken. Rapid changes occurred throughout society, and the reshaping affected all art forms too, as people looked for new ways to express themselves and their attitudes. The Vietnam War undeniably had much to do with the social unrest and outright anti-establishment rebellion which blew up in the USA. The younger generation was not used to lack of money or freedom, unlike their parents during the Great Depression and World War II. Instead, a philosophy of 'I'll live the way I want to live' reigned.

Pat was upset by the whole situation, distressed by the war in Vietnam and concerned about the anarchy which was threatening his country as draft cards were burned in the streets and unrest seemed to be rising. As a means of expressing his feelings, he wrote and recorded the song 'Wish You Were Here, Buddy!' 'None of the soldiers liked being in Vietnam,' he explains, 'but it seemed to me that back home too many people were pulling out from under their feet the rug of national support. So I wrote the song more as an anthem of support for those in the mud dodging the bullets, rather than as a jingoistic pro-war song. It was in stark contrast to the popular themes of other songs in the charts at the time, penned by dreamers like Bob Dylan, Peter, Paul and Mary, Barry McGuire and others.'

Amid all this social unrest there emerged a completely new pop sound from the downtown streets of Liverpool, England. The Beatles – John Lennon, Paul McCartney, George Harrison and Ringo Starr – met the revolutionary spirit of the age artistically, turning music industry norms upside down. The band's invasion of the American music scene had a dramatically adverse effect on many indigenous artists, and Pat was not excluded. The phenomenal publicity that preceded the Beatles' first USA release caught the imagination of the public and guaranteed that the record became a smash hit, bringing in its wake wave after wave of British rock acts during the years that followed.

The knock-on effect on established singers like Pat and Elvis was catastrophic. Previously, Pat had enjoyed continuous record success, along with the guarantee of handsome royalties as well as lucrative bookings worldwide, which included the enthusiastic UK market (Pat played at the London Palladium in 1962, for example). Inevitably, he saw his royalties suddenly and dramatically reduced by those 'foreign invaders' from Liverpool, and found himself pushed down the list of priorities for those who arranged concert tours. 'If you can't beat 'em, join 'em,' he decided, and branched out into the world of art. Calling on the services of Dutch portrait-painter Leo Jansen, he commissioned group and individual paintings of the Beatles and sold the pictures to the thousands of Beatles fans in the States with a great deal of success.

Just prior to the Beatles' invasion of America, Pat had been enjoying a period of great success with his two hits 'Moody River' and the very different 'Speedy Gonzales'. Now he had to think quickly and decide on a strategy for the future. The keynote to his continuing success had always been his variety of repertoire. Now he felt a need to go back to his roots, at least to a certain extent.

Despite his early Nashville tag, there was nothing really 'country' about his life, persona or performing style. Dozens of fellow Nashville-based artists were yet to come to international fame in the decade after Pat's groundbreaking start. Tennessee was, of course, the seedbed of much rock and gospel music as well as country, and Pat had absorbed much of those genres at an early age. He never embraced the rough-and-ready hillbilly style, preferring a more sophisticated package in terms of sound, dress and general image. He did not want to change that, but he had to look for a new niche, and there were aspects of that Southern background which offered promising opportunities.

In the end, what slowly started to evolve was a highly commendable role as a kind of 'Christian spokesman'. Pat took the decision to leave Dot after many years of successful collaboration and entered nervously into new arrangements with several record producers, including Kurt Kaiser, Buck Herring and Paul Mickelson from the Christian music arena. One result of these changes was the *Departure* album, which came out on the Tetragrammaton label in 1969. It was in vogue to be 'socially aware' at that time, and this was Pat's personal 'social awareness, folk-style album'. Its intense orchestration was not, however, a feature normally identified with folk albums, and it certainly stood out from the crowd. The album included a couple of Biff Rose songs, 'What's Gnawing At Me' and the melodic 'Molly'. Country songwriter John D. Loudermilk contributed 'No Playing In The Snow Today', 'Bad News' (originally recorded by Johnny Cash) and the George Hamilton IV hit 'Break My Mind'.

For Pat, the late sixties was a rather odd time career-wise. There were great highs and lows, but he tried to keep working steadily and thinking of new routes to explore. It was not, of course, entirely a case of the old-timers being forced to make way for the newcomers. In some ways there was space for both, but adjustments had to be made, and it was never going to be the same as it had been before.

As for the Beatles themselves, they always held in high regard the myth-makers of the classic rock'n'roll era, including Pat, Elvis, Carl Perkins, Little Richard, Buddy Holly, Chuck Berry and many others. Many years later, on 1 June 1990, Pat joked about it all during an interview with BBC Radio Kent. Discussing the steam-rolling effect of the Beatles on the rest of the popular music industry, he went on to mention a show he had done in Folkestone in 1989. 'You know,' he said, 'I'm told something – I don't know if it's true for sure – but apparently Sir Paul McCartney eased into the back of the auditorium the last time I was here. Perhaps he just wanted to check on that old Boone fella who was already singing and well established when he and the mopheads got going...'

CHAPTER 8

THE GREAT PRETENDER

My need is such, I pretend too much!

Buck Ram

As the 1960s progressed, Pat remained heavily involved in movie-making, not all of it in Hollywood. *The Main Attraction* was made in England's Shepperton Studios in 1962 and was to provide Pat with the perfect opportunity to prove his prowess as a maturing songwriter. Originally the film-makers were intending to ask the famous songwriter Jules Styne to compose the theme song, but Pat suggested that he should write it instead. They gave him the go-ahead and he wrote the catchy title song used in the movie, a feat of which he is very proud. The film itself was nothing much to be proud of, however, despite assurances from producer Ray Stark that it would open new horizons for Pat. At the time Pat was concerned with trying to balance out his 'goody-goody' image, and this film – about a young man falling for an Italian circus entertainer – seemed to offer a chance to do just that.

The Boone family rented accommodation near the Shepperton Studios in Middlesex, and filming began in earnest. Pat's leading lady was the attractive actress Nancy Kwan. At the start, Pat had insisted that the film should not contain any bed scenes between himself and Nancy, but scriptwriter John Patrick included one nonetheless. Pat admits that by today's permissive standards the scene would not be considered at all extreme, but he was unhappy with the result. He was already contracted, however, and could not get out of it. In the event, the film had little effect on his career, positive or negative. It was a huge flop, and disappeared from cinema screens very rapidly.

The other movie Pat made in 1962 was *State Fair*, a Rodgers and Hammerstein classic from the forties. The sentimental family film charted the adventures of a farming family attending the annual Texas State Fair. The light-hearted score included several popular songs such as 'It Might As Well Be Spring' and a Pat Boone/Bobby Darin duet in 'It's A Grand Night For Singing'. Disappointingly, however, the film failed to produce any hit songs for Pat, and was not a notable box-office success, despite the all-star line-up which included Ann-Margret, Alice Faye, Tom Ewell and Pamela Tiffin alongside Pat and Bobby Darin.

Undaunted, Pat continued to show a preference for the more light-hearted movies throughout the sixties, including the adventure-farce *The Perils of Pauline*, which came out in 1967. The British production (with a screenplay written by Albert Beich) starred Pat, the English comedian Terry Thomas and Pamela Austin. The crazy story charts the love of two orphans brought up together in a foundling home. Hero George (played by Pat) pledges his love to Pauline (played by Pamela Austin), promising to make a million dollars and return to the home to rescue Pauline. Pauline eventually tires of waiting, and leaves the orphanage to become a schoolteacher to an Arabian prince. George duly chases across continents in pursuit of his lost love – through bizarre adventures in Africa, the sewers of New York, a trip into space and a happy ending in Venice. Pat remembers the whole thing being enormous fun to make.

Not everything ended so happily, however, and there were some less light-hearted moments to deal with too. Pat may have been attempting to shed his cleaner-than-clean image at this time, but he did sometimes experience a crisis of conscience over things he was asked to do as a performer when they touched directly on his religious convictions. One such difficulty occurred when Buddy Adler, head of the Fox Studios, asked him to play the lead role in *The St Bernard Story*. Pat's character was meant to be a Roman Catholic monk, and Pat found himself struggling with some hard questions. Could a person whose strong Protestant beliefs were well known play such a character? How would playing such a character go down with Pat's fans? Could he honestly play the part of a monk who falls in love with one of his parishioners? What was 'right' in this situation?

The answer came from his old high-school principal Mack Craig, who phoned Pat out of the blue one day. His opinion was that this role would not be right for Pat. Respecting Mack's advice, Pat withdrew from the movie, despite having already signed a contract. Buddy Adler hit the roof: how could Pat be so 'bigoted and narrow' in his beliefs? He threatened to sue Pat for breach of contract. In spite of threats about union walkouts and non-appearances on TV as a consequence of his actions, Pat stuck to his guns. The threats never materialized into anything, and Mr Adler sadly died from cancer soon after, so the incident came to a natural close.

Regardless of the awkward moments, however, Pat would say without hesitation that he thoroughly enjoyed his Hollywood movie days. To him it was a fantasy land. 'The idea that a schoolkid from Tennessee who'd thought he was going to be a teacher should wind up making movies was preposterous to me! I think Elvis must have felt the same way, because neither of us had any drama training. My movie parts were not demanding from a dramatic standpoint, however, so I really enjoyed them. I deliberately didn't take on any heavy roles, as I hadn't been trained in that way. Luckily, the roles that came my way were all easy and fun.'

Ironically, he went on to undertake some formal acting training some time after his Hollywood successes, at the Sandy

Mysengers Neighbourhood Theatre, a New York school that produced many great actors. Pat, having already experienced Top 10
box-office success, found himself working alongside a group of
aspiring young actors. 'There was I, a rank beginner-student,
doing scenes and improvisations with people who hoped to get
where I had already been. They had more reason to be there. I had
already earned much money making films, yet I didn't know any
more about it than they did – except that I'd actually been in front
of a camera!'

There is little doubt that for several years Pat was captivated by
the prospect of a high-flying Hollywood career, lured by the spell
of the bright lights. Yet, although he made regular top-of-the-bill
movie appearances, a truly big-time career seemed not to be his
destiny. The greatest difficulty he encountered was in finding
wholesome stories in which he was happy to be involved. Time
and again, he refused parts in the biggest movies (including one
part playing opposite Marilyn Monroe) because, as he explains,
'the story line tended to glorify some evil without showing its
adverse consequences. I was convinced that such movies would
give the totally wrong impressions, so I turned them down.'
Hollywood was not the best place in which to hold on to high
principles, however, and in time even Pat found his standards
slipping. Surrounded by temptation and a very worldly culture, it
was all too easy, he says, to find oneself joining in rather than
staying safely out on the fringes.

Hollywood may have been a fun and exciting arena, but there
were many pitfalls and temptations amongst the glitz, and Pat was
not immune. Serious problems arose in his personal life – above
and beyond the usual stresses and strains of a show-biz life – and
they were, he says, directly linked to the Hollywood culture.
Things really started to change for the worse after the Nancy
Kwan film bombed at the box office in 1962. During the early
years of their marriage, Pat had always been 100 per cent faithful

to Shirley, but he began to get increasingly involved in the show-biz lifestyle. It was inevitable that during his frequent absences on tour he would find himself spending time alone with other women. Conversation backstage and at parties was often ribald and Pat, with his ready wit, was often in the thick of it, telling dirty jokes along with the rest.

Shirley expressed her concerns over the double standards that began to appear in Pat's life. On the one hand he appeared to be the faithful husband and father, while on the other hand he was doing things which were clearly not consistent with someone who professed to be a Christian. In spite of her remonstrations, however, he continued to pursue the kind of lifestyle that once would have horrified him. It was so hard not to get swept along by the crowd, says Pat, and the constant round of parties and heavy drinking did not help. He remembers consciously trying to shrug off his 'goody two shoes' image. The party to celebrate the end of filming for *Goodbye Charlie* in 1964 (in which Pat starred oppo-site Debbie Reynolds) was a case in point. Pat arrived home very late afterwards, appallingly drunk on champagne, and Shirley was confronted by a man who seemed to be a complete stranger to her. This was not the man she had married. Sometimes Shirley accompanied Pat to launch parties and other social functions, but she often found the atmosphere, conversation and content of the performances offensive. Increasingly she preferred to stay at home with the children rather than go out with Pat.

In time Shirley found herself facing a battle with her own principles. She was intensely weary of the constant friction between her and Pat. Their marriage was suffering badly. To make matters worse, she found out that she was pregnant again. Depressed and convinced she would be unable to cope with another baby, she prayed that God would take the child. In the fifth month of her pregnancy, she miscarried. It was a truly desperate time, she says. Finally she told Pat that she would not be arguing with him any more. She would do whatever he asked her and the family to do. Suddenly she began to act totally out of character, attending parties and going out whenever she could, flirting with other men in order to make Pat jealous – something he had never had to contemplate before. Things turned quite rapidly from bad to worse.

It was a sorry season in their life together, and Pat puts it all down to the fact that he was moving away from God, away from his faith, and had lost that 'clear telephone line to heaven'. He had started out so well, trying to keep to the simple faith his parents had taught him, even as his career intensified. Yet his Christian convictions were tested to the extreme in the gaudy, alluring world of show business – and this was especially true of the sixties era, with its culture of rebellion and permissiveness. For Pat and his peers, those years concealed enormous moral snares. Many of his contemporaries fell into the traps, which led to misery at best, tragic ruin and death at worst. Pat undoubtedly teetered on the edge, although the worst excesses of drugs and drink passed him by. In the late sixties, however, he did find himself vulnerable to the sexual temptations that abounded in Hollywood and Las Vegas.

Perhaps he should have seen it coming. Pat and Shirley had married young and their four baby daughters arrived in quick succession, giving the couple very little time to cement their own relationship. Very early on in their marriage, therefore, they were fully occupied in quite separate spheres, Shirley with the children and Pat with his burgeoning career. There was scant opportunity for meaningful communication. After an evening concert or TV special, for example, Pat would come home exhilarated after an adrenalin-filled performance to find a house already asleep – the girls bathed and bedded and Shirley either in bed too or ready to collapse. During the long separations, Pat no longer always called home every day, and when he did the girls took first priority, telling him about school and friends and leaving little time for any affectionate chat between husband and wife.

Pat admits that he was not always sensitive to his wife's needs, only thinking selfishly of his own frustration at being shut out by her time-consuming involvement with the demands of a young family. Shirley, not surprisingly, always seemed to be tired, and she was also coping at that time with ill-health due to an ovarian malfunction. The couple's love life dwindled. Shirley was in considerable pain because of her illness, and intimacy was out of the question. As Pat recalls, it was a frustrating and testing period of their lives and blame came to be apportioned where it was not deserved. 'Shirley had, it seemed, lost all interest in the sexual activity that had created our children. Her illness caused her pain and nausea whenever I embraced her, and it seemed that my love-making was causing her to be sick. I felt a deep sense of personal rejection.'

It is well documented that such a feeling of rejection often leads the 'injured' party to search for affection elsewhere, and that is precisely what happened to Pat and Shirley. Pat says sadly, 'I knew I was appreciated elsewhere, and I succumbed to temptation.' Occasional hints would be dropped by colleagues or in show-biz gossip columns about Pat's attachments to certain ladies. At first, Shirley did not know whether to believe them or not. She was aware that Pat was lonely and matters were certainly not good between them, but then again, Pat's image made him an easy target for journalists' imaginations. Finding out the truth led to many tears and much anger. Shirley felt completely betrayed. She had put her career on hold to raise Pat's four daughters, and now he was cheating on her.

During that dark period of his life, Pat confesses that for several years he made more and more compromises with his previously high principles. 'Heaven became more and more distant.' He discovered that, after all, he could fit perfectly well into the glamour of the Hollywood community. Today he confesses that he did some things which shocked other people and damaged his life and family relationships. 'I felt I needed to do things like the other Hollywood guys were doing. I began to feel that I *belonged* in the entertainment business and went on to make one compromise after another to try and maintain my position.' He did a great deal of social drinking, got involved in gambling and succumbed to the temptations of various attractive women. He also began to take on screen roles which were totally out of character with his previous squeaky clean image. In the end, however, the compromises cost him dearly.

It was the lure of 'big-time money' that originally persuaded him to venture into Las Vegas. His first performance took place at the famed Sahara Hotel, where many other big names had appeared, and for a couple of years his regular dates there drew record-breaking crowds. At first he did not gamble in the casinos, but he was nevertheless fascinated by the whole scene – and by the kudos provided through being identified with some of the biggest names in the business. During Pat's stints in Las Vegas, the family rented a house owned by the zany comedienne Phyllis Diller. The house was full of leopard-skin rugs and outlandish furniture, but it was fun, and there was plenty of space for the whole family. In time Pat's fascination with the gambling world led to him learning his way around the craps and blackjack tables. Eventually, however, he gave up visiting the casinos, having come to the sensible conclusion that it was a fool's game to gamble away his hard-earned cash in that way. He never lost huge amounts of money on the tables, but it was enough to teach him the lesson. Other troubles were soon looming on the horizon.

Shirley became increasingly lonely, staying at home with the girls while Pat played the tables night after night. Also, his childish pranks were beginning to cause her great embarrassment. He had always been a joker, but for a while he seemed to lose his sense of what was appropriate. One such incident occurred when he and his friend Nelson Sardelli visited a TV station to appear on Forrest Duke's *Tonight Show*. Nelson persuaded Pat to pose as his young, mixed-up brother Washington Sardelli, dressing him up in a hat and dark glasses, with a big cigar as a prop. Driving into the studio on a Vespa motorcycle, Pat played his part to the full, spitting on the floor, blowing clouds of cigar smoke everywhere, and finally starting a mock fight with Nelson. Forrest Duke and the programme producers were at a loss, uncertain how to stop these violent characters ruining the show, until Pat removed his glasses and hat to reveal who he really was. There was great hilarity in the studio and the stunt became the talking point in Las Vegas for a while.

Shirley, on the other hand, was far from amused. She was furious about the whole stupid escapade, and refused to talk to Pat for a long time afterwards. He was supposed to be a principled Christian, a responsible father, but his walk was far from matching his talk. Events finally came to a head in 1965 when Shirley collapsed through fatigue and stress. A period of hospitalization led to a diagnosis of glandular fever, and recovery would take some time. Pat willingly paid the hospital bills and arranged for help to look after the girls, but instead of sticking around to support his wife as she lay ill, he continued with his own selfish pursuits. He visited her, but did not curtail his busy schedule to make her a priority.

Once she was well on the road to recovery, Shirley decided that she had endured enough and took some time out for herself, travelling to New York to visit some friends. One of these was Lloyd Hand, who was the Chief of Protocol to President Johnson. He was able to introduce Shirley to the ambassadors and diplomats who made up his social circle, and she enjoyed the sensation of being courted by some of the eligible young attachés. Carried away by an unaccustomed feel-good factor, she bought some new and fashionable clothes and coloured her hair. Meeting her at the airport on her return, Pat failed to recognize the beautiful blonde as his wife!

The changes were not only on the outside. The realization finally hit them both that they had changed in their feelings towards one another. The closeness they once enjoyed had dissipated, and they hardly knew each other any more. Pat was not, of course, the first entertainer who reached the summit of his profession and then plunged to the depths, losing everything that was really important. His now fragile marriage had clearly arrived at a crisis point. 'Shirley and I just didn't love each other any more. We lived together in the same house, but there was little between us except anxieties, animosities and mutual blame.'

The domestic crisis was also beginning to take its toll on Pat's daughters. As Pat explains, 'Unfortunately, because of the compromises I had made, my girls saw one Pat Boone at home, another Pat Boone at church, and yet another Pat Boone on TV. Rightfully, they wondered how many Pat Boones there were! I'd lost much of their respect. It was just a matter of time until the whole family disintegrated.' The couple kept up the appearance of being a happy family in public, but at home everything turned sour. Shirley, deeply hurt by Pat's infidelities, no longer made any attempt to persuade him to change his ways, but in retaliation flirted with temptations of her own. She and Pat could barely bring themselves to be civil to each other in front of their children.

It could not go on. Even if they were not talking to each other, both Pat and Shirley were privately feeling increasingly desperate about the situation. Quite apart from a personal reluctance to see his marriage disintegrate, Pat had another worry: he never had managed to shake off his 'Mr Nice Guy' image, and he was painfully aware that any hint of marriage problems or infidelity would be disastrous to his reputation and career. 'I knew that my fans and the general public would be shocked to discover the plain truth about our marriage, and my successful career would suffer. In my mind there was no way I could allow this situation to become obvious to everyone. Shirley knew this too – although her motivation was no doubt different. To her credit, instead of merely trying to keep up public appearances while we were still living a lie at home, she decided the situation was serious enough to warrant seeking help.'

In 1967, Shirley finally turned back to God in desperation. She decided to put herself and the fate of her marriage into the hands of the only person she knew could help. She poured out to God her deepest feelings and needs, pleading for Him to take over her life and rekindle the love she felt for Pat. And, she says, He did just that. She knew that she had become lukewarm towards her faith in recent years, but understood that God had not become lukewarm towards her, and that day she recommitted her life to Him. Then, as she sat reading her Bible, she felt increasingly convinced that she should ask God to fill her with His Holy Spirit.

She prayed her request very simply, and testifies to how wonderful it was when God answered her prayer. 'The Lord did fill me with His Holy Spirit, and I became a totally changed woman.' It was hard to quantify just what had changed, but she was no longer despairing, and her altered outlook was clear even to Pat. He was initially sceptical about her enthusiastic rediscovery of faith, believing it to be a fad that his unhappy wife just happened to be going through. As he watched her become stronger and happier, however, he recognized that she had experienced something from God that he desperately needed too.

Pat's back was now firmly in the proverbial corner, and he saw at last that only a miracle from God *could* put his family and marriage back together again and give his career new meaning. Divorce was never an option, he says, because even in the worst times they were still aware of the vows they had made at their marriage ceremony. But now he realized that there could at least be a way out of the ice that had formed between them. So it was that, with an enormous sense of personal failure, he found himself one day earnestly talking to God about his situation. It was, he says, a revolutionary day. 'Suddenly, without warning, I discovered myself on my knees crying out to God, whom I had long deserted. I didn't expect to cry, but an emotional dam just broke inside me. I began to ask God to come into my wayward life, save my broken marriage, bring my family back together, and give my career some purpose again. I also asked him to solve my financial problems.' (Pat had invested in several business ventures in the 1960s, including a real estate outfit and a basketball team, which turned out to be less than successful.)

When Pat told Shirley about his prayer, she wept for joy and they found themselves embracing with the kind of love they had not experienced for a long time. The ice had already started to melt. Pat says that at the time he identified very closely with the first verses of Psalm 40:

> I waited patiently for the LORD; and he inclined
>   unto me, and heard my cry.
> He brought me up also out of an horrible pit …
>   set my feet upon a rock, and established my
>   goings.
> And he hath put a new song in my mouth, *even*
>   praise unto our God.
>
> Psalm 40:1–3

The rebirth of a deeper relationship between Pat and Shirley had a dramatic effect on family life. Pat's daughters got their father back, and he and Shirley once again followed God together. 'God answered my prayer,' Pat says. 'He saved my marriage, brought my family back together, and gave my career new meaning. People often ask me whether I ever felt tempted to stray again from my marriage. With all honesty, I have to admit that I've been tempted, but I have never strayed again. I know too well what the cost of giving in would be. And besides that, I do not feel the need to leave my restored and happy relationship with my wife.'

Shirley's experience of being filled with the Holy Spirit and the exuberant joy she exhibited as a result caused serious concern amongst the elders of the Church of Christ which the Boones attended. They were suspicious of the whole thing, and feared that Shirley's description of her experiences went against the strict teaching of their Church. Matters finally came to a head when Pat was approached by one of the elders. A long-time doctor friend, he expressed his concern that Shirley's experience might be the start of a nervous breakdown. Pat tried to assure him that in fact it was really quite the opposite, but the elder left still puzzled and concerned. Shortly afterwards, the elders decided that Pat and Shirley had been deluded by false doctrine and should no longer be admitted as members of the Church of Christ.

Their judgement was made public to the entire congregation one Sunday evening, when the reasons for their decision were given. The announcement came like a bombshell. Most of the congregation had no idea what was afoot. Many were visibly distressed, and pleaded with the couple not to leave. By contrast, however, Pat and Shirley were filled with an immense sense of peace. It seemed, explains Pat, that it was God's will for them to move on at that time. 'We clearly understood the concerns of the Church of Christ. In their eyes, they were just trying to straighten us out, but on the evidence of Scripture and our own experience, we were convinced of the legitimacy of our testimony. Other Christian friends also helped to bolster us.' The story soon made it into the press, of course, stimulating much debate, but Pat and Shirley were not worried about other people's opinions. They simply began seeking a new place of worship.

Renewed commitment to God led to dramatic changes in Pat's lifestyle as he set himself apart once again from the Hollywood glamour. His family and career were back on the right track again and he began to look with fresh enthusiasm at work he could do in the future. He prayed every day and read the Bible, returning to the habits he had formed much earlier in life. Something was missing, however. Could he find the joy that Shirley was so obviously experiencing? One day in 1969, sitting alone, he prayed that God would baptize him with His Holy Spirit. As he describes it, he found himself all at once overtaken by an intense feeling of joy.

He poured out his feelings to God, but was aware that he was not speaking in English. He had been given the gift known as 'tongues', and from then on this special prayer language formed a vital part of his worship every day. Such gifts apart, he had rediscovered the strong faith of his childhood. The pretence with God was over.

It felt like a new beginning. Soon he was involved in Bible study groups and prayer groups held in other people's homes, meeting Christians of different denominations. They opened up whole new dimensions of faith, and Pat was thrilled by what he heard. 'The time had come in my life when I just asked the Lord to take over,' he explains. 'I said to Him, "I give up trying to place limits on it; you do it!" I realized this might mean me giving up my career and material things, but I just asked God to take me.' Soon the Boones had opened up their own home for Bible study, prayer and fellowship meetings. Visits from other celebrities were not unusual, and those who came included Glenn Ford, Doris Day, Priscilla Presley and Zsa Zsa Gabor. Pat believes that they welcomed the non-threatening and non-hyped private surroundings.

The change in Pat's spiritual life caused his parents some concern, however. His father had been a pillar of the local Church of Christ for many years and was very firm about his doctrine. When his son came to him and told him of his experience of the Holy Spirit, therefore, Archie decided to prove from Scripture that Pat was wrong. The more he studied, though, the more it became clear to him that the Bible taught that this experience was indeed available for the Church today. In the end, Pat's parents decided to ask God to reveal the truth to them in some real way. One morning Pat received a phone call from his father, who told him that the Lord had answered his prayers and he too had received this gift of the Holy Spirit. Pat's mother experienced the same thing a few days later. Just like Pat and Shirley, the experience meant that they were disfellowshipped from their local Church of Christ (which Archie's company had built). Nonetheless, the couple continued to attend the church every Sunday morning as guests rather than members. In time they found fellowship in a different church in Nashville, with people who shared the same convictions.

By the end of the sixties, it was clear that Pat's recorded music had started to reflect his deepening faith. Much of the semi-religious pop material recorded at this time had a searching or mystical theme, reflecting society's ongoing search for something to satisfy a strong sense of emptiness. Pat's music, by contrast, was not so much expressing a quest as offering a statement of truths already discovered. Pat had found his deeply satisfying faith, and he now wanted to share it with tens of thousands of people across the globe.

The Pat Boone Family, the family's first gospel album on Word Records which came out at the turn of the decade, was nominated for a Grammy award. At around the same time Pat wrote his book called *A New Song*, which recounted the family's rediscovery of God and the miracles in their lives and relationships. The book attracted much public attention, prompting numerous invitations to appear on talk shows. Pat and Shirley were only too happy to explain how God had rescued their failing marriage, reunited their family and completely changed their outlook on life.

Pat's newfound enthusiasm for his faith did not endear him to everyone, however. In fact, in public relations terms it was a disaster. One agent told him, 'You're committing suicide, and I don't want to be part of it!' Many people no longer wanted to be associated with this 'born-again Boone'. He was too intense, too God-centred, and it made people uncomfortable. He became the butt of several comedians' gags once again. The baptism theme was a rich vein: Red Buttons joked, 'I went swimming over at Pat Boone's house – and he dunked me three times!' Pat was determined, however, and continued to tell anyone who would listen what had happened to him.

Like many other things, the focus of Christian music had begun to change radically during the sixties. Suddenly, innovative sounds were appearing from artists such as Andrae Crouch, Second Chapter of Acts, Barry McGuire and many others. Before this time, gospel music had mainly appealed to the older generation, but now there was something to catch the attention of youngsters too. Significantly, after 1969 Pat took a leading part in facilitating these changes. Contemporary composers, arrangers and producers (among them Michael Omartian, David Clydesdale, Bruce Herring and Jimmy Owens) started writing material which was much broader in its appeal and Pat enthusiastically absorbed the new songs into his repertoire.

Soon he was being considered as one of the most progressive of the professional Christian artists. Keen to encourage the development of new Christian talent, Pat went on to form his Lamb and Lion record label, which began in 1971. Most of the label's early projects were recording in the hit-making studios of Los Angeles or Nashville. Hundreds of recordings were to follow from many talented Christian artists, including the Boone Girls themselves, Dogwood, Betty Jean Robinson, Arthur Smith, George Hamilton IV, Andrae Crouch and others.

Pat's reawakened faith and baptism in the Holy Spirit led to him experiencing things that he described as supernatural – by which he meant God-given experiences of divine power. This was the inspiration behind his work on *Something Supernatural*, a Lamb and Lion album released in 1975 with backing from the outstanding trio Second Chapter of Acts. Recorded in Hollywood, it featured contemporary Christian songs on the theme of the supernatural, each one pointing in some way to the second coming of Jesus. Produced by Buck Herring, it contained songs such as Malcolm and Alwyn's 'Fool's Wisdom', Chuck Girard's 'Something Supernatural' and Larry Norman's 'UFO'.

After the near-disaster of the 1960s, Pat made the 1970s a fruitful decade, travelling from east to west and north to south to record the best Christian material available. Additionally, he was active in encouraging others far and wide. British folk-rock star

Garth Hewitt has fond reminiscences of the boost given him by the visitor from Beverly Hills at the launch of his album *Under the Influence* at London's Claridge's Hotel. All sorts of people were there, including Cliff Richard and Pat, and it turned into a memorable occasion. Garth found himself chatting at length with the two famous figures about his album, then they moved on to the joys and pains of concert touring. The animated trio was snapped by an opportunist photographer and *Music Week*, Europe's premier trade music magazine, printed the photo of Garth, Cliff and Pat in its next edition. Garth says he could not have asked for a better piece of publicity.

Next on the programme for Pat was a visit to Charlotte, North Carolina. The Arthur Smith Studios there, booked for Lamb and Lion, were soon full of the sound of Pat recording some classic bluegrass Southern gospel. Arthur 'Guitar Boogie' Smith was a multi-instrumentalist who had shared top billing with Hank Williams on the prestigious MGM label. 'Many key country and Christian artists came under his skilled studio direction as an album producer,' Pat says. 'Avoiding the magnetic pull of Nashville, he set himself up in Carolina as a successful businessman and quality songwriter. He was an outstanding Christian gentleman, too.' Among Arthur's best known songs were 'Acres Of Diamonds', 'The Fourth Man' and 'I Saw A Man'. That day in the studio he helped Pat lay down some famous gospel songs, long associated with Roy Acuff, Benny Martin, the Louvin Brothers and the Stamps Baxter Quartet, as well as some new songs written by Pat's friend Johnny Cash.

Another song from that time, with lyrics penned by Pat's friend Pastor Jack Hayford, was 'Majesty', which went on to become a highly popular modern-day Christian anthem. The lyrics speak of Christ's kingship, and Pat loved the song from the first time he heard it. '"Majesty" is a wonderful, regal song that declares very powerfully the truth of Christ's sovereignty. It looks forward to the day when "every knee shall bow before Him".'

On several occasions Pat has found himself concerned with an entirely different kind of sovereign. Most artists are delighted to receive one invitation to perform for Her Majesty Queen Elizabeth II of England. Pat has been the proud recipient of not one but *two* invitations to the annual Royal Command Performance. He found the second occasion, he says, more than a little embarrassing.

Standing in the line-up after the performance in London, sandwiched between the movie actors Claudia Cardinale and Peter Finch, Pat was trying to appear calm and blasé. After all, this was his second Royal Command Performance. He even joked with the others. 'Why are you all so nervous?' he asked them. 'The Queen is just a human being like us.' Pride, as they say, comes before a fall. The Queen eventually reached Pat's place in the line-up and stopped in front of him. Pat bowed, suddenly more nervous than he had thought.

'We've met before, Mr Boone!' said Her Majesty.

He had not expected her to remember him. Completely thrown, he said the first thing that came into his head. 'We did, Your Majesty?'

'Yes,' the Queen replied, a twitch of a smile appearing on her face. 'Yes, you came over for another Command Performance and, if I remember correctly, you interrupted your studies at school to do it!'

This was true, but Pat's mind went entirely blank and he could think of nothing intelligent to say in reply. 'I'm glad you're here!' he burst out at last.

'Oh, what a dumb thing to say to the Queen of England!' he moans now, still squirming at the memory. The next day, his discomfiture was complete when his picture appeared on the front pages of the London newspapers: there was the Queen standing before him, and the proud Mr Boone was staring back at her, mouth hanging open and a completely dumbstruck look on his face.

In 1991 Pat (with his daughter Debby) was once again singing at a Royal Command Performance. This time it was for His Majesty the King of Thailand, to raise money for the Thai troops protecting refugees escaping from Cambodia. A gifted musician himself, the King asked Pat and Debby to sing a song he had written specially, entitled 'Candelight Blues'. The royal connection may have enhanced people's appreciation of the performance, but they won rapturous applause from the distinguished audience.

Pat's royal command performances taught him an important spiritual lesson, as he explains. 'People everywhere are still awed by royalty. Nobody stirs excitement or demands respect like a king or a queen. I've sung for kings, queens and presidents several times. I can tell you that it's an exhilarating and frightening experience! No matter how many times you tell yourself, "They're just people like I am," when you're confronted with a direct view of royalty or presidential power, your heart pounds. All normal behaviour is suspended and you press forward with everyone else to see more clearly. The psalmist King David, great as he was, recognized the importance of honouring God, who is the King of Kings. In Psalm 100 he said, "Enter into His gates with thanksgiving, and into His courts with praise: be thankful unto Him, and bless His name. For the LORD is good; His mercy is everlasting; and His truth endureth to all generations." '

CHAPTER 9

I GOT CONFIDENCE

I got confidence my God's gonna see me through!
Andrae Crouch

A MAJOR TURNING POINT in Pat's journey back to a strong Christian faith came when he read David Wilkerson's seminal book *The Cross and the Switchblade*. Pat describes the book as 'the true story of a man who truly believed in miracles and staked his life on the proposition that God would perform supernatural things in the lives of those who are really committed to Him'. In 1970 the book was adapted for the silver screen, and Pat was honoured to be given the starring role of small-town preacher David Wilkerson. It was, he says, the most demanding and memorable part he ever played (it was also the last big-screen film he made).

The hard-hitting movie tells the story of one man's crusade to bring Christianity to the lives of the teenage gangs who roamed the streets of New York City, and in particular charts his encounter with gang leader Nicky Cruz. Produced by Christian director Dick Ross, the film sought to capture the reality of life in a Brooklyn tenement, and the violent, hopeless lives led by the young gangsters. Wilkerson started up Teen Challenge Ministries and took the message of the gospel into the very darkest places. After initial hostility, many of the gang members found faith in

Christ and turned their lives around. Nicky Cruz himself later became a church minister. The screen action pulled no punches, and with its contemporary music score by Ralph Carmichael and generally stark imagery, the film was undeniably attention-grabbing. Wilkerson's book had already caused waves around the world, and the inspirational film did just the same. Pat's strong performance won him much acclaim from public and critics alike.

Having been so closely involved with *The Cross and the Switchblade*, Pat was delighted to discover a special David Wilkerson connection with contemporary Christian musician Andrae Crouch. Excited by the new developments occurring in the Christian music sphere, Pat was particularly impressed by Andrae's compositions, which included 'I Got Confidence', 'Through It All', 'The Blood Will Never Lose Its Power' and 'Bless The Lord O My Soul'. He was one of the first to recognize the true quality of Andrae's writing. Like Pat, Andrae was a resident of LA. He came from a family of pastors, but was reluctant to follow in their footsteps and went to college to train as a schoolteacher instead. He hated it, however, and left to work for the LA branch of David Wilkerson's street-level ministry Teen Challenge.

It was an extraordinary experience, he says. Andrae saw for himself the powerful effect his music had on people who were not Christians, and he began to write new songs especially for them, such as 'A Broken Vessel' and 'I Find No Fault In Him'. Thrilled by the dramatic change-around he saw in many desperate people's lives, he found himself after all in full-time ministry. He formed a choir from among the drug addicts he worked with and they were soon performing regularly, winning enormous respect for themselves and their director Andrae. Andrae told Pat, 'My aim is to reach as many people as I can with my ministry and music. I want to take my music to people who have never heard the gospel. They have a right to hear it and choose for themselves.' Some of Andrae's songs are now firm favourites worldwide, many of them given prominence through regular performances by popular singers such as Pat.

Pat was not the only famous performer causing a stir with his Christian beliefs at the time, of course. Cliff Richard's commitment to Christianity also occurred in the 1960s – another similarity in their careers. While Pat was enjoying his fifties' hits such as 'Love Letters In The Sand' and 'April Love', Cliff was moving successfully up the European charts with 'Living Doll' and 'Travelling Light'. Both men have also had successful secular and Christian movie careers (Cliff's box-office hits include *The Young Ones* and *Summer Holiday*) and for many years now they have both appeared regularly at Christian concerts. Cliff's conversion to Christianity came to public attention on 16 June 1966 when he appeared at a Billy Graham Crusade meeting in London's Earls Court Arena. There he sang Stuart Hamblen's 'It Is No Secret' (which he had first heard on recordings by Pat and Elvis) and spoke openly of his commitment to Christ. It prompted huge media attention, with many eager to find out more about Cliff's life and beliefs. Pat would experience a similar level of interest a few short years later. In 1967, Cliff starred in the Billy Graham Evangelistic Association's film *Two A Penny* with Dora Bryan and Nigel Goodwin. He also went to the Holy Land in 1977 to film *His Land*, with Billy Graham's choir conductor Cliff Barrows as co-narrator. Later on, Pat produced a musical travelogue on a similar theme. In more recent years Cliff has worked unstintingly for Tear Fund, to whom he donates the proceeds of his annual gospel concerts.

There is one more connection of particular note between Pat and Cliff Richard: Cliff is an honorary member of the UK's Pat Boone Appreciation Society, alongside other distinguished names such as the BBC's David Jacobs and Irish singer Val Doonican. Pat is one of the very few American artists of his age and era who can boast an active and supportive British fan club. Founded in 1990, it actually has members right around the globe, and is headed up by the hard-working Judy Donald (Club President) from her office in Sunderland and Alan Coates (Vice President), a retired senior police officer.[1] Pat is keen to express his thankfulness for their tireless work: 'I can never express enough gratitude to Judy and Alan for all they have done for me over the years to help keep the balls in the air over in the UK!'

Boone fans and admirers come from all walks of life worldwide. In America, the Pennsylvanian Christine Bujnovsky is the current President of the National Pat Boone Fan Club. As a victim of childhood polio, she is confined to a wheelchair and reliant on a carer, but she administrates the USA Fan Club with flair and unending enthusiasm. Chris moved on to the national presidency of the club in 1960, having previously been a chapter president. Forty years on, the club continues to go strong. Chris says that co-operation from Pat and a range of staff over the years has made her labour of love a joy. 'I have spent many pleasant hours rooting for Pat, and I'll continue to do so as long as I'm able!' So far she has met Pat 13 times (and counting). Once he dedicated 'April Love' to her at a live performance, and she confesses she was quite overcome.[2]

From very early on in his career, Pat's popularity was not confined to an American audience, and he rapidly became a major star in many parts of the globe. He was one of the privileged few American artists who could guarantee an automatic overseas release for their product – and in his heyday, more often than not, those releases turned into hits. It was not always simply a case of releasing the original US recording, either. Pat's producer at Dot, Randy Wood, was keen to capitalize on Pat's early overseas successes by experimenting with some foreign language recordings.

It was, remembers Pat, a very tricky undertaking! The first venture, in 1961, was to be in Spanish, with some direct translations

1 For more information, contact the Pat Boone Appreciation Society, PO Box 63, Sunderland, England SR1 1PN.

2 For more information, contact the National Pat Boone Fan Club, 1025 Park Road, Leesport, PA 19533, USA.

of several of his most popular songs. Pat had never learnt Spanish in any formal way, and he had to take some training from a Spanish-speaker before any recording began. The interpreter also sat in on the recording session itself, to offer further advice as they went along. Pat did not want to do anything by half measures. Using the original backing tracks, he duly put down the new vocals, just two or three lines at a time. It was hard work. Pat was concerned to get the words and intonation just right, and constant retakes ate up a great deal of studio time. It was achieved at last, however, and Pat went on to make similar recordings in other languages, including Italian and German. He likes to think that his fans in other countries appreciated his efforts.

He had perhaps let himself in for more than he had bargained for. Trying out his foreign language skills in the safety of an American recording studio was one thing; risking it in front of a foreign audience was quite another! Late in 1965, Pat was invited to the famed San Remo Song Festival to sing several songs in Italian on TV. The anticipated audience was set to reach 100 million viewers, Pat was told. Cue cards were not offered as an option and, as he recalls, 'It turned out to be one of the most terrifying experiences of my life. I felt very panicky throughout. When the results came in, "*Mi, Mi, Valentina*" was a very commendable third, however, so I guess it was worth it! I remember that the song "*E Fuori, La Pioggia Cade*" was a nightmare to remember. No matter what I did, the lyrics just would not register. Eventually I borrowed a ballpoint pen and wrote the lyrics on the palm of my hand. But I was so nervous that my palms sweated dreadfully and the words turned to an inky blur. When it came to the performance, however, the fear seemed to focus my mind and I managed to remember the words after all!'

By 1966, the short-lived practice of English-speaking artists recording in foreign languages was receding in favour. Pat believes it was a worthwhile experiment, however, and continued to do his best to communicate with overseas fans in their own language whenever he could. One of the hardest languages he tackled was Japanese. His *Tokyo '64* concert album was Pat's only live concert recorded and released on LP, and it was also his only release containing material sung in Japanese. He learned the Japanese words to 'April Love' phonetically, hoping against hope that they would be understood by his Japanese audience! They seemed perfectly happy with his rendition, and over the years Pat maintained his popularity in that country. In 1977 he returned to Japan on an unprecedented evangelical outreach tour with Pastor Jack Hayford, visiting a number of big cities to sing and speak about his faith.

Since the seventies, eager to make the most of his worldwide popularity and standing, Pat has single-mindedly devoted much time and effort to proclaiming the gospel via a wide diversity of media – including radio, TV, movies, recordings, books, videos and concerts. He has continued to tour extensively, believing in the effectiveness of conducting Christian ministry through song, and over the years has attracted huge audiences, many of them full of people who otherwise may not have heard the Christian message in a way that appealed to them.

He generally enjoys the experience of touring, although it is inevitably exhausting and it is always hard, he says, to be away from the support of family, friends and church for any length of time. He believes passionately in what he is doing, however, and values his encounters with audiences across the globe. Finding a right balance between show-biz glamour and Christian ministry is a serious undertaking.

There is always room for a joke, however, and touring has provided Pat with moments of great fun over the years. Musician David Diggs recalls an incident in 1976 that illustrates the Boone humour and reckless enjoyment of adventure that persists into his more senior years. During a busy tour Pat and his musicians were waiting for their luggage at an airport's baggage reclaim area. David's amplifier case got stuck in the elevated conveyor belt system and no official came to release it. Eventually, patience exhausted, Pat set off up the conveyor belt, announcing that they would just have to shift the thing themselves. All eyes in the terminal were fixed on Pat as he crawled upwards, finally disappearing from sight through the rubber slats. David and his colleagues were just starting to worry about his safety when he reappeared, breathless, red-faced and dusty. 'I've got it!' came a cheerful cry, and applause and laughter rattled round the terminal as the wayward amplifier and its rescuer made their way back down the luggage belt. Less amused were the airport police who arrived to investigate the transgression of safety rules. Pat got away with it that time, however, when they recognized him and were persuaded to see the funny side of the incident.

By the early seventies, some 20 years after Randy Wood had signed Pat for Dot, the Boone sound was still hitting the charts, although by then the entries were predominantly in the country charts. His signing with Motown's country outlet Hitsville marked an exciting new turn in Pat's long recording career and his first issue on the label was a single released in October 1974. Although it was classified as a 'country' song, to some ears 'Candy Lips' was not unlike some of Pat's mid-1950s recordings. They had also had a country feel about them, so perhaps it was not such a new departure after all. His subsequent album *Texas Woman*, released by Hitsville in 1976, included songs such as 'Indiana Girl', 'Oklahoma Sunshine', 'It's Gone' and 'Don't Want To Fall Away From You', as well as the title track. Also on the disc were two self-penned songs, 'Won't Be Home Tonight' and 'Young Girl', plus a duet with Shirley called 'I'd Do It With You'. Sales of the album were encouragingly healthy.

By then Pat was the owner and operator of the Lamb and Lion record label, as well as several music publishing companies. Variety was still the spice of life and he was also busy recording with his Boone Family group (the album *All in the Boone Family* was released by Lamb and Lion in 1973), and with the First

Nashville Jesus Band. Indeed, it was through his Lamb and Lion recordings with the First Nashville Jesus Band that his country music really matured. Produced by Martin Haerle, the FNJ Band featured some high-ranking sessioners, including Jeff Newman (steel and dobro guitars and banjo), Jimmy Capps (bass, rhythm, electric and gut guitars and banjo), Johnny Gimble (fiddle, guitar and electric mandolin), Jerry Whitehurst (piano), David Reese (piano, organ and celeste), Billy Linneman (acoustic bass) and Paul Charron (percussion and drums). The respected Curtis Young was among the backing vocalists.

Pat was first brought into association with the FNJ Band when MGM arranged for the partnership to record the country album *I Love You More and More Every Day*, released in 1973 and containing some truly classic country favourites. Pat remembers that first on the recording schedule was Hank Williams's tongue-twisting 'Jambalaya'. He just could not get his tongue around the lyrics and after a number of aborted takes, each apparently worse than the last, the studio was full of hysterical musicians, a speechless Pat and a very irritated sound engineer. After an untold number of false starts, they did get the song laid down successfully and were able to move on. The rather more manageable words of John D. Loudermilk's 'Blue Train' and Hank Snow's hit song 'Golden Rocket' followed, among other classics.

Before their association with Pat, the FNJ Band had recorded instrumental versions of some of the great Southern gospel songs, and when Pat asked if he could do some vocal work with them, they were delighted to agree. Another session was arranged, and they spent a memorable day minting a bumper collection of Southern gospel favourites, all featuring the distinctive Boone voice and released on the album *Pat Boone and the First Nashville Jesus Band*. Stuart Hamblen's splendid song 'My Religion's Not Old-Fashioned But It's Real Genuine' was the first to be recorded. They followed that with well-known numbers such as 'The Great Speckled Bird' (a big hit for Roy Acuff), Hank Williams's 'I Saw

The Light' and 'Tramp On The Street', along with more contemporary songs such as Tom T. Hall's 'Me And Jesus'. Last in the marathon session came Albert Brumley's 'Turn Your Radio On', a song with a very catchy chorus which had the backing vocalists repeating the title rapidly in a kind of echo.

'Turn Your Radio On' is, in Pat's view, 'a jewel of a song, simple yet profound – well done to Ray Stevens for rediscovering it!' Albert Brumley was born into a farming family in Oklahoma in 1905. In his teens he attended a community singing school in his home town. He and his wife Goldie had five sons and one daughter, and one son, Tom Brumley, became a famed West Coast steel guitarist, spending many successful years with Buck Owens's band, the Buckaroos. Albert himself was only the second living individual to be voted into the Gospel Music Hall of Fame. A number of true gems came from Brumley's pen, including 'I'll Fly Away', 'River Of Memories' and 'Jesus, Hold My Hand', several of which Pat recorded.

The success of that gospel album led Pat and the FNJ Band to collaborate on further projects, and later FNJ Band ventures featured the whole Boone family. In the seventies Pat toured and recorded very successfully with the pop/folk/gospel-based Pat Boone Family Show, which included his wife and all four of their daughters. The Boone Girls as a quartet also became an extremely popular group, appearing on TV shows with celebrities such as Glen Campbell and Dinah Shore. Debby, with her naturally strong voice, went on to solo stardom when her song 'You Light Up My Life' became a worldwide hit later in the seventies.

Pat's daughters took to show business like ducks to water, enjoying every aspect of being together on the road and on stage. When the whole family was on tour they would hire a big bus to travel in. On one memorable occasion, Pat managed to get the bus stuck in the 'drive-thru' lane of a fast-food restaurant. 'He wanted to see if it would fit!' Shirley explains, rolling her eyes. In the process of releasing the vehicle, Pat was forced to leave behind various fixtures and fittings! Shirley was not amused, but it was all just part of family life, and at least they were all together. The fact that the Boones were a 'real' family endeared them to the general public and ensured their popularity on TV shows.

Meanwhile, Pat's solo country music prowess continued to gain international acclaim. In 1976 he made it into the Top 30 of the country charts with 'Texas Woman', remaining there for 10 weeks. This success was followed by 'Oklahoma Sunshine' and 'Colorado Country Morning'. Pat also continued to use his exploration of country music to reflect his renewed faith. One day in the summer of 1976, under the auspices of producer Martin Hearle, a glittering array of sessioners assembled at the Arthur Smith Studios in Old Monroe Road, Charlotte, North Carolina. The singers and instrumentalists included Arthur Smith and his brother Ralph, Margaret Griffin, Lois Adkins, Tommy Faile, Benny Martin, blind Don Ange, Gerry Dionne, Carl Hunt, David Brakefield and Gene Martin. They were there to record the album *Down Home with Pat Boone* for the Lamb and Lion label. Gems recorded during the session ranged from Arthur Smith's beautiful 'Acres Of Diamonds' to Kris Kristofferson's 'Why Me, Lord?' A couple of songs by Hazel Houser were also included, as well as one by Wayne Raney, amusingly titled 'We Need A Whole Lot More Of Jesus And A Lot Less Rock And Roll'.

Their first song was Louisiana Governor Jimmie Davis's 'Someone To Care'. Jimmie had been the State Commissioner of Public Utilities before World War II, then he surprised everyone by co-writing the song 'You Are My Sunshine', which rapidly became a wartime favourite, popularized by Bing Crosby, Gene Autry and Vera Lynn. Jimmie served three terms as Governor after the war, and is also unique in being cited in both the Country and Gospel Halls of Fame. Even towards the end of the century, Jimmie was still fulfilling the occasional singing date, most notably his annual Jimmie Davis Homecoming at a church in

Louisiana. On 10 September 2000, Jimmie celebrated his 101st birthday party. He died two months later.

Pat relished the renewed family closeness the Boones experienced from the late sixties onwards, and was immensely proud of his talented daughters. He loved the family tours they did together. Meanwhile, of course, he and Shirley were always concerned about the welfare of their children. Hollywood was perhaps not the easiest place in which to protect a young person's innocence, but the Boone parents did their best to see that their daughters were safe and sensible, while trying not to limit their lives unreasonably.

As the four girls grew into beautiful teenagers, the inevitable crowds of young men flocked to their door. Pat and Shirley, however, were adamant that there was to be no one-to-one dating until the girls reached their sixteenth birthdays. Such rules were practically unheard of in the permissive atmosphere that pervaded Hollywood at that time. Boyfriends were apparently undeterred, and continued to beat a path to the Boones' front door to spend evenings with their 'dates' watching TV or playing pool or basketball in the back yard under the watchful eye of one Boone parent or the other.

Troubles of another kind arose when Cherry developed anorexia nervosa, the so-called 'slimmers' disease'. Looking on helplessly, the Boones observed their daughter becoming thinner and thinner, exhibiting an irrational aversion to her body as she felt, for whatever reason, that she was failing to measure up to her own impossible standards. A cure for Cherry seemed out of reach, even though they tried one thing after another. The answer to everyone's prayers eventually came in the form of a young Youth With A Mission missionary named Dan O'Neill. Dan and Cherry had been introduced by their mutual friend George Otis. They were both students of the Hebrew language and would converse with each other in the ancient tongue. In time they grew very close, and Dan prayed long and hard for Cherry to recover from the anorexia. Cherry did indeed begin eating again, gaining weight and returning to her normal self in a remarkably short time. The young couple went on to become engaged.

Pat's youngest daughter Lindy was herself already engaged by then, bringing home a fellow student named Doug Corbin from Pepperdine University. The Boone parents were at first dismayed by the intensity of the couple's feelings for each other, Lindy being just 19 and Doug not much older at 22. During the year that followed, however, Doug won the hearts of everyone in the family and, when the two still felt the same about each other after a year, permission was given for them to marry.

Cherry and Dan married first, on 4 October 1975 at a ceremony at the Church on the Way conducted by Pastor Jack Hayford. This was followed by a traditional Jewish blessing, prayed over them by Rabbi Hillel Silverman of Temple Sinai in Los Angeles. Pat had agreed to sing 'Sunrise, Sunset' from *Fiddler on the Roof* for them, but confesses that it was far from being his best performance because he was so overcome by the emotion of the day. Cherry and Dan later presented Shirley and Pat with no fewer than five grandchildren between 1981 and 1992, named Brittany, Brendan, Casey, Kevyn and Kylie.

Doug and Lindy were married on 29 October 1975, again in a ceremony at the Church on the Way conducted by Jack Hayford. Pat struggled with his emotions once again as he tried to sing 'Father of Girls' at the wedding reception. It seemed at first like the perfect marriage. Doug left his teaching post for a career in the Christian music recording industry and was soon a successful junior executive. The couple had two children, Ryan Patrick and Jessica Lynn, but various pressures were beginning to take their toll on the marriage. Pat and Shirley were eaten up with concern and prayed earnestly for the troubled young family. In the end, however, the marriage did fall apart, and divorce followed. Happier times returned for Lindy when she met and married attorney Mike Michaelis. She and

Mike gave Pat and Shirley another grandchild, Tyler Michaelis, born on 19 September 1987.

Meanwhile, Pat's daughter Debby was following in her father's footsteps, making her own distinctive mark on the pop music world. In 1977 she recorded the ballad 'You Light Up My Life' which took her into the Billboard Hot 100, where the song remained for 10 weeks, selling over 4 million copies worldwide. Entrepreneur-producer Mike Curb had been the first to recognize Debby's solo potential, and it was he who introduced her to the song, the title track from a low-budget independent film. A demo copy was made and played for producer Joe Brooks, who promptly sent Debby, accompanied by Shirley, to New York to record it as a single.

The song's lyrics impressed themselves very deeply on Debby and she became increasingly convinced that they could be sung in a sacred way, addressed to Jesus, even though the song had originally been conceived as a love song and could still be interpreted in that way. In the studio, Debby put all her emotion into the song, trying to communicate the strength of her faith as she sang. The result was a recording that many people felt had a 'special touch' to it. It earned her an Oscar at the Academy Awards Show. By its very nature, the song was also received well in country music circles, where it entered the charts and rose to number four, opening up the chance for Debby to follow in her Grandfather Foley's footsteps too and make her name in country music. Like Pat, she now had her feet firmly in both pop and country circles.

On 1 September 1979 Debby married Gabriel Ferrer at the Hollywood Presbyterian Church, with Pastor Jack Hayford invited to conduct the ceremony. Their home church, Church on the Way in Van Nuys, was not considered large enough to contain all the many guests! Gabriel is the son of actor Jose Ferrer and singer Rosemary Clooney (the movie star George Clooney is his cousin), and he and Debby had first met in 1976, when Gabriel had been among a group of neighbours invited to the Boone family home for Bible study classes. Debby says that she had privately always wanted to marry someone with the same qualities she observed in her father, namely 'a person with traditional values and morals', someone who cared about others and was even-tempered. Gabriel, brought up as a Catholic, confesses to a rebellious period as a teenager, but by the time he met Debby he had developed a strong and renewed faith and had undertaken a year's Bible study course with a view to becoming a church minister, so he was deemed to fit the bill!

Debby's second release, 'God Knows', also made it into both pop and country charts, and she followed it in 1979 with a remake of the Connie Francis 1950s hit 'My Heart Has A Mind Of Its Own', which took her to number 11 in the country charts. Her number one hit 'Are You On The Road To Lovin' Me Again?', penned by Bob Morrison and Debbie Hupp, came not long afterwards in May 1980. Produced by Larry Butler, this was the title track on Debby's Nashville-recorded solo country album.

At the time of the recording sessions she was expecting her first child, a baby boy born on 8 July 1980 and named Jordan Alexander. Debby fitted in a two-week concert tour of the Far East with her father in December that same year, but family priorities took over after that. Twins Gabrielle and Dustin arrived in September 1983, and two and a half years later came baby Tessa. Debby decided to abandon the pursuit of a country music career for the time being, preferring to concentrate on her family instead. She does find time, however, to make occasional forays into TV movies and concerts. One notable appearance came in 1992, when Debby and her family were guests on a show called *White Christmas Party* hosted by Gabriel's mother Rosemary Clooney. Together they sang Christmas songs such as 'Do You Hear What I Hear?' and young Gabrielle and Dustin sang the Andrews Sisters' big hit 'Sisters'. Rosemary told the children a Christmas story, and the show ended with the whole family singing 'White Christmas'. Rosemary, of course, had played a memorable part in the original hit movie, singing 'White Christmas' alongside co-stars Bing Crosby, Danny Kaye and Vera Ellen. Rosemary had enjoyed her first big hit in the early 1950s with 'Come On-A My House', and many more hits had followed in her long career, including Stuart Hamblen's 'This Ole House' and Hank Williams's 'Half As Much'.

Debby was not the only Boone daughter to display solo flair when it came to singing. Her sister Laura's debut CD *Thursday's Child* was released in 1990 by Lamb and Lion. Produced by Roby Duke, the title song was written by Robyn Frazer. The album as a whole has a soulful, warm jazz feel which enhances Laura's engaging voice. One outstanding track is a duet with Bryan Duncan for the James Taylor classic 'Shower The People'. Other excellent songs on the album are 'Carpenter' and the majestic praise anthem 'Come Lift Him Up'. Along with her husband Harry Browning, whom she married in August 1980, Laura had previously recorded several impressive albums, including *Push Back the Darkness*. Minted in 1984 on the Lamb and Lion label, it was produced by Roby Duke at Mama Jo's studio in North Hollywood and featured songs written mainly by Harry.

Laura and Harry have presented Shirley and Pat with three grandchildren, Michael and the twins Sara and Rachael. All in all, their four daughters' offspring add up to quite a number, but Pat and Shirley love them all and Pat says he is insanely proud of every single one of his now well-extended family.

CHAPTER 10

THE EXODUS SONG

Though I am just a man, when you are by my side,
With the help of God, I know I can be strong –
To make this land our home.

Pat Boone

PAT AND SHIRLEY HAVE travelled to many foreign countries over the years, but they were unprepared for the effect that Israel, the Holy Land, would have on them. They first visited the country in 1972 and have returned on a regular basis ever since, sometimes privately, sometimes as leaders of a tour party. The entire family have been involved, often alongside their good friend George Otis, who shares their passion for the historic place. Pat believes that Christians are able to share a deep awe for this special land with the Jews, because of Christianity's obvious Jewish roots. Israel has had a profound effect on all his children too, with Cherry studying Hebrew and both Debby and Laura attending a Youth With A Mission training programme.

Long before he became more closely involved with Israel, the land of the Bible had a grip on Pat's imagination and led directly to his composition of the lyrics for 'The Exodus Song'. The original music, a hit for pianists Ferrante and Teicher, was purely instrumental, and the melody gave orchestral conductor Ernest Gold an Oscar for the best scoring of a dramatic movie in 1960. The movie was the impressive epic *Exodus*, which starred Paul

Newman and depicted the return of the Jews to Palestine in the 1940s when the new independent state of Israel was created. During Christmas 1960, Pat listened repeatedly to the majestic theme tune. He could not get it out of his mind. Suddenly, the beginning of a song lyric popped into his mind: 'This land is mine...' Words piled up in his head, fitting the haunting tune, and he grabbed the nearest thing he could find to write on, which proved to be the back of a Christmas card. He had composed the entire lyrics within 30 minutes. The emotive song went on to become known around the world and even entered the US charts, going as high as number 64 in 1961. It has, Pat says, kept a very special place in his heart ever since.

Over the years Pat's growing empathy with the nation of Israel gave him a special connection with the country. In 1979 the Israeli government honoured him with the Israel Cultural Award, the highest award available for non-natives, in recognition of his artistry and humanitarian work. Later, the Israeli Tourism Department in the USA named him as a Christian Ambassador to Israel. In this capacity he has led many tours for the Christian Broadcasting Network. During one such visit he filmed the video *Israel, O Blessed Israel*, a collection of his favourite sacred songs sung at different sites, with some commentary explaining those sites' biblical importance. In 1994, Pat and his daughter Debby teamed together with Jewish leaders to sponsor the initiative called On Wings of Eagles, providing funds for thousands of Russian Jews to emigrate to Israel.

Pat has relished every visit he has made to what he describes as a fascinating and awesome country. There have been some special moments along the way which, he says, have helped to deepen his faith and bring the events of the Bible very much closer. He has particularly vivid memories of the first time he and Shirley visited the Garden Tomb in Jerusalem, walking along the narrow streets of the Old City until they arrived at the Tomb, not far from the hill of Golgotha where Christ's crucifixion took place. On the plain timber door marking the entrance to the Tomb was the declaration, 'He is not here, He is risen!'

The Boones immediately caught sight of a small chapel in the Garden. The chapel, as they discovered, was an unpretentious stone structure and as they entered they heard familiar worship choruses being played on an electronic keyboard. Pat remembers that as soon as they sat down, they were aware of an extra sense of God's presence in that humble place. An English pastor welcomed the small congregation (there was no room for more) with enthusiasm and proceeded to lead them in singing a few hymns. The sound echoed from the stone walls, and Pat felt he had never heard such a rich and wonderful sound. Given the small numbers present, the effect was, he says, quite extraordinary. The pastor preached a moving sermon on the empty tomb and gave a convincing gospel message, inviting people to ask the risen Christ into their lives if they had not done so already. It was such an emotional and meaningful experience, Pat says, that he and Shirley were most reluctant to leave when the service came to an end. They spend some minutes just sitting quietly, drinking in the atmosphere as the rest of the congregation left.

When they finally left the Garden, they walked back through the streets discussing the miracle of the empty tomb. Ever since they had renewed both their faith and their marriage in the late 1960s, Easter and its resurrection news had been a special time for Pat and Shirley. Pat explains: 'I love the Easter time of the year because it speaks of new life. It's the time when the whole of nature stirs. Everything begins to blossom, bloom and turn beautiful again after winter. But Easter is also a spiritually important time of year, of course. It's a time of *spiritual* new life, celebrating the rebirth of each individual human spirit. Each of us can experience that, through faith in Christ. It's the most important thing that can ever happen to anybody.'

An unforgettable experience during another visit to Jerusalem served to demonstrate for Pat both the current tensions in the country and the timeless aura of holiness which seems to remain as strong as ever around the ancient places of worship. It was an April morning and he and Shirley were strolling along a crowded cobbled street on the way to the Damascus Gate entrance to the Old City. Beaming at his wife, Pat burst into song with the words of his old hit 'April Love', once again attracting curious stares from passers-by.

Down ancient stone steps they went, passing street vendors by the score, then through the historic Gate and into the Old City. Within that ancient metropolis, now generally outlawed to motor vehicles, the sunshine turned abruptly to shadow and the narrow market thoroughfares were crowded with tourists purchasing souvenirs, mingling with Jerusalem locals seeking bargains.

Pat was conscious of the need to protect his wallet and beware of pickpockets. Buttoning up his jacket, he whispered in Shirley's ear, 'Keep close to me, Honey! I don't want us to be parted in this crowd.'

Shirley nodded. 'Pat, have you looked up on the rooftops? There are armed police officers up there watching over these streets. They make me feel more secure!'

Pat glanced up and surveyed the skyline – grimy parapets lined with silhouetted figures, clearly alert and vigilant, automatic rifles in hand. 'Shirley, they're not police officers, they're Israeli soldiers … We've seen them everywhere, haven't we? It shows how fragile the peace and security of this land is.'

Pat and Shirley continued to wander along the dark alleys of the bazaar, taking in the exotic sights, sounds and smells. Finally they arrived at a grim-looking Israeli checkpoint, manned by young Jewish military conscripts, their automatic rifles ready to hand or slung across their backs. Politely, and without conversation, the soldiers searched the Boones' bags and motioned the couple to pass through a metal detector. As Pat walked through, the silence of the checkpoint was pierced by a loud whine from the security machine. He stopped abruptly. The soldiers remained silent, but indicated that Pat should empty his pockets onto the counter. Then they frisked him, thoroughly and professionally. It was obvious from the items on the counter that Pat's pocket calculator had set off the alarm. The nervous couple breathed sighs of relief as the soldiers waved them on through the checkpoint. Having a famous face counted for nothing here.

Shirley was visibly shaken by the experience, and Pat tried to give her a smile of reassurance – although in reality he was very relieved to have got through without further trouble. Seeing that the strain did not leave his wife's face, Pat broke the silence. 'Well, Mrs Boone, we don't get this much drama where we normally shop! Really, we need to be thankful that the Israelis are this careful. They need to be.'

Suddenly the shadowy alleys came to an end and the couple emerged into gleaming sunshine again, finding themselves in a large square. There before them was a scene that seemed to have popped straight out of biblical times. The huge square – the size of a couple of football pitches – was alive with people. Some individuals were earnestly making their way to one specific place, a place of devotion and prayer. Pat and Shirley looked on in awed silence. The Wailing Wall, or Western Wall as it is now called, is a dramatic sight, the only remnant from the Jewish Temple destroyed by the Roman armies in AD 70. Today a concrete barrier wall separates worshippers from sightseers. The Jewish worshippers lined up behind the low wall, facing the Western Wall. It turned into quite a crowd that morning, and Pat and Shirley wished they could understand the prayers. The sense of reverence in that place was very strong.

Looking back today, Pat remembers the scene with much emotion. 'It was very deeply meaningful and a moving experience. There is no doubt that God spoke to us that day in the square.' Pat was acutely aware of the sincerity of the worship he was watching, and he was profoundly touched by it. He has been visiting Israel regularly for some decades now, but is struck every time by that unique atmosphere. 'After all these years, despite the tragedy of their history, they still worship the God of their fathers, the God of Abraham, Isaac and Jacob … These are a very special people.' It was obvious to Pat, that day at the Western Wall, that he was seeing a spiritual sincerity and depth of commitment now sadly rare in his affluent homeland.

Back in America, following on from his own rediscovery of faith in 1969, Pat was increasingly involved in working to spread the good news and to encourage others to take up a fresh commitment to Christ. In 1972, both sides of the Atlantic saw a special innovation in gospel music with a show called *Come Together*, led by composers Jimmy and Carol Owens and enthusiastically assisted by Pat. It had an extraordinary, galvanizing effect in both America and Britain during the years that followed.

Jimmy Owens and Pat first met in 1966 when Jimmy, an experienced choir conductor and music arranger, was working as music director for the David Wilkerson Youth Rallies in California. Jimmy went on to produce two of Pat's albums in 1970 and 1971, *Golden Hymns* and *Pat Boone Sings New Songs of the Jesus People*. (Jimmy was one of the key people involved in the 'Jesus People' movement in the 1970s.) Jimmy, his wife Carol and their two teenage children, daughter Jamie and son Buddy, were soon all attending the Church on the Way in Van Nuys, pastored by Jack Hayford. The Boones were already regulars there, happy to have discovered a new worship home after their controversial departure from the Church of Christ. They still attend the church today, after some 30 years, and Pat is one of the elders.

Pat's association with the Owens lasted for many years, and he went on to be closely involved in three of their gospel musicals – *Come Together*, *If My People* and *Come Together Again* – as well as taking the part of 'The Command-ant' in their brilliant children's work *Ants'hillvania*. The latter was co-written by the Owens and Cherry Boone. When it was recorded, it became the first Christian album ever to be nominated for a Grammy award in a secular category, 'Best Album for Children'.

The ground-breaking musical *Come Together* had a rather dramatic inception. In the early seventies, Jimmy believed he was being told by God to cease writing music until he was given clear instructions to begin again. It was a drastic decision, because his writing was really the family's source of income, but they followed what they believed to be the right course, and watched their resources dwindle as the months passed. Eventually they resorted to selling their furniture to make ends meet. Even their piano, the tool of Jimmy's trade, had to go. The testing time lasted for 18 months. Then one day, after a church service, the Owens were chatting with Pastor Jack when he said, 'Jimmy, I believe I've had a word from the Lord for you. I feel that He's asking you both to write a new musical expression based on the life of our church here.'

He made exactly the same suggestion over supper a few nights later. 'Why don't you write about what we're doing here at the Church on the Way?' Jimmy and Carol were initially unconvinced, but by the next morning, after long prayer, they were sure that this was indeed their next assignment. The musical would not strictly be 'about' the church, but would set out the principles of ministry they had learned, to be shared with other churches.

They started work immediately, Jimmy using all his expertise as a composer, with Carol also contributing fully to the creative process. Even their daughter Jamie wrote one of the songs, 'May I Introduce You To A Friend'. *Come Together* was duly published by Lexicon Music of Texas and was soon in demand across the States. At first the Owens, with musicians and singers from the Church on the Way led by Pat, presented all the performances themselves, but as the take-up of *Come Together* began to spread right around the US, it became impossible for them to be physically present at every production. Each local church was therefore encouraged to provide its own musicians and worship leader. The only stipulation was that the musical should be presented in its full, given form. Sometimes, of course, the lack of direct involvement by its creators led to the show taking on a rather different character from what had originally been intended, but Jimmy says he and his colleagues came to see that they simply had to 'give it away' to God and allow things to happen.

The impact of this innovative gospel presentation began to make itself felt in other parts of the world too, including the UK. In the summer of 1973, the Owens family were invited to England by Jean and Elmer Darnell (an American couple living in the UK) to promote *Come Together* there. Pat was in the thick of the tour plans from the beginning, and had agreed to go to Britain with the show even before Jimmy crossed the Atlantic to start the preparations. Supported by the Evangelical Alliance in England, Jimmy duly travelled to the UK to arrange venues and train local groups. In 1974, 30 such groups did some 400 presentations around the country, many of them in the largest halls and cathedrals. Such was the success of *Come Together* that many of the groups collaborated again the next year on the follow-up show *If My People*.

It was a pivotal time in the Church – those were the early days of the charismatic and house church movements, and the two gospel shows became vehicles that helped spread these new departures. Many people could also see that the UK was facing spiritual and social crises at that time. Churches were often small and full of contention. Inflation, unemployment and strikes were rampant. *Come Together* and *If My People* somehow offered a chance to bring people together. Certainly the presentations caused previously estranged churches to work together in their local areas. As for those who came to see the shows, it was a rare chance to participate directly and freely in a new approach to worship, and the effect was inspirational.

For the 1974 performances of *Come Together*, the Owens and Pat were the nucleus of the show. Backed by guitarists, drummers, a pianist, solo singers and a small choir, Pat was there to lead the worship and ministry at each venue. There was no doubt that initially, he was the show's greatest drawing card, but as the momentum began to grow, *Come Together* became so popular that they had no trouble attracting record crowds to each venue. Edinburgh's Usher Hall was full to capacity, and in Birmingham they turned away as many as were admitted due to lack of space. Coventry Cathedral and two other buildings in the city were full to capacity each night, and Belfast was just the same. Everyone taking part was excited about the way the show was being received, but Pat particularly recalls the dedication of those in charge of the sound system. Packing the sophisticated equipment into a huge van after each performance, they would often drive through the night in order to set it all up again at the new venue in time for the next rehearsal and performance.

Nearly 30 years on, Carol Owens still enthuses about the *Come Together* days – and about Pat's crucial involvement. He was a very encouraging and positive person to have around, she remembers. 'When we flew into Belfast to get ready for the show, one runway at the airport had been blown up the day before and the streets were full of barbed wire and armed men! Our auditorium had a boarded-up window where a British soldier had been killed by a sniper a couple of days earlier, and some of the factions out there had let us know they didn't like our message (we were, after all, calling for unity amongst Christians). Besides all that, we think the pilot of our chartered plane was drunk: we had practically taxied to Dublin by the time he was stopped. While the rest of us were white-knuckled and dreaming of home, however, Pat and Jimmy were having a wonderful time, just singing away and chatting. We never heard a single gripe out of Pat about accommodation, travel or food, either!'

The show's London venue, Westminster Central Hall, was packed to capacity on the first night, with over 1,000 people unable to get in. Undaunted, the crowd outside stuck around in the pouring rain and held their own worship celebration while the show continued inside the hall. The next evening the organizers were able to open up the Lower Hall and relay the show to over 3,000 people. London's enthusiasm for *Come Together* seemed to be inexhaustible. In December that same year, an unexpected opportunity arose to use the Royal Albert Hall for several shows. Miraculously, with only four weeks notice, Pat and Jimmy were both able to fly over to London for the occasion. The same musicians and singers were also available, boosted by groups of extra choir members bussed in from Edinburgh, Bristol and even Belfast. Every show played to capacity audiences, with 11,000 tickets issued 10 days before the first night. As with all the shows, expenses were covered by free-will offerings.

For those who have never attended a *Come Together* presentation, it is a little difficult to explain exactly what it was like, although Pat has a good description of it: 'Some folks have likened it to Handel's *Messiah* – and, as it had its own 'Hallelujah Chorus', perhaps the similarity is there! Like the *Messiah* in its day, the music of *Come Together* was contemporary. The show sought to involve the whole congregation or audience in worship, eventually splitting everyone up into small prayer groups to pray for individuals.' Most of the narration, read by Pat at the original performances, was taken from Scripture, though not all of it. There was also an informality and freedom in the worship, without it being allowed to become frivolous or sacrilegious in any way. South London pastor Gordon Thomson clearly identifies the impact the show had: 'Many attendees found a new freedom in their style of worship that still carries on today. *Come Together* also promoted the use of contemporary songs as well as older hymns in church services.'

In 1975, following the success of *Come Together* and recognizing the profound impact it had made on many churches, Jimmy and Carol were inspired to build on that foundation with a new show. 'We both felt that this time the emphasis should be to call on Christians to unite and pray for their nation, which had turned its collective back on God. Our inspiration came from a verse in the Old Testament which said, "If my people, which are called by my name, shall humble themselves, and pray, and seek my face, and turn from their wicked ways, then will I hear from heaven, and will forgive their sin, and will heal their land" (2 Chronicles 7:14). The aim was to help bring about both the healing of old wounds and revival.'

Calling on Pat's skills as MC once more, *If My People* followed a similar presentation style to *Come Together*, using local church people in each production. Other singers from the US, such as Jamie Owens, Annie Herring, Barry McGuire and the group Second Chapter of Acts, joined the production as it toured, with Jimmy conducting. Once again the innovative style caught the imagination of churches around the world. Carol describes the show as 'an interactive musical prayer meeting', and Jimmy says, '*If My People* wasn't a thrill-a-minute musical. Anyone who came just wanting to be entertained would go away disappointed, but those who really captured the message weren't worried that it hadn't been a time for laughing and dancing. Because of its serious message, we used music which was heavier, more traditional. A couple of numbers were Wesleyan hymns. There was also a good deal of teaching, and we included four prayers, one of which was four minutes long. We really got down to business! It was a kind of wake-up call to Christians everywhere.'

Songs from *Come Together* and *If My People* were rapidly absorbed into the mainstream of musical resources used by churches, and are still sung today. Jimmy and Carol Owens went on to write two more musicals – *The Witness*, which toured the UK in 1978, and *Come Together Again*, written in 1987. *Come Together Again*, which gain involved Pat, toured extensively, and the emphasis of the show was a call for people to become missionaries and take the gospel to everyone on earth who had not yet heard it.

The Owens and the Boones remained firm friends. Looking back, Jimmy and Carol say they value very highly the chances they had to work with Pat. Carol has just one complaint: 'Pat was a consistent 40 minutes late for everything! Although I have to say that he was never late for a *performance…*' When the Owens went to live in Kona, Hawaii, Pat came for a visit. 'This place is OK…' he remarked when he had looked round the area, '…if you like nirvana!' Jimmy and Carol moved away from Hawaii in 1980 and Pat and Shirley bought the house they had owned there, keeping it as a vacation home ever since.

The Owens may have been the main creative engine behind the gospel musicals, but Pat was no mean songwriter himself. Over the years he developed a gift for penning songs that touch the heart. The internationally known 'Exodus Song' was just one example of this talent and certainly the most famous. Later he composed the plaintive 'Let Me Live: The Anthem Of The Unborn Child', which was adopted by some pro-life organizations as their theme song. In June 2000, Pat was especially delighted to be the author of a biographical song in tribute to Dr Billy Graham. 'For my money,' he says, 'I would name Billy Graham as the greatest individual of the twentieth century. I wrote my song as a tribute to him in time for the Nashville Crusade in the summer of 2000, as I knew that it would likely be one of his last big preaching engagements. My plan was to surprise Dr Graham and have the song sung by a host of big names from the music community.'

Songs were not the only way in which Pat communicated his thoughts and convictions. He discovered early on a certain ability for prose writing, and went on to become the author of a number of books. He had, after all, received a full education and had always enjoyed reading whatever literature was available. At college he had majored in English and Speech, and liked to think that he was able to articulate his thoughts effectively, whether live to an audience or through the written page. Perhaps an urge to teach also still remained, despite the very different direction his life had taken.

Several of his books proved to be highly successful, as the famous singer proffered 'down home' advice to his readers. His first book was the chatty guide for teenagers, *Twixt Twelve and Twenty*, written in 1958 when he was himself still a very young man, and which sold more than a million copies. The book maintained an emphasis on Christian morals and principles, but it was written in an accessible manner and young people picked it up in droves. The royalties from the book were donated to the North Eastern Institute of Christian Education, with Pat confirming his recognition of the importance of on-going education throughout people's lives. The college built and named Boone Hall in honour of its benefactor.

Pat continued to write with a strong homespun, philosophical emphasis. His later books included *The Real Christmas* (1961), *Between You, Me and the Gatepost* (1966), *The Care and Feeding of Parents* (1967), *A New Song* (1970), which topped one million in sales and was published in six languages, *A Miracle a Day Keeps the Devil Away* (1974), *Joy* (1973), *My Brother's Keeper* (1975) and *Pray to Win* (1980). He and Shirley also co-authored several books about family life, including *The Honeymoon Is Over* (1977) and *Together: 25 Years with the Boone Family* (1979).

Most of these books are easily comprehensible guides regarding various issues of concern to adults and young people, all written from a Christian perspective. Pat says he has always tried to practise the principles he expounded in his books, particularly *Pray to Win*, which he wrote at the invitation of New York publishers G.P. Putnam. They were planning a series of books on meeting goals for success-motivated people and had heard that Pat believed prayer to be an effective method of achieving one's goals. Would he write a book on 'prayer and the secular man'? His imagination sparked, Pat set to work with particular enthusiasm. He had seen the effectiveness of prayer in his own life, and wanted to make the most of his chance to encourage other people to take that leap of faith too and trust God with their needs. 'As the

Bible says,' he explains, '"What thing soever ye desire, when ye pray, believe that ye receive them, and ye shall have them" (Mark 11:24). Jesus encouraged His followers to ask anything in His name and promised that, if they believed, they would receive it. I practised those principles in my own life and my main aim in writing the book was for readers to discover for themselves how God could help them every day.'

Pat was always keen to find new ways of putting his faith into practice, and all his work, whether literary or musical, gradually came to reflect this. One important message he had absorbed for himself during the exhilarating time spent touring with the Owens' musical *Come Together* was that unity among Christians was something worth working for. A recording project he undertook in 1980 was specifically designed to reflect this idea.

Pat surprised many people when he travelled to the Underground Studios in Indianapolis to record a Christian album for the North American Liturgy Resources label. The album, called *The Time Has Come*, featured contemporary songs composed by artists well known in the Catholic community, including songs penned by The Dameans (four priests from Louisiana) and by priests Donald Reagan, Carey Landrey and Michael Joncas. It also used the vocal talents of members of the Indianapolis Evangelical Orthodox Church, with additional backing vocals from two up-and-coming Christian artists named Steve Green and Sandi Patti (who went on to become outstanding stars in their own right). Pat's album was something very out of the ordinary in the gospel music scene of that time. Normally recordings drew predominantly on Protestant artists and repertoire. In an article in the Catholic *Twin Circle* journal, Pat gave his reasons for undertaking the project:

The whole purpose is to build a bridge and enlarge on the commonality we do have between Catholics and Protestants in the body of Christ ... We hope it will be the beginning of much cross-pollinating between Catholic and Protestant music. There's so much rich contemporary music in what's thought of as Protestant circles, and a lot of work is being done in Catholic circles as well … We hope to do a fresh, new album, the Catholic equivalent of some of the songs that we like to think of as milestones in … Protestant music.

In another, rather different kind of push for inclusiveness and unity, Pat began a popular radio series called *The Pat Boone Show*, which initially went out worldwide on nearly 170 stations. Broadcast from his home in Beverly Hills, the show was full of a wide-ranging selection of contemporary Christian music and attracted a huge, broad-based audience. Even though it was clearly a Christian show, it managed to attract a collection of sponsors which included top secular advertisers as well as those with specifically religious interests. That was an unusual mix in the prevailing media market place, and was largely thanks to the wide, 'crossover' audience appeal that Pat possessed.

CHAPTER 11

MR NICE GUY?

I gotta bad reputation and I don't know why!
Michael Bruce and Alice Cooper

PAT BOONE'S HOLLYWOOD OFFICE is located at the Beverly Hills end of Sunset Boulevard, which runs parallel to the star-spangled Hollywood Boulevard with its pavements full of 'gold star' tributes to the greatest names in the entertainment business. Pat is honoured with two star tributes, located at 6262 Hollywood Boulevard and 1633 Vine Boulevard. June 1984 saw him being honoured in a more private way, as he reached the milestone of his fiftieth birthday.

Having a business meeting to attend on the day of his birthday, Pat was at his office promptly in the morning, and at first the day seemed like any other. A few people wished him a happy birthday, but that was about it. Little did he know that his faithful staff had been laying plans for weeks, organizing a surprise party for him. When Pat disappeared into another part of the building for his meeting, everyone else downed tools and hurried to prepare the office. They had exactly one hour to hang streamers, blow up balloons, arrange the furniture, put out the food (including a huge gold record-shaped cake), mix the punch and generally prepare for the sudden arrival of 50 secretly invited guests. A 30-foot banner saying 'HAPPY BIRTHDAY PAT' was strung around a parking sign and a lamppost in the street outside.

Pat emerged from his meeting to be met by administrator Maureen Mata, who steered him on some pretext towards the main office area. There was a 'Happy Birthday' balloon floating in the entrance lobby which caught Pat's eye, but he still did not suspect anything. When he stepped into the normally sedate main office, he was astonished to be greeted with the deafening sounds of 'Happy Birthday To You' being thumped out on the piano by Dave Siebels. Suddenly he found himself surrounded by a crowd of people – his staff and the 50 guests had been hiding out of sight. Pat was overwhelmed, flabbergasted to see so many of his friends and business associates gathered there in the middle of a working day, especially for him. The celebrations went on for some time, and little work was done that day.

Some time before his birthday, Shirley had asked her husband what he wanted to do to mark 'the big 5-0'. Pat was adamant that he did not want anything as a present (they had agreed some time before not to buy each other specific birthday gifts any more). What he *would* like very much, he told her, was to have as many family members as possible around for a party on the weekend nearest his birthday. That would mean a lot to him. Shirley had pulled a face, however, and warned him that it might not be possible – she thought many of the far-flung family were already committed elsewhere for that weekend.

And so it proved. Cherry and her family lived in distant Seattle, and Cherry explained sadly that they had already agreed to something else that weekend, so would not be able to make the trip, even though Pat had offered to pay their fares to LA. Lindy was relocating that weekend to a new house, so there was no question of her being there. Her husband offered to bring the children by himself, which raised Pat's hopes a little, but then he sent a message to say that they could not make it after all. By this time, Pat was beginning to feel more than a little disappointed. Was *everyone* going to be busy or away? Then Shirley reluctantly told him that Laury and her husband Harry would away be on the road doing a gospel concert elsewhere in California and would not be able to get back to Beverly Hills. That only left Debby and Gabriel.

In the end, Shirley suggested to Pat that he spend the day playing golf with his friend Jack Spina and Gabriel. At least that would be something to enjoy. But even this did not go so well on the day. An ABC TV team arrived at the golf course to interview Pat, interrupting the threesome's game. Pat was not impressed, and in any case it meant they were out for longer than they had intended. Pat, Shirley, Gabriel and Debby had arranged to go out to a favourite Italian restaurant for a celebratory meal that evening, and Pat was aware of time running out. When he returned home from the golf course, he saw that there was barely time for him to rush into the house and grab a clean jacket before they were all due at the restaurant. Ominously, Shirley was already waiting on the doorstep.

To Pat's surprise, however, instead of urging him to hurry up as she normally did, she said there was something she wanted to show him. It was not a birthday present for him, she said, as she knew he had not wanted one. This was something for both of them, so she thought he would approve – but he had to come and see it *now*. Brushing aside Pat's objection that they would be late at the restaurant, Shirley told him to shut his eyes and guided him round to the back of the house. Pat remembers bumping into several bushes in the process! They finally stopped on the patio, and Shirley checked that Pat had not been peeking. 'OK then,' she said, 'you can open your eyes now!'

To Pat's utter amazement, he opened his eyes to see two big tables set for about 15 people, candles ablaze, balloons every-where. Suddenly the door from the house opened and Laury and Harry appeared, then came Debby, Gabriel and their children. They were followed by Lindy, Doug and *their* children. More surprises were in store. Turning round, Pat saw his little grand-daughter Brittany come running round the corner, followed by her mother Cherry and the rest of the family from Seattle. Even Pat's parents turned up. Nobody's excuses had been genuine after all, and Pat could only marvel at the skilled planning that had gone into the arrangements, leaving him completely oblivious to the whole scam during the weeks leading up to the great day. It was, he said, the perfect birthday present.

Pat was immensely touched by the lengths people had gone to in preparing those special surprises for his birthday. Particularly moving had been the thoughtful efforts of his office staff in organizing that secret party for 50 people. Through the years, Pat has had frequent cause to be grateful for the skills and loyalty of his staff.

Administrator Maureen Mata, he says, has been a pillar of strength, as has his personal assistant Janet St Pierre (née Fix). Janet has worked with Pat for over 10 years and has helped him weather quite a few storms, not least the rush of correspondence which followed the publicity surrounding his discovery of spiritual renewal in 1969. Pat's own church, of course, had strongly disagreed with his experience of baptism in the Holy Spirit, and many people from around the world wrote letters of rebuke and condemnation. Pat answered as many as he could, but says he would never have coped with the load had it not been for Janet. Janet, in turn, says that she was astounded by Pat's ability to respond to such opposition (many of the letter-writers quoted chapter and verse from the Bible to support their detailed arguments) with well-informed clarity and articulateness. (His correspondence on the matter with some of the Church's thinkers later became a book called *Dr Balaam's Talking Mule*.)

The bearded and personable Charlie Shaw is another valued member of staff. Charlie's business experience in the music industry is priceless. He has been involved in the development and sales of Pat's recordings for over 17 years, and today sees 'no time in the near future when Pat's ideas will stop flowing or the need to market his recordings will slow down'. Also on the musical side of his activities, Pat relies a great deal on the expertise of David Diggs. Occupying the office next to Charlie, David has an active musical imagination and an extensive education in orchestration and conducting. He has collaborated with Pat on many projects and is always available to be consulted about new ideas.

New ideas, new activities, have always been important to Pat, and this spills over from his musical interests into the sphere of business ventures. Supported by his close-knit staff team, Pat has pursued a number of varied business projects over the years. He has always been fascinated by business and its processes, and confesses that in the past he has tended to 'jump in where angels feared to tread', sometimes taking chances on business propositions that turned out to be unwise. Certainly, not all his enterprises have been profitable and several have been downright disastrous. Sometimes, of course, he has not received the best advice, and fluctuating market forces affect everybody, but he would be the first to admit that his own judgement has not always been sound.

In the 1960s, for example, Pat invested in several difficulty-beset businesses, including a direct-mail film company that went under and an automated restaurant chain that also went out of business. The struggling Oakland Oaks team in the now defunct American Basketball Association were briefly owned by him, but he narrowly avoided losses in that particular deal by selling the franchise. In the 1970s, he lost over $20 million when some of his investments failed. As he says, however, the bad times did not deter him for long. 'I've always enjoyed being an entrepreneur. I suspect I inherited that from my Dad! I'm constantly thinking of all kinds of ideas for businesses, and I'm always willing to consider ideas other people put to me. I've had my fingers burned on more than one occasion, but I still keep on looking for those great ideas!'

The record label Lamb and Lion, which Pat regards as one of his most important enterprises, was founded in 1971. In the late 1970s, Pat bought out his original partner in the venture, Irv Kessler, after a difference of opinion about the kind of music they should be producing and the overall approach of the business. Pat believed Lamb and Lion should be a ministry first and a business second. Of course, the record company had to be operated as a business, but he felt that only Christian music should be on the label, and he also wanted the freedom to be able to give records away to people who could not afford to buy them. It was, he believed, important to expose as many people as possible to the music and the message, even if it was not profitable to the company.

In 1989 Lamb and Lion did indeed find itself in difficulties and sought protection by going into Chapter 11 bankruptcy (in the US this enables a business to reorganize and stay in operation). The company came out of that worrying time whole and healthy, with everything settled and with the strength to continue as a creative recording company. The label is still going today. Pat had much love and faith invested in the Lamb and Lion enterprise and, looking back, he is philosophical about the difficulties the business experienced. Overall, he says, he has been very fortunate. After all, he has enjoyed a tremendously long career in what is a notoriously fickle industry. Peaks and troughs are to be expected over such a length of time. Besides, he adds, 'Earthly successes come and go, but God's truth endures for ever. That's where my treasure is truly to be found.'

Today the offices on Sunset Boulevard are a hive of activity, the focus of the business and charity affairs of Pat Boone Enterprises. Pat is still busy thinking up great ideas and new ventures. Among his many current interests is the KDOC TV station in Orange County, of which he is president.

Pat, of course, is often away from the centre of his business interests, still performing a wide variety of music. In 1994, always happy to try out something different, he spent seven months starring in the title role of the musical stage comedy *The Will Rogers Follies* at the Will Rogers Theater in Branson, Missouri. He relished the chance to appear once again in a 'proper' theatrical production, as a change from the one-off shows and concerts he had become used to in more recent years. The acclaimed musical depicted the life story of Oklahoma philosopher Will Rogers, one of America's modern legends, and had won six Tony Awards for choreography, costumes, score, lighting and direction during its run on New York's Broadway.

Pat was fascinated by the story of Will's extraordinarily varied life. He was born on a ranch in 1880 and was taught complicated rope tricks by one of the ranch employees at an early age. Schooling was intermittent, one of his teachers commented wryly that Will's passion for rope-throwing was to blame for his poor grades. Sensing that his son could do with a little military discipline, Will's father packed him off to a military academy in Boonville, Missouri, in 1897. Will caused a sensation at the academy with his flamboy-ant cowboy clothes. He left to become a cowboy in the Texas Panhandle, then he travelled on to Buenos Aires and later South Africa, where he was hired by Texas Jack's Wild West Circus troupe.

Returning to the USA in 1908, he carved out a lucrative vaude-ville career, joined the Ziegfeld Follies in 1918 and started to appear in motion pictures. In 1922 he began a series of weekly articles, syndicated to over 400 US newspapers. He went on to write a daily newspaper column for the *New York Times*, which he did for the rest of his life, from wherever he happened to be. He became very wealthy, donating large amounts to charities like the Red Cross and the Salvation Army. Will was also fascinated with flying, and this enchantment took him on numerous flights with aviation pioneers Billy Mitchell, Eddie Rickenbacker and Charles Lindberg. This pastime, however, eventually cost him his life. In July 1935, Will and fellow Oklahoman Wiley Post flew to Matanuska Valley, Alaska, as part of a trip to Russia. Taking off from Point Barrow, the red monoplane plunged into the river bank, instantly killing both men.

The musical set out to reflect all the different facets of Will's life and character, so it turned out to be quite a spectacle! Pat thoroughly enjoyed the part, and says he was glad to have had the chance to pay tribute to one of America's more flamboyant and noteworthy figures.

Hot on the heels of Pat's lengthy participation in *The Will Rogers Follies* came a very special foreign tour in 1995, to mark the fortieth anniversary of his first million-seller, 'Ain't That A Shame'. To commemorate the occasion, he put together a nostalgic concert programme, during which he sang almost exclusively from the list of his hit tunes. Indeed, Pat says, he had enormous difficulty deciding which songs *not* to include. With no less than 60 charted singles, there was far too much material to be performed in one go! Every concert on the tour of New Zealand, Australia and the UK was sold out.

It was satisfying to look back with nostalgia at all the popular songs he had performed so often since the 1950s, but even in the mid-1990s Pat was still on the lookout for new ideas, new material, new experiments. 'I was never content to rest on the laurels of past chart success or the security of the status quo. I have always needed to push back the horizons, and I've never been enamoured with labels. I've always tried to re-examine what I've done and evolve my skills.'

In 1997 Pat certainly pushed back the horizons with his controversial album release *Pat Boone in a Metal Mood – No More Mr Nice Guy*. His aim was to spark new life into songs first recorded by heavy-metal artists with some new, jazzy, big-band arrangements. Released in January 1997 by MCA, the album stunned critics and public alike. This was not the Pat Boone everyone knew and loved, and he found himself the talk of the town. Heavy metal? What *was* the Christian crooner thinking of?

Conductor Dave Siebels was the first to encourage Pat in the idea, enthusiastic about the prospect of bringing heavy metal songs to a new audience through more accessible band arrangements. He taped a selection of famous heavy metal songs for Pat to listen to, including Deep Purple's 'Smoke On The Water' and songs by Led Zeppelin and Van Halen. Pat says that he soon became fascinated by the sheer musicianship on those recordings, and was hooked by the notion of adapting them for himself. 'I went through literally hundreds of heavy metal songs. Like Captain Kirk in *Star Trek*, I always considered myself to be the kind of person who likes to go where no one else has gone before. A heavy metal album was certainly exploring new territory for Mr Boone!'

The idea may have seemed absurd at first, but Pat and Dave got to work and soon realized that the arrangements were sounding far too good to laugh at. They worked on. Of course, there were many songs that Pat just would not consider because of their content, which went against his Christian principles, but there were plenty of others that he was happy to develop. The first experimental tracks they recorded in Dave's studio were 'Enter Sandman' and 'Stairway To Heaven'.

During this period, Rhino Records released a music video entitled *40 Years of Hits*, a compilation of Pat's top songs taken from his TV performances. While he was talking to publicist Dave Dom to promote the video, Pat happened to mention the heavy metal project. He was met with incredulity, but Dave Dom's subsequent write-up of the interview sparked considerable media interest which even reached other countries. German documentary producer Hennings Lohner was busy making a documentary on heavy metal at the time and he invited Pat to accompany him to an Ozzy Osborne concert at the Thomas Mack Arena in LA. It was Pat's first experience of a heavy metal concert, and he says it blew his mind! He later saw Alice Cooper and the Scorpions perform live, and went backstage to persuade Alice to join him on the Boone version of 'No More Mr Nice Guy'.

News of this coup soon escaped, and MCA's head man Bruce Resnikoff asked Pat to let him have the recording. Pat agreed and, with award-winning producers Jeff Weber and Michael Lloyd on board alongside Dave Siebels, the project took off again. The creative juices hummed. Along with electric guitars, drums, trumpets, trombones and saxophones, even a string quartet was used to great effect. News of the unusual recording buzzed around the heavy metal world and the studio was visited by a variety of interested parties, including Mick Fleetwood, Lindsey Buckingham, Billy Preston, Paula Kelly and Ronnie James. Later on, Richie Blackmore of Deep Purple had Pat sign a copy of the CD for his father. Mr Blackmore Senior was a big Pat Boone fan, and Richie hoped that the CD would finally bring his father to express approval for Deep Purple's music!

'We knew before we ever got to the recording session that we were going to have tremendous music,' says Pat. In July 1996, at Ocean Way Recording Studios, a hand-picked group of backing musicians and guest artists assembled, including Greg Bissonette on drums, and hard-rock veterans Ronnie James Dio, Ritchie Blackmore and Dweezil Zappa on guitar. The tracks were cut in much the same way as Pat had recorded his early hits. 'We did them live to two-track, which is almost never done any more. The musicians and the singers knew that we were going for a final mix with each song, and it gave the whole session a special sense of excitement. It was a party! I've never had a better time in a recording studio in my whole life, and I've never been more proud of a finished album than this one.'

The album was released, and made something of a splash. Ripples turned into waves, however, when Pat turned up on stage at the American Music Awards on 27 January 1997. Gone were the white bucks and golf sweater of the traditional Boone look: he was in full heavy metal garb, complete with leathers, chains, tattoo and ear-ring. Before the show, DJ Dick Clark had contacted Pat and Alice Cooper, asking them both to present the

'Best Hard Rock Heavy Metal Group' award. He had also – or so he thought – persuaded the two of them to dress up in each other's style of clothes. Pat, always game for a laugh, had gone to town on his costume. Alice, however, had clearly had second thoughts about the white shoes and the golf sweater, and appeared dressed in his normal style.

Pat was unfazed and went ahead with his own part of the joke, swaggering out onto the stage in his uncharacteristic gear. His appearance was met with gasps of surprise and even disapproval from some of the audience. Many caught on to the joke and laughed with Pat as he strutted about, but some clearly thought he had gone completely 'off his rocker', renouncing his Nice Guy image for real. Was he going through some kind of mid-life crisis?

No one quite anticipated the trouble that followed. The shock waves proceeded to reverberate around the conservative Christian community and the little joke soon stopped being a laughing matter even for Pat. His syndicated TV Show *Gospel America* on the Trinity Broadcasting Network was banned from the airwaves: large sections of the Christian public were now convinced that Pat was no longer what he seemed, and nobody at Trinity asked his opinion before taking their decision about the programme.

Pat insisted that he had forewarned the Trinity bosses, *and* his church pastor, about the plan and all, he said, gave their initial approval. He was therefore doubly disappointed that some chose to believe that he had actually changed in some radical way and 'sold out' to those 'wicked rockers'. Ironically, while many TBN viewers were – wrongly – outraged by Pat's actions, the reaction from college students, bikers and heavy metal fans was entirely different. Pat found himself swamped with calls from TV and radio stations all over the US, wanting to interview this 'new Pat Boone'!

On 15 April 1997 Pat stood before a cluster of representatives from Trinity Broadcasting Network for a hearing, along with his pastor. He was there to explain the reasons for his appearance at the American Music Awards. What had begun for Pat as a light-hearted attempt to poke fun at his own image had been blown out of all proportion and turned into a kind of trial by television. Pat said he was deeply hurt by the negative reactions and vicious letters he had received, and strongly objected to the way his programme had been taken off the air. Where was trust and loyalty in all this? He had forewarned them, after all. In any case, he added, 'Christians have got to deal with this judgemental, self-righteous, opinionated attitude that if somebody doesn't dress like we dress, or doesn't like the same music ... he must be a heathen. That mindset ... is a turnoff to the very people we would like to reach.'

Eventually a two-hour discussion programme went out on the Trinity network, featuring parts of the hearing and tracks from the CD (probably the one and only time heavy metal has been played on American Christian TV!), and a vote was taken from the viewers. They voted overwhelmingly that Pat's programme should be reinstated at once. The fuss eventually died down, but Pat says he still has people commenting on the unforgettable episode even now!

Pat will never really be known as a heavy rocker, of course, and the foundation of his huge popularity lies in other spheres. In 1997, *The Fifties Complete*, a boxed collection of 12 CDs containing a massive 324 tracks, plus a hefty accompanying book, was issued under the direction of Richard Weize of Germany's Bear Family label. It contains all of Pat's Dot and Republic recordings from his heyday, and the book documents his life with many nostalgic photographs.

Pat's latest big venture, begun in the late 1990s, is likewise concerned with nostalgia. The stated aim of his Gold Label is 'to establish itself as the principal source of multimedia entertainment products for the age-50-plus market'. Partnering Pat in the venture is Jim Long, an experienced ex-DJ and record producer. Using every multimedia means at its disposal, Gold Label concentrates on meeting the needs of the growing number of so-called 'Pre-World War II Baby Boomers', who are now the senior citizens of the new century. With an emphasis on quality not quantity, the qualifying criteria for inclusion on the label are that artists should be over 45 years of age and should have a track record that includes gold-album status – 'the original kids on the block', as Pat puts it.

In 1999, Pat compiled an impressive list of artists who were willing to record under his new label – among them Glen Campbell, Connie Francis, Jerry Vale and Patti Page. Pat himself issued several albums on Gold Label early in its development. First was the double CD *Golden Treasury of Hymns*, consisting of 40 hymns and gospel songs. Then came *The Gold Collection*: 14 revamped Boone hits including 'April Love' and 'Speedy Gonzales'. He also planned to revive recordings from the Lamb and Lion label, reissuing some country gospel recordings to be made available through Cadence Records in the US. Two video and CD releases entitled *The Crooners Collection: Volumes I and II* were issued, featuring tracks by Sinatra, Belafonte, Mathis and other luminaries. Tracks included 'For The Good Times', 'Dream A Little Dream Of Me' and 'Fools Rush In'.

Jack Jones was another fine name to join the Gold list. In January 1999, unbeknown to each other, Pat and Jack were on the same flight to Dallas from Los Angeles. They were simultaneously trying to contact each other by phone to discuss arrangements for Jack's recording session when they bumped into each other in the Dallas airport lounge! Arrangements were soon finalized and the Gold Label album *Jack Jones Paints a Tribute to Tony Bennett* was duly issued and nominated for a Grammy Award. Plans and discussions are continuing with a number of quality singers from the rock era, including Huey Lewis. Glen Campbell's Gold Label CD *Love Songs* is already available, offering a sparkling array of standards including 'Ebb Tide', 'And I Love You So' and 'What A Wonderful World'.

In the interests of promoting the gems available on Gold Label, Pat agreed to take part in a TV commercial. Arriving rather late at the Hollywood studio for the filming session on 13 April 2000, Pat found the set already prepared and director Chuck Blore, photographic director Hal Trussell and producer Wendell Weathington all patiently waiting for him. There was clearly no time to be lost, so Pat donned the special yellow sweater with the Gold Label logo on it and sat down on the stool provided for him.

'He's too tanned!' said Chuck Blore suddenly, gazing critically at Pat. Make-up artist Nancy Ferguson jumped forward and got to work until Chuck was happy with Pat's complexion. Chris Haughom, the creative director, then ran Pat through his lines and moves for the three one-minute commercials, noting each gesture with an eagle eye and asking for several minute adjustments. Filming began at last, with Pat mouthing the script to a pre-recorded soundtrack. Many takes were filmed, and in each one Pat had to try to sit in exactly the same position and move his hands in precisely the same way. Sometimes he forgot and did something slightly different, in which case another cry of 'Cut!' would come, and they would start all over again. Attention to fine detail was apparently essential for continuity, even down to the hairs on Pat's head! It took all day before the director and producer were satisfied that they had sufficient quality material for the final edit. Eight hours of exacting work had been needed to make just three 60-second commercials. Pat says he was awed by the effort that had gone into the production!

Pat's standing in the music world remains as high as it has ever been. As something of an 'elder statesman' now, he is honoured for his experience and his long-lasting success. It is not only the music fraternity that holds him in respect, either. Pat has a certain status in general public terms too. Part of this is due to his high profile in Christian circles, but perhaps a broader appeal comes from his obvious and active patriotism. Pat Boone loves his country. 'I admit to getting goosebumps down my spine whenever I hear "The Star-Spangled Banner"!' he says. 'Some cynics may mock, but for me, patriotic songs such as "America The Beautiful" and "God Bless America" are songs to be proud of. I believe they speak eloquently of the beauties and quality of life in our country.'

A regular face at the White House in Washington DC, Pat has enjoyed the rare privilege of meeting every American president since Dwight D. Eisenhower, not to mention many well-known names in government ranks, including the former Secretary of State Henry Kissinger. Pat initially met President Eisenhower when he was acting as entertainment chairman for National Bible Week. Ike, he said, was a very gracious, friendly man, and warmly received the Bible which Pat presented to him. He also visited ex-President Harry Truman at his library in Independence, Missouri. President Truman had reproduced the famous Oval Office there, complete with a replica desk displaying the plaque stating 'The buck stops here'. Pat remembers sitting proudly, if a little gingerly, at the desk while Mr Truman looked on. In July 1980, Pat appeared at the Republican Convention in Detroit in support of Ronald Reagan's bid for the presidency, and continued making appearances in support of the campaign whenever his schedule allowed. He was invited to President Reagan's Inaugural Celebration in January 1981.

During President Bush's incumbency, shortly after the Gulf War, Pat was invited to attend a Presidential Prayer Breakfast. These annual events are held on the first Thursday in February, and special prayers are said for the whole country. At the time Pat was a spokesperson for the company who make the famous 'Precious Moments' figurines, and one of these, entitled 'God Bless the USA' (a figure of Uncle Sam on his knees in prayer) was to be presented to Mr Bush at the breakfast. The President announced that he was receiving the gift on behalf of all those who had served in Operation Desert Storm during the Gulf War.

More recently, Pat has expressed his sense of betrayal in the light of the controversies surrounding the presidency of Bill

Clinton. 'The USA was saddled with an X-rated presidency,' he says. 'Whether all the charges were true or not, our nation became the butt of dirty jokes around the world. The astonishing thing was that, at least according to the polls, a majority of Americans didn't think these sordid indiscretions and the transparent cover-ups seemed to matter, at least not enough to have demanded that someone else be placed in the Oval Office. It became obvious that serious changes had occurred in many people's concept of morality.'

Pat's commitment to his country was given musical and artistic expression in July 1996 when his *American Glory* video was released. Accompanying the shots of some of America's most breathtaking landscapes were rich renditions of the nation's favourite anthems, sung by Pat to the strains of the majestic Ralph Carmichael Orchestra. In the early days of the new millennium, he travelled round the USA delivering a speech which he entitled 'Losing Liberty', which warned of the dangers of America losing her identity and character. 'America's people,' he said, 'are in danger of becoming homogenized, washed out, intimidated and bland. Our people are surrendering our hard-won ... freedom to express ourselves, including our differences. Our political, religious and ethnical differences are liberties that the Constitution promised to protect. Americans are in great danger of losing blessings people fought and even died for. The danger comes from being apathetic, passive, non-involved and not using the power of the ballot box to bring about change ... We must never forget that God says, "If my people, which are called by my name, shall humble themselves, and pray, and seek my face, and turn from their wicked ways; then will I hear from heaven, and will forgive their sin, and will heal their land." Prayer and repentance will keep our nation free and prosperous.'

Pat is one of the few singing stars to have remained a household name over a couple of generations. Nowadays he commands undeniable respect among many of his show-biz peers – although some will always tend to mock him as a 'holy roller'. His lifestyle and obvious contentment, however, attract more admiration than anything else. Record producer Larry Scott, for example, comments, 'Pat is a man whose deeds speak far louder than words – although he's always ready to talk about his convictions when he's asked!' Pat has always had a concern for matters outside the narrow world of show business, and over the years has been involved in a number of political and social campaigns. As an articulate person with both strong convictions and a public profile, he says, he has always felt a responsibility to put those attributes to use for the good of the society around him. Politicians seem to value the presence of such a popular figure on their rostrums, and Pat has also been closely involved as a spokesman for pro-life and anti-pornography campaigns.

He is also fervently anti-racist, and takes every opportunity to attack racism in any shape or form. To this end, he gave his whole-hearted support to the cause of Willy T. Ribbs, a man many think is destined to be the Tiger Woods of auto-racing. Pat helped him secure full sponsorship on the NASCAR racing tracks, and said he was proud to be involved in 'breaking the last racial barrier in professional sports in America'. Like many local residents of Southern California, Pat was deeply shocked by the Los Angeles riots of 1992 and joined Rodney King in the crusading song 'Can't We All Get Along'.

As a Christian citizen, Pat believes that support for the enforcement of law and order is essential for the wellbeing of his country – and he is not frightened to say so publicly. This kind of outspoken support for the work of the police force has not gone unnoticed. In 1998 he was the first person to be awarded the Michael the Archangel Award by the National Association of Chiefs of Police. The Association works hard to support police officers and their families, particularly in times of stress or when officers are injured or killed in the line of duty. Pat became involved after the civil riots of the 1960s and '70s, composing the song 'Won't Be Home Tonight' about an officer killed in a drugs bust. Some of his songs, accompanied by a message of consolation, were later sent to the grieving families of officers who had been killed. 'I wanted to help humanize the police,' says Pat. 'I wanted those songs to be played on the radio, to counteract the thinking that law enforcement is our enemy.'

In the sphere of specifically Christian work, Pat also continues to be an enthusiastic supporter of evangelistic projects. In 1994, he acted as co-chair for an extensive crusade in California's San Fernando Valley. There he spoke and sang to a total of 54,000 people, encompassing 200 churches and 25 denominations. 'I need to remember that even my fans require my witness,' he says. 'They need Jesus too! I have an important message, and I count it a privilege that I have the job of talking about my faith to many people around the world.'

For several years, Pat co-chaired America's annual National Day of Prayer, held in May. He is a strong believer in the power of prayer, both for individuals and for the country as a whole. The National Day of Prayer has roots stretching right back to the founding of America, as Pat explains: 'Prayer played a prominent part even at the first Continental Congress in 1775. In 1952, Congress passed a joint resolution, signed by President Harry Truman, establishing an annual National Day of Prayer. This was later amended in 1988 and signed by President Ronald Reagan. It permanently set the Day of Prayer as the first Thursday in May. My own commitment to this Day of Prayer reflects my strong agreement with the beliefs of America's founding fathers. President Abraham Lincoln once said, "The only assurance of our nation's safety is to lay our foundation in morality and religion." General George Washington prayed at the end of the Revolutionary War, "Almighty Father, if it is Thy holy will that we shall obtain a place and name among the nations of the earth, grant that we may be enabled to show our gratitude for Thy goodness, by our endeavours to fear and obey Thee."'

CHAPTER 12

FREELY, FREELY

Freely, freely you have received:
Freely, freely give!

Jimmy and Carol Owens

PAT'S POLITICAL AND SOCIAL campaigning has been accompanied over the years by generous gifts of time, money and enthusiasm to a whole variety of charitable projects. He has never just wanted to donate money, however: he loves to get involved in the action and says he finds it enormously satisfying to give something back to his community in such a way.

One of the charities with which he is most deeply involved is the Easter Seals organization, for which he is spokesman and chairman as well as host of their annual telethon appeal. The thousands of dollars raised each year go towards research to help disadvantaged and disabled people, and Pat is tremendously excited about the charity's work. 'This charity exists to bring hope to handicapped – or, as I would have it, handi*capable* – children and adults.' Pat wrote a book in support of the charity, *The Human Touch: The Story of Easter Seals*, which contains stories about 'the Easter Seal children' from 1947 up to 1991, as well as introducing the adults who have worked as Easter Seal representatives, and the charity's founder Edgar F. Allen. About 800,000 Easter Seals volunteers are at work in any one year, helping over one million people. Pat has hosted the annual telethon since 1981 and fundraising has increased every year, recently passing the half-billion-dollar mark. The telethon itself takes up just one weekend in the year, of course, but Pat is involved with the charity all year round, making appearances at Easter Seal centres, conventions and corporate sponsorship events.

Bethel Bible Village in the suburbs of Chattanooga, Tennessee, exists to support underprivileged young people of a different sort. Pat has been involved with the Village since 1978 and says that until that time, although he had always had an interest in supporting prison ministries, he had never previously thought much about what became of the *children* of prisoners. Bethel Bible Village, founded in 1954 by Rev. F.L. Hipp, is a non-denominational Christian home for boys and girls whose parents are in prison. With only seven per cent of the funding the Village needs coming from government resources, they rely heavily on donations. Pat helps to contribute to the cause by fronting an annual golf tournament in Chattanooga, followed by a 'Pat Boone and Friends' concert. The Village is run on a family basis, with six children and a couple acting as house-parents in each cottage. The children attend local Christian schools and churches, and are generally helped to try to overcome the enormous emotional wounds they inevitably carry.

Pat's involvement in the rehabilitation and treatment of people who are drug-abusers or who have psychiatric problems is also well documented. In 1991, for example, he opened a treatment centre as part of the Community Hospital in Van Nuys, run with the help of Christian psychiatrists, psychologists and doctors. The Van Nuys Rapha Centre is one of many in a chain now operating around the USA. Founded by Robert McGee, the name comes from the Hebrew word *Rapha*, which means 'our God heals'.

On a rather larger scale is Pat's involvement with a worldwide humanitarian concern. In 1979, Pat, Shirley and their son-in-law Dan O'Neill hosted a special meeting in their home which led directly to the founding of Mercy Corps. The Corps is now an internationally acclaimed organization which targets crisis hunger spots around the world, fuelled by a growing annual budget exceeding $30 million. The funds are used to provide aid programmes for needy people who are victims of famine, poverty and war, particularly in the Third World. Pat's particular role is to promote and publicize the activities of Mercy Corps through the media.

In an entirely different sphere, Pat has also been a lifelong supporter of the Boy Scout movement – his adult involvement having been kickstarted by his Den Chief days with the Denton Cub Scouts. These days he often finds himself writing individual letters to encourage young Scouts in their endeavours, often at the request of a parent hoping to mark some particular achievement or commendation. Pat is always happy to dispense such encouragement, telling the boys that they will not regret their Scouting experiences and urging them on to demonstrate to others their newfound abilities to lead rather than follow.

As well as giving time and money to a whole range of charities, Pat has also never stopped giving to the Church. He has always been free with his time, taking on leadership roles in terms of music and worship whenever his schedule has permitted, and he and Shirley continued to contribute financially to the Church of Christ, despite the doctrinal and cultural differences which arose in the late 1960s. One particular innovation is of special importance to Pat, as he explains. 'Mack Craig, my high school principal, and his wife Dottie both had strong influences on Shirley and me in our teenage years and for years afterwards. When Dottie died of cancer, we helped to sponsor a Dottie Craig Memorial Fund that still continues today at Lipscomb College in Nashville.'

On 13 April 2000, Pat was invited to the Canyonville Christian Academy to witness the rededication of the Men's Residence, which was formally renamed as Boone Hall. The Academy was originally founded as an orphanage in 1924 by A.M. Shaffer, an itinerant preacher who had been on his way to Los Angeles' Azusa Street revival when his car broke down in Canyonville. He started one of the first pentecostal Bible schools on the West Coast there and, when it became too dangerous for young people to accompany their missionary parents abroad during World War II, the school became home to many for the duration. Today there are still missionary children in the student body. The renaming of the hall was part of the school's desire to honour living Christian personalities who had 'made a difference', serving as role models for the young people passing through the academy. The school also helped to launch a three-year study programme on the history of Christians in the arts.

Charities are not alone in praising Pat for his generosity, and there are countless fans who would also happily testify to his open-handed, friendly nature. He has always had time to give to his fans, and has always shown his appreciation for them. Many respect him for it, and hundreds now have treasured memories of a personal encounter with him at one time or another in his long show-business career.

British tour organizer Jeffrey Kruger remembers an incident that illustrates the point very well. 'After a show one night the weather was atrocious. There was the usual long line of fans standing patiently in the streaming rain, waiting for Pat to leave the theatre and hoping to get his autograph. I was concerned that Pat would catch a cold if he stood outside signing autographs that night, so I suggested it would be in his best interests if he allowed me to sneak him out by a side entrance and get him back to the warmth of his hotel as soon as possible!' Pat thanked Jeff for his concern, but insisted that he must meet his fans. He could not leave them standing outside in the rain for nothing, he said. Pat duly spent some time chatting to his admirers and signing auto-graphs for anyone who wanted one, but he did agree to sit in the stage doorman's cubbyhole out of the rain, while fans filed in a few at a time. 'In all my years of promoting,' comments Jeff, 'I've discovered that Pat is one of the very few artists who *really* cares for his fans.'

Pat continues to attract admirers from many diverse sources. Not all, however, come on board as a result of his songs or movies. In 1988, Jim Malkin and his family were on their way home to California after a trip to Washington DC which they had won in a competition. Jim was relishing the experience of travelling first class on the plane, and was delighted to find himself in a seat across the aisle from Pat. The two men passed the flight deep in conversation. In the bustle of the baggage reclaim hall at Los Angeles, Pat and the Malkin family said a cordial goodbye, both happy to have travelled in congenial company.

The Malkins were standing outside, waiting – apparently in vain – for the car they had ordered to take them home, when Pat passed them in his sports convertible. Much to their surprise, he pulled up, seeing they were stranded. 'Where are you headed?' he asked. When he heard that they needed to get to San Fernando Valley, he said that was exactly where he was going – would they like a lift? Pat would not take no for an answer, and they spent a hilarious few minutes trying to make three adults, two children and a mound of luggage fit into Pat's small and snazzy car. They had just about shoehorned everyone in when the Malkins' original ride appeared. Everyone said goodbye again, and the Malkins sped away in their rather larger car, waving enthusiastically. Now Jim Malkin says he will not have a word said against Pat Boone, having been so impressed by his kindness and generosity.

Some of Pat's fans have been long-distance admirers for decades. Until 20 February 2000, Alan Farr of Sacramento, California, had never written a fan letter in his life, although he had followed Pat's career since the 1960s. He and his friends had been to see *Journey to the Centre of the Earth* so many times that they had known the script off by heart. When he was 14, he was looking up articles about Pat in the Cheyenne Library in Wyoming. He read *Twixt Twelve and Twenty* twice, and the first album he bought with his own money was *Pat's Great Hits*. He even bought some white shoes! In the letter he finally wrote to Pat, he said he wanted to acknowledge the positive influence Pat had exerted on his life, an influence which had lasted into his adult years and through several troubled times.

Alan had been prompted to write his letter after meeting an insurance client of his. The client was an elderly gentleman called Hal, and he had spent his working life as a behind-the-scenes manager in show business. Seeing that Alan was interested, he brought out some scrapbooks and photo albums, featuring shows and stars dating back to 1931. Hal turned the pages, stopping to tell the odd anecdote, until he came to 1958 and a show given by Pat Boone in Las Vegas. Hal brightened up considerably and spoke enthusiastically about Pat and his crew, describing the fun they had had during rehearsals and saying how much respect he had for Pat's talent. Then, from a dusty wooden box which he brought out from his bedroom, he produced an obviously prized possession. It turned out to be a Christmas card, personally written to him by Pat and dated 1958. It was now the late 1990s, and Hal had carefully preserved the card for all those years. Out of all the many stars he had met in his career, he told Alan, Pat Boone had been the performer he had most liked to work with. Afterwards, Alan had felt prompted to write to Pat and tell him the remarkable story. 'You have thousands of Hals out there,' he wrote. 'You are truly rich.'

It is not only Pat's talent and friendly character which have had such an influence on his fans. His Christian beliefs have also changed many people's lives. Cynthia Wright, from Pembrokeshire in the UK, was one such person. She had been a fan since her teenage years, and had continued to follow Pat's career through a busy life as a mother of three children. In 1981 she discovered that Pat was going to be appearing at the Apollo Victoria in London for one night only. Leaving her children with her husband, Cynthia travelled to London and got to meet her idol in person. She had been particularly struck by the way he sang a gospel song during the performance, and soon afterwards she purchased Pat's book *A New Song*, which told the story of his rediscovery of faith. That was the kind of faith she wanted too, she decided. Eighteen months later, Cynthia found herself in hospital, giving birth to a stillborn baby. It was at this low point that she finally found her own personal faith in Christ. A year later she gave birth to a healthy baby girl, and in 1995 she took her 11-year-old daughter to one of Pat's concerts. Her daughter was chosen from the audience to receive the 'April Love' bouquet that Pat gave to the youngest female at every show. It was a moment of special meaning, Cynthia says, adding, 'I will always be grateful to Pat for the influence he has had on my life, and for bringing me to faith in Jesus.'

Pat may love his fans, but even as he continues to work hard and perform well for them in this new millennium, most important of all to him is his family. This is increasingly so, he says, as he comes to realize ever more clearly how special they all are to him – wife Shirley, four daughters and their husbands, grandchildren and now great-grandchildren.

His favourite word in the whole world, Pat says, is 'Daddy'. 'I always refer to my father as "Daddy". My four daughters all still call *me* "Daddy", and even my grandchildren call me "Daddy Pat"! In our society, family relationships are struggling and it's projected that at least 50 per cent of our children born at the turn of this new century will be raised in single-parent families. The word "Daddy" takes on enormous new significance in this situation. I believe that God likes the word "Daddy" too. In the Bible God actually says He wants us to know Him not just as "Father" but, even more intimately, as "Daddy" (the Hebrew word is *Abba*). For me, every association and connotation of the word "Daddy" is good. It speaks of parental care and support, fun and friendship, wise counsel and stirring example. God offers all that, and more, and my parents reflected Him by being wonderful role models for their children.'

He has always, he says, tried to do the same for his own off-spring, and now looks back with some regret at the length and frequency of his absences from home while his daughters were growing up. 'I regret that we never really had enough fun time together, for a start!' he comments. Nonetheless, he believes that he and Shirley did their best to meet their responsibilities as parents – not so easy in the midst of Hollywood – and recognizes that his close-knit family was considered something of an oddity in that shifting, fickle environment. Today he expresses pride in all four of his daughters, with their different talents and their own expanding families. He is completely soft on all his grandchildren.

Even in his sixties, Pat remains a child at heart. 'Right up to the time they died, I loved to go home to Nashville to stay upstairs in my parents' house. Although I feel like a grandfather when I'm with my grandchildren, I was just Mama and Daddy's boy again when I stayed upstairs in the house where I grew up. It was a great feeling!' Pat admits to having felt rather reluctant when the idea of being a grandfather first cropped up. He was only 42 when he and Shirley were presented with their first grandchild by their daughter Lindy. Naturally, he says, they were thrilled with little Ryan, but they were also adamant that names like 'Gramps' and 'Grandma' were taboo! Instead, they instituted the names 'Daddy Pat' and 'Mama Shirley', still in use today by all their grandchildren. Some months after Ryan's birth, Lindy arrived for another visit with her parents, and Pat remembers going out to the driveway to welcome them. Baby Ryan saw Pat straight away and started to wriggle about, trying to reach him. 'Something melted inside me,' Pat says, 'and I thought to myself, "Oh! *This* is what a grand-daddy feels like!" There's been no looking back since…'

At the last count the Boones had 15 grandchildren, including two sets of twins, as well as a growing band of great-grandchildren.

Pat and Shirley bought each family a video camera so that they could capture both special and day-to-day events in the children's lives, all to be collected for the 'Boone Family Archive'. The extended family often meet for Christmas and Thanksgiving, and the grandparents frequently find themselves in charge of visits to Disneyland and other treats. Family life, says Pat, is very happy.

The central pillar of the family, of course, is Pat's wife Shirley. Such a long marriage as the Boones have enjoyed is all too rare in show-business circles – although it has not always been plain sailing. Pat thanks God for the fact that they have come through the difficult times still together: 'We've found great comfort and reality in the promise found in 2 Corinthians 13:9 – "My grace is sufficient for thee: for my strength is made perfect in weakness."'

After the problems in their relationship during the 1960s, difficult times returned more recently when Shirley spent most of the 1990s fighting an extended battle with fibromyalgia (a crippling muscle ailment) and clinical depression. The Boones sought every kind of help, starting with prayer and fasting and working through all kinds of self-examination, as well as seeking professional and medical consultations. 'Nothing seemed to help,' says Pat, 'and Shirley just seemed to get worse, withdrawing from all but the closest family circle and just a couple of dear friends.'

Then, in late September 1999, they were visited by some missionaries to Ghana, a man and his wife called Faithful and Mary. They prayed with Pat and Shirley, and told her that they believed God wanted her to press on through the pain and look for ways in which He might use her to help others. Shirley took this to heart and began to go out and about a little more. Soon after that, she heard that evangelist Benny Hinn, whom the Boones had known for years, would be preaching in a big arena in Anaheim, just a few miles from their home. Desperate for some spiritual encouragement, Shirley decided that she should go. She made the arrangements herself, only telling Pat shortly before she left. He was only too happy to see her taking such an initiative.

At the arena, Shirley accompanied a friend up to the platform during a time of prayer for healing. Benny recognized Shirley and prayed for her in front of the huge audience. She had had no expectation of healing, and was astonished when all the pain disappeared from her body and the depression vanished overnight. 'For several days,' says Pat, 'we both wondered if the symptoms might return, but they didn't. Shirley really was healed!' Suddenly she was full of energy again, no longer crippled by the muscle pain that had afflicted her for so long. She organized the first big family Christmas they had been able to have for a dozen years, and is now keeping everyone at Pat's office very busy setting up and administrating a new women's ministry called WeWin (Women Empowering Women In Need).

Sad times returned in the spring of 2000, however, when Pat's parents both died. Pat is quick to explain that he may be sad because he misses their presence here, but at the same time he is happy knowing that they are safe in heaven. He is not at all embarrassed to say that he believes in the certainty of heaven, although it may be an often ridiculed notion these days. The funeral services were magnificent celebrations, he says, 'each an emotional review of a life beautifully lived and a joyous recognition of their homegoings. The funerals focused almost as much on my parents' future as on their past. There *is* a future ahead, an eternity with God, and with all the loved ones who have put their faith in Him. We'll see them and rejoice with them again, never to be separated. I know some will say this sounds like romantic fantasy and wishful thinking, but it's as real to me now as my own reflection in the mirror – and a lot more beautiful!'

Of course the Boones' family life has not always been easy. There has been much pain and heartache at times. Nonetheless, looking back at his life and career so far, Pat acknowledges the ups and downs with equanimity and quotes one of his favourite passages from the Bible: 'And we know that all things work together for good to them that love God' (Romans 8:28). He finds this an enormous comfort, he says. 'I do believe that "all things" include the sweet *and* the bitter experiences of life, the good, the bad and the ugly. It's all part of God's plan, and we just have to trust Him.'

Pat is proud to be still active at the head of what is rapidly shaping up to be something of a Boone dynasty. The family can now boast three generations of professional singers – from Shirley's father Red Foley to Pat's musical daughters (many of his grandchildren also sing) – and that, Pat believes, must add up to some kind of record.

At the start of the new millennium, Pat is fast heading for his 'golden jubilee' – half a century as a professional singer! Although he made his first recordings way back in 1954, he is still enthusiastic about performing and recording, and it is difficult for him to think of music as work. He is excited about future plans, always hoping to build on the many years of success he has already enjoyed. Pressed to explain the reasons behind his lasting success, Pat puts it all down to 'hard work and spiritual optimism', and to a willingness to explore new styles and different music. Critics may mock his generally 'easy listening' sound and choice of material, but, says an ebullient Pat, nobody can really say what the public likes except the public themselves – and they have been only too happy to buy his records and pack out his concerts year after year. That is what matters to him, and he is profoundly grateful for the support and popularity he has enjoyed for nearly fifty years.

Although Pat spends much of his time singing and recording secular music, he is still dedicated to the cause of Christian music. His performing career, he says, was always a kind of ministry, even in the early days when he was feeling his way while trying very hard to reflect his life's principles in the way he behaved and the things he chose to do. 'These days, my music is my testimony to my faith in Jesus,' he says. 'If music is the food of love, then it must be doubly true for Christian music! There's some great music out there and I love to sing it. Fads come and go, even in sacred music, but my direction is always the same. I've had some shaky moments, but that direction started right back with my parents, who trained us children to follow God. They trained us, and we trained our children. Hopefully that train of blessing will continue on to our grandchildren and great-grandchildren.'

As busy as ever, Pat has no plans to retire just yet. He is committed to a full and active schedule of concerts and Christian work both at home and abroad, to say nothing of his myriad business and charity interests. 'Too many things are going on even to allow me to slow down!' he says with a grin. 'I'm old enough now to do whatever I want, and still young enough to do it... My poor wife Shirley *had* hoped that I would retire somewhere around the 65-year mark, but she says I'm like one of those old vaudeville plate-spinners: I've got about eight or ten plates whirling on sticks, and I'm running back and forth like crazy trying to keep them all spinning. She's about right!'

APPENDIX

MOVIES, VIDEOS, BOOKS AND DISCOGRAPHY

Movies

1957   *Bernadine* Twentieth Century Fox
       April Love Twentieth Century Fox

1958   *Mardi Gras* Twentieth Century Fox

1959   *Journey to the Centre of the Earth* Twentieth Century Fox

1961   *All Hands on Deck* Twentieth Century Fox

1962   *State Fair* Twentieth Century Fox
       The Main Attraction Severn Arts Production, Shepperton Studios

1963   *Yellow Canary* Twentieth Century Fox

1964   *Goodbye Charlie* Twentieth Century Fox
       The Horror of It All Twentieth Century Fox
       Never Put It in Writing Severn Arts Production, MGM British Studios

1965   *The Greatest Story Ever Told* MGM (re-release due 2001)

1967   *The Perils of Pauline* Universal Pictures

1969   *The Pigeon* Thomas/Spelling

1970   *The Cross and the Switchblade* Gateway Films

Videos

(All produced by Pat Boone Enterprises Inc.)

A Better Way
American Glory
Christmas Memories
Greatest Hits
Hits the Road
Israel, O Blessed Israel
Let Me Live
No Alibis
The Real Me

Books

1958 *Twixt Twelve and Twenty* Prentice-Hall Inc
1961 *The Real Christmas* (reprinted 1972) Revell
1966 *Between You, Me and the Gatepost* Prentice-Hall Inc
1967 *The Care and Feeding of Parents* Prentice-Hall Inc
1970 *A New Song* Creation House
1973 *Joy* Creation House
1974 *A Miracle a Day Keeps the Devil Away* Creation House
      Dr Baalam's Mule Bible Voice Inc
      (original title: *Dr Baalam's Talking Mule*)
1975 *My Brother's Keeper*
      (original title: *Dr Baalam's Talking Mule*)
      Get Your Life Together Bible Voice Inc
1977 *Devotional Book* Bible Voice Inc
      The Honeymoon Is Over (with Shirley Boone)
          Creation House/Thomas Nelson
1979 *Together: 25 Years with the Boone Family* Thomas Nelson
1980 *Pray to Win* Putnam/Fawcett
      Coming Out (reprint of *Joy*) Bible Voice Inc
      Miracle of Prayer Zondervan
1984 *Pat's Favourite Bible Stories for the
          Very Young* Random House
1988 *A New Song* (updated edition) Creation House

Discography

Top 20 Hits

GOLD SINGLES

1955	'Ain't That A Shame'	Dot 15377
1956	'Tutti Frutti'	Dot 15443
	'I'll Be Home'	Dot 15443
	'I Almost Lost My Mind'	Dot 15472
	'Friendly Persuasion'	Dot 15490
1957	'Don't Forbid Me'	Dot 15521
	'Love Letters In The Sand'	Dot 15570
	'Bernadine'	Dot 15602
	'Remember You're Mine'	Dot 15560
	'April Love'	Dot 15690
1958	'A Wonderful Time Up There'	Dot 16035
1961	'Moody River'	Dot 16209
1962	'Speedy Gonzales'	Dot 16368

PLATINUM SINGLES

1957	'Love Letters In The Sand'	Dot 15570
1962	'Speedy Gonzales'	Dot 16368

GOLD ALBUMS

1957	*Pat's Great Hits*	Dot 3071/25071
	Hymns We Love	Dot DLP3068***

Vinyl Albums

(Listed in alphabetical order. Not all compilation releases are included.)

12 Great Hits	1964	Hamilton HL60010
16 Classic Tracks	1982	MCA MCL 1676
Ain't that a Shame	1964	Dot DLP33573
All in the Boone Family	1973	Lamb and Lion 2008
The American Way	1981	Thistle TR-1002
April Love	1957	Dot DLP9000

The Best of Pat Boone	1982	MCA2-6020
Blest Be the Tie that Binds	1965	Dot DLP3601
The Boone Family Christmas	1975	Thistle TR-1001
Born Again	1973	Lamb and Lion 2007
Boss Beat	1964	Dot DLP3594
Canadian Sunset		Pickwick SPC3123
Christian People	1973	Lamb and Lion 2004
Christmas is a-Coming	1966	Dot DLP3770
Come Together	1972	Light LS-5592
The Country Side of Pat Boone	1977	Motown MC6501S1
Crisis America Bible		Voice
Days of Wine and Roses	1963	Dot DLP3504
Departure	1969	Tetragrammaton 18
Down Home with Pat Boone	1976	Lamb and Lion 2024
The Family who Prays	1973	Lamb and Lion 2006
The Favourite Hymns of Pat Boone		Pickwick SPC3145
Golden Era of Country Hits	1965	Dot DLP3626
Golden Hits – 15 Hits of Pat Boone	1967	Dot DLP3814
Golden Hits – 15 Hits	1973	Dot-Paramount SLPD504
Golden Hits – 16 Hits	1974	Dot-Paramount SLPD504
Golden Hymns	1983	Lamb and Lion 1060
Great Hits of 1965	1965	Dot DLP3685
Great Millions	1959	Dot DLP3181
Great! Great! Great!	1961	Dot DLP3346
He Leadeth Me	1960	Dot DLP3234
How Great Thou Art	1967	Dot DLP3798
Howdy!	1956	Dot DLP3030
Hymns We Love	1957	Dot DLP3068
I Love You More and More Every Day	1973	MGM SE4899
I Love You Truly	1962	Dot DLP3475
I Was Kaiser Bill's Batman	1967	Dot DLP3805
If My People	1972	Light LS7026
I'll See You in My Dreams	1962	Dot DLP3399
It's Time to Pray, America		House Top
Just the Way I Am	1979	Lamb and Lion 2039
Let's Get Cooking, America		Hunt-Wesson
Look Ahead	1967	Dot DLP3876
The Lord's Prayer	1964	Dot DLP3582
Love Me Tender		Pickwick SPC3101

Love Songs	1986	MFP 5758
Memories	1966	Dot DLP3748
Miracle Merry-Go-Round	1977	Lamb and Lion 2024
Moody River	1961	Dot DLP3384
Moonglow	1960	Dot DLP3270
My God and I	1961	Dot DLP3386
My Tenth Anniversary	1964	Dot DLP3650
Near You	1965	Dot DLP3606
The New Songs of the Jesus People	1972	Lamb and Lion 2002
The Old Rugged Cross	1977	Pickwick SPC3568
Originals	1974	ABC ABSD
Pat	1957	Dot DLP3050
Pat Boone	1956	Dot DLP3012
Pat Boone	1965	Hamilton HL60081
Pat Boone and the First Nashville Jesus Band	1972	Lamb and Lion 2003
The Pat Boone Family	1967	Word WST-8536
The Pat Boone Family in the Holy Land	1972	Lamb and Lion 2000
Pat Boone Gold		Thistle TR-1003
The Pat Boone Gospel Collection		Word 1012
Pat Boone Sings	1959	Dot DLP3158
Pat Boone Sings Golden Hymns	1972	Lamb and Lion 2001
Pat Boone Sings Guess Who?	1963	Dot DLP3501
Pat Boone Sings Irving Berlin	1958	Dot DLP3077
Pat Boone's Golden Hits	1962	Dot DLP3455
Pat Boone's Greatest Hits	1975	K-Tel 1473
Pat Boone's Greatest Hits	1978	Pickwick SPC3597
Pat Boone's Greatest Hits		Famous Twin Sets 1043
Pat Boone's Greatest Hymns		Famous Twin Sets 1024
Pat's Big Hits	1956	London HAD 2024
Pat's Big Hits Volume 2	1957	London HAD 2024
Pat's Great Hits	1957	Dot DLP3071
Pat's Great Hits Volume 2	1960	Dot DLP3261
A Pocketful of Hope		Thistle TR-1005
Rapture	1972	Supreme Prod. 2060
Reads from the Holy Bible	1962	Dot DLP3402
The Romantic Pat Boone	1969	Pickwick PTP2006
S-A-V-E-D	1973	Lamb and Lion 2013
Side by Side	1959	Dot DLP3199

Sing Along without Pat Boone	1963	Dot DLP3513
Sixteen Great Performances	1972	ABC ABOP4006
Something Supernatural	1975	Lamb and Lion 2017
Songmaker	1981	Lamb and Lion 1058
Songs for the Family of God	1983	BDMC Records
Songs for the Jesus Folks	1973	Supreme Prod. 2085
Songs from the Inner Court	1974	Lamb and Lion 2016
Stardust	1958	Dot DLP3118
The Star Spangled Banner	1963	Dot DLP3520
State Fair	1962	Dot DLP9011
Tenderly	1959	Dot DLP3180
Texas Woman	1976	Hitsville H6-405S1
Thank You, Dear Lord	1973	Lamb and Lion 2011
Thank You, Dear Lord	1974	Supreme Prod. 481
This and That	1960	Dot DLP3285
Tie Me Kangaroo Down, Sport	1963	Dot DLP3534
The Time has Come	1980	Lamb and Lion PB805
The Touch of Your Lips	1963	Dot
Tokyo '64 Concert	1964	Dot SJet 7465
True Love	1968	Pickwick SPC-3079
We Wish You a Merry Christmas	1968	Pickwick SPCX1004
What I Believe	1985	Lamb and Lion 3004
When I Fall in Love	1966	Pickwick SPC3167
White Christmas	1959	Dot DLP3222
Winners of the Reader's Digest Poll	1965	Dot DLP3626
Wish You Were Here, Buddy	1966	Dot DLP3764
Yes Indeed!	1958	Dot DLP3121
You've Lost that Lovin' Feeling	1970	Pickwick SPC3219

Compact Discs

(Listed in alphabetical order. Not all compilation releases listed.)

16 Great Songs: Pat Boone & Don Williams	CD11018
20 Golden Pieces	Bulldog Records BDCD2053(UK)
20 Greatest Hits	EMI 30CP26

A Date with Pat Boone	MCA MSD-35254
April Love	Pat Boone Enterprises BPECD1402
Baby Oh Baby	Bear Family BCD15645 (Germany)
Collection (5 CDs)	Dot MVCS-34-38 (Japan)
Come Together Band	Word WSTCD 9729
Echoes of Mercy	Word IMCLCD001 (UK)
The EP Collection	SEE CD487
The Fifties Complete	Bear Family BCD15884 LK (Germany)
Going Back Home	Word TIMED021 (UK)
Gold	Thistle TRC-CD1974
The Gold Hits of Pat Boone	Lamb and Lion TRCD99991974
The Golden Collection	Bulldog Records BDCD2053 (UK)
Golden Greats	MCA MCLD19182 (UK)
Gospel	Lamb and Lion GPB40001
The Great Pretender	CeDe 66064 (EEC)
Greatest Hits	Curb Music ROJOC 1011
Greatest Hits	Curb Records D277298
Greatest Hits Dot	MCA D-10885
Greatest Hymns	Curb Records D2-77808
His Greatest Hits and Finest Performances	Readers Digest Music MCA 3 CD set
Hits of the 60s	Stetrum 544097-2
I Remember Red	Laser Light 12384
I Remember Red - My Tribute to Red Foley	Pat Boone Enterprises PBECD1401
In a Symphonic Mood	Pat Boone Enterprises
Love Letters	K-Tel ONCD5106
Love Letters in the Sand	Entertainers ENTCD238
Love Letters in the Sand	Pat Boone Enterprises PBECD1401

More Greatest Hits	Dot VSD-5522
My God is Real:	
the Inspirational Collection	Varese Serabarde
No More Mr Nice Guy	Hip-OHIPD 40025
Old Fashioned Christmas	Word TIMED011 (UK)
Our Re-collections	Word 7013544361
Pat Boone in a Metal Mood	Hipp-O HIPD40025
Rare and Great Hits	Rock in Box Records
	RIBCD015 (Hungary)
Starlite	CDS5102AAD
The Star Spangled Banner	Lamb and Lion
	LLCD8725
The Sweetest Song	Word TIMED001 (UK)
The Ultimate Hit Collection	Laserlight 12387
Unforgettable	Castle Communication
	UNCD023
The Very Best of Pat Boone	Pickwick PWK074
White Christmas	MCAD-22049

INDEX

227

Also by Paul Davis and available from Zondervan

GEORGE HAMILTON IV

AMBASSADOR OF COUNTRY MUSIC

George Hamilton IV's chart successes and long career, spanning half a century, are an integral part of show business. He has worked and appeared with some of the greatest rock 'n' roll artists – Elvis, Little Richard, Buddy Holly, Chuck Berry, Brenda Lee and the Everly Brothers – although his first love was country music and the Grand Ole Opry.

This full-scale authorized biography goes behind the events in George's life to discover the unique people and remarkable influences that have helped shape the singer today. From his birth in North Carolina the book traces his rising fame and the resulting pressures on his family life, the tough times in Nashville when George turned his back on 'pop' to concentrate on country music, and the years spent coasting along in token Christianity before he nailed his colours to the mast in a remarkable way.

This inspiring book makes essential reading for adherents of country and gospel music alike, and tells of a winsome personality of skill and integrity, worthy to be the role model he has become.

We want to hear from you. Please send your comments about this book to us in care of the address below. Thank you.

GRAND RAPIDS, MICHIGAN 49530 USA

WWW.ZONDERVAN.COM